Unholy War for An Islamic Empire

Ron Cantrell

Published and distributed by
Bridges for Peace
Tulsa, Oklahoma

Unholy War for an Islamic Empire is not meant to incite hatred against Muslims. Its purpose is to define the difference between a Muslim and an Islamist.

Islamists suffer the delusion that non-Muslim people and non-Muslim governments are out to destroy their faith.

Islamists also believe that Islam is the only valid faith and that all others have been superseded. Muslims and Islamists hold differing interpretations of certain terms. An example is the term *jihad*. A Muslim might interpret it as a spiritual struggle to become a better Muslim, but an Islamist sees it as a license to kill infidels.

With that belief, comes violent behavior against people outside the Islamic household of faith.

In today's diverse world, this activity is unacceptable.

© 2002 by Ron Cantrell, Jerusalem, Israel
All rights reserved

ISBN 0-9704083-2-3

Published and distributed by Bridges for Peace
P.O. Box 33145
Tulsa, OK 74153
800-566-1998
First edition: August 2002

Scripture quotations from *The Holy Bible, New International Version*, ©1973, 1978, 1984, by the International Bible Society, unless otherwise noted.

Scripture marked KJV is taken from the *King James Version* of the Bible.

Scripture marked NRSV is taken from the *New Revised Standard Version*.

Cover Photo: Ron Cantrell

This book is dedicated
to victims
of Islamic terror, whom
we must not treat as
mere statistics.

Table of Contents

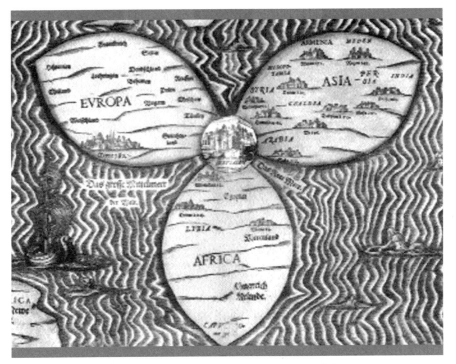

An ancient map was inspired by
the silk and spice routes from the far east
to Europe and Africa,
and the frankincense and myrrh routes,
from Africa to Europe and Asia.

Jerusalem was perceived as the hinge of the world.
In the map she is depicted as the
center of the earth.

Another export is currently renewing the
concept of the centrality of the region—
Islamic terrorism.

Moreover I will appoint a place
for My people Israel, and will plant them,
that they may dwell in a place of their
own and move no more; nor shall the
sons of wickedness oppress them anymore,
as previously.

II Samuel 7:10

Kurdish Jewish immigrants return home to Israel - (1936)

Vortex

We had just entered the central London traffic circle at Hyde Park when, suddenly, two unmarked, white Volkswagens cut us off from both sides in a "V" formation, stopping us in our tracks. In what seemed like a scene from a movie, four gun-wielding policemen jumped from the two cars, shouting for us to get out of our van. From what followed, I presume that we did not move fast enough for them.

The policeman did not even bother to slide open the side door of our van for me to exit in a dignified manner. After the first policeman pulled my two friends from the driver's and passenger's seats, another grabbed me by the front of the shirt and pulled me over the front seat and into the street.

I had just arrived in London from the Middle East where I had been covering news on Israel's war in Lebanon. At first, I thought we had inadvertently entered an area where a bomb scare was taking place. But, standing there like a criminal in the street, legs spread eagle and arms up on the side of the van, I noticed that no one else was being stopped, and people passing by were staring.

Puzzled, I turned to the policeman who was frisking me and asked as calmly as I could manage, "Do you mind telling me what is going on?" White-lipped, pale-faced and trembling, he almost shouted for me to shut up. I complied. I quickly realized that the best course of action was to flow with what was happening.

Soon, we were being questioned by the sergeant at the police station in the London suburb of Golders Green. I relayed my story while my friends, who had been escorting me around London, stood by. We were all in shock from our rather rough apprehension.

Working as the Jerusalem correspondent in the early eighties for an Australian magazine, I had been in and out of Lebanon during, what the media had labeled, "Israel's invasion of Lebanon." Witnessing for myself the exaggerations in news coverage, consistently slanted against Israel, I had decided to travel to the U.S.A. on a speaking tour in an attempt to counter what the media was reporting. Israel's Ministry of Foreign Affairs had provided me with information videos to use. Some of the video titles were straight forward, such as, "Terrorism in the Middle East" and "The P.L.O. in Lebanon."

9

Unholy War for An Islamic Empire

At the last minute, before leaving Jerusalem, I had been contacted by friends in England, who requested that I stop there first and let them in on the report I had prepared for the United States.

Purchasing tickets so late, I had to settle for a circuitous route. I landed in Brussels, Belgium on a Saturday, took the train to Calais, France, and from there, crossed the channel to England and traveled by train on to London.

Thornton Heath in Surrey, south of London, was my destination. Upon arriving, I realized I had made sure to have NTSC videos that would work in the U.S.A., but England uses PAL, and I was stuck. Frantically searching for an alternate plan, I contacted WIZO, the World International Zionist Organization. They assured me that one of their departments had at least some of the videos that I needed. They directed me to their offices in Golders Green, north London to pick up the material.

My two friends, who had invited me to come, were teachers at a Christian Bible School there. They graciously offered to chauffeur me through London to Golders Green.

When we arrived at the address I was given, it was very obvious that we were not at the headquarters of WIZO. Instead, a small dilapidated structure, with its windows boarded up, confronted us. We sat in the van bewildered. I got out and paced for a minute, trying to come up with an explanation and a plan. Standing on the sidewalk, I could see, what I thought to be, Hebrew letters on a building at the end of the block. Reentering the van, I instructed my friends, Ted and Freddie, to drive to the corner so that we could see what was there.

We entered the parking lot, and I grabbed my briefcase, making my way to the door. It was a Hebrew school. I knocked on the door to ask directions to WIZO. The door opened a very small crack, and I could see only one eye looking at me.

"Can you tell me where the World International Zionist Organization is?" I queried.

"No!" came a brusk answer.

"Is it possible for me to come in and made a phone call?" I asked. "I am lost."

"No!" came the answer again, and the door closed.

More bewildered than ever, I joined my friends in the van. They suggested we drive further along the street to see if the numbers changed. "We could be in the wrong borough," they offered. Sure enough, the numbers changed. We found WIZO, and I completed the business I had set out to do.

We were headed back to Thornton Heath in Surrey when the unmarked police cars intercepted us at Hyde Park.

After about fifteen minutes of questioning by the sergeant, we sat in three separate jail cells in the Golders Green Police Station. No explanation had yet been given for our arrest. About two hours later, a police officer came and inquired which one of us could be considered the "ringleader." I volunteered since it was my mission we were on. I was removed from my cell and appeared before the sergeant once again. He wanted to clarify some details. With still no offer of explanation, I was returned to my cell.

Soon after, we were all summoned. The sergeant was softer this time, but asked why we had refused to stop when the police had first tried to pull us over. His statement shocked us, as none of us had any idea we were being asked to stop. I am sure it had to do with us all being Americans. It would never have occurred to us that Volkswagen hatchback vehicles were police cars.

"Our next step was to shoot one of you!" the sergeant informed us. We stared at each other in awe. Pointing to me he said, "Your head was in the sights of our automatic rifle."

"Last week a terrorist phoned a bomb threat to the Hebrew school you stopped at." He continued, "Stepping up security, we were watching you on closed circuit television from the school. The synagogue in Brussels, Belgium was bombed Saturday of last week as well. In your briefcase, we found videos on Middle East terror as well as a plane ticket, showing you were in Brussels last Saturday. All the pieces of the puzzle were there," the sergeant explained. "The only thing that kept you from being incarcerated is that you actually did make it to the World International Zionist Organization, who could vouch that your story is true."

My friends were spluttering, but I could see that the London police were doing their job, and quite well. To the shock of my friends, I thanked the officers for doing a good job of protecting the Jewish community of Golders Green. That, in fact, was my mission anyway.

Though this incident happened two decades ago, the West was then becoming acquainted with Islamic terror and beginning to realize that there would be a high price to pay for terror in every way. They were beginning to understand that it would not be confined just to the Middle East.

It was a sobering way to be introduced to something which would escalate into a worldwide scourge over the next twenty years. It is a lesson I have never forgotten.

Training Hijackers in Iran

I relate the story, because at that time, terrorism was already in full swing. Iran maintained two major airports, dedicated to terror training. The latest Western equipment was purchased and transferred to the training facility. Iran Air maintained a Boeing 707 and a Boeing 727 jet in the airport and would send a Boeing 747 for special classes. Iran Air also contributed an A300 Airbus for training.

According to an ex-trainee, one of their exercises included having an Islamic Jihad detachment seize (or hijack) a transport aircraft. Then, trained air crews from among the terrorists would practice crashing the airliner—with its passengers—into a selected objective.

This information was available to U.S. government authorities as early as the first few years of the 1990s. At that time, Yossef Bodansky served as Director of the House Republican Task Force on Terrorism and Unconventional Warfare of the U.S. Congress. Bill McCollum (R-FL) served as the Chairman of the Task Force. Together they warned of the potential targets and real dangers posed by highly trained and deadly international terrorists.

The Balkans

The present wave of terror has surprising roots—and they are in surprising places. What do the Mufti of Jerusalem, Hitler, and Osama bin Laden have in common? The Balkans. What does this have to do with Islam and the Middle East? It is indicative of the broad scope of today's crisis.

The wave of Islam, spreading throughout Europe between A.D. 1451 and A.D. 1566, under the Ottoman Empire, stopped just short of Vienna, Austria. The demographics of Europe were upset generally, and the area of the Balkans, specifically. Lying on the border of that once massive empire, the Balkans still suffer residual ethnic conflicts. Areas once Christian, conquered for Islam, have tried to right the imbalance. In the course of their actions (many of them very wrong), they brought the world's wrath upon themselves.

Why was the media inept at interpreting the Balkans? Newspapers repeatedly reported on Osama bin Laden's Albanian-trained and drug-money-supported Kosovo Liberation Army as early as 1998. Much earlier, the Mufti of Jerusalem aided Hitler in his quest to rally the Muslims of the Balkans to his anti-Semitic, anti-Christian program in 1941.

The Islamist's Scheme

It is convenient to lay blame for the critical condition of the world at the feet of Israel, but in the final analysis, it is not justified. Israel has become a whipping boy in a much larger drama.

That drama is part of a broad-based power struggle between *Islamists* and democracy. Israel, unfortunately, happens to be caught in the middle. Whether Israel existed or not, the struggle would be waged. Before Israel became a nation in 1948, the struggle was going on. Blaming Israel has been in vogue, but is quickly becoming an earmark of an uninformed source.

The end of the cold war between the former U.S.S.R. and America laid the foundation for Islamists who are violently pitted against a monopolizing superpower, hawking Western values. Their revolution aims at the resurrection of an Islamic Empire. Should their plans be realized, it will make Japan's attack on America and Hitler's plans for Europe seem provincial.

The dynamic power of the present struggle is a vortex that will suck much of the world, both East and West, under its power. How we deal with the elements of the problem determines how out of control it will become.

What can we do, and how do we live, now that the curtain has been drawn back exposing the Islamist scheme?

Fair Warning

America was given fair warning. Mr. Bodansky has written

several books. One of them, *Target America: Terrorism in the U.S. Today,* is exhaustive in detail and scope, warning of the looming specter on the horizon known as "international terrorism." According to Bodansky, this information was gathered and gleaned from many sources over a period of more than twenty years. It was not cloistered away from the people who needed the information to prepare themselves for terror attacks. It was available for purchase by 1993.

The burning question then is, what did the appropriate government authorities do with this information when it was coming to light?

Once the scope of Islamists' intentions are understood, Americans will no longer allow their government to sit waiting for the next terrorist attack to take place. The cost will be too high. The searching for and rooting out of terrorism, before it can cross a border, will be the *modus operandi* the American public should press for—and we cannot move too soon.

Where Do We Come In?

I believe that a two-part mandate from heaven is upon us. First, a mandate of repentance for how we have treated Israel, tying their hands behind their backs, thus restricting their ability to deal effectively with terror in their own land. After all, the shame is that Islamic sources (the Hadith) predict a decisive massacre against Jews:

> Abu Huraira reported Allah's Messenger (may peace be upon him) as saying: The last hour would not come unless the Muslims will fight against the Jews, and the Muslims would kill them until the Jews would hide themselves behind a stone or a tree and a stone or a tree would say: Muslim, or the servant of Allah, there is a Jew behind me; come and kill him; but the tree Gharqad would not say, for it is the tree of the Jews.[1]

The second part of the mandate is strong support for Israel. The tiny nation is a microcosm of terrorist activity. Israel is the incubator in which new methods of terror are hatched and tested. Western governments unfairly urge Israel to "restrain" herself from carrying out defensive measures in order to secure safety for her citizens.

14

This scenario is being played out for us daily on our news media. It is not about Muslims against Jews and Christians. It is about Islamists against "moderate" Muslims, Hindus, Buddhists, and every other religion. It is not about Palestinians against Israel; rather, it is about Islamists against Israel, India, the Philippines, and Egypt, and, in fact, Islamists against the entire West.

Unless we change our present course of hobbling the only democracy in the Middle East, the just reward will be that terror will rear its ugly head and devour the West. The test cases, tried and proved in the petri dish of the Middle East, are moving outside that laboratory and into our world. The future is certain to contain serious terrorist strikes that will make what we have seen so far seem elementary. Just as the first attempt to bomb the Trade Center was eclipsed by the second strike and destruction of the Towers on September 11, 2001, so will succeeding terror strikes be increasingly horrific, unless we firmly and decisively stop them where they are being birthed. Nuclear and biological terror is unthinkable, but becoming a likely possibility.

As Christians, we want to respond appropriately to our enemy. In this context, we may have trouble interpreting Jesus' command to turn the other cheek. I believe Jesus was teaching this principle on an individual personal level. There is also a national level where response is different, but we will deal with this more later.

Our job is not to take matters into our own hands as vigilantes, but to use all means available to us within biblical principles—including prayer and the due process of law, in order to move our government to action.

The Vortex

I stood high on the Narrows Bridge connecting Tacoma, Washington and the Olympic Peninsula, the beautiful Pacific Northwest vacation spot. Warm weather was on its way in the city where I co-pastored a good sized congregation. A bout of spring fever had driven me from our house for awhile. I had wandered out with my three children just to clear my mind before other responsibilities demanded my attention.

Never having walked across the bridge before, we all decided to make the adventure ours. I parked our car on the Tacoma side, and we wandered out. The height was dizzying. It was so much more impressive than crossing in a car. I had never before noticed, from a vehicle, that the bridge surface was constructed of metal grid that you could see through. Below our feet, the powerful currents emptying and filling the Puget Sound with tidal surge twice daily, moved with amazing power.

The bridge we were standing on was aptly named. The narrow channel through which millions of metric tons of water passed daily was more than dangerous during those two surge periods— it could be deadly. Small craft in the area knew to stay clear during those unstable power surges of rushing water. The forces of the current were too strong for the motor of a small boat to navigate successfully. Disaster was a distinct possibility if your timing was wrong.

Standing perhaps a hundred feet above the water, we watched the turbulent forces under our feet. I felt small and helpless. Instinctively, I gathered my children closer to me. We stood near the support structures of the bridge and watched the riveting scene below. The water, meeting tons of concrete footing, swirled with overwhelming force, creating a vortex of opposing currents, which sucked all debris that came near enough, down and out of sight beneath the dark water. My excited children were not bothered by the scene below and pointed out numerous things that I should look at, but I found the water hypnotizing.

In hindsight, that day now seems to have stood as a harbinger of another kind of vortex I would observe from another kind of bridge—this time in the Middle East.

My wife, three children, and I were preparing to leave America and return to the Middle East on an extended career opportunity. With a background in journalism and newspaper publishing, I was going to rejoin an organization called Bridges for Peace, headquartered in Jerusalem, Israel. I looked forward to taking my skills to a faraway country and using them to the best of my ability.

Bridges for Peace has been active in building Jewish-Christian relationships for over thirty-five years. We recognize the need to educate Christianity at large as to why they should be supportive of Israel and the Jewish people wherever they might be found. Education, coupled with practical aid to homecoming Jewish immigrants from the former Soviet Union and other countries, has made Bridges a cutting-edge ministry for these present times.

Having lived in Israel earlier, in the eighties, we knew the political climate. What I did not know was how powerful the vortex would become between those early years and the present. The countercurrent would reach beyond the borders of the Middle East and begin to suck all that concerned themselves with it, as well as many who did not want to be concerned with it, beneath the dark waters.

In the years following our outing on the Narrows Bridge, this visual experience would be brought back to my mind many times. It seemed symbolic of the events we would witness in the following years of our residence in Jerusalem.

Notes

1. Hadith: Book 041, Number 6985; Book 041, Number 6983;
   Volume 4, Book 52, Number 177; Volume 4, Book 56, Number 791.

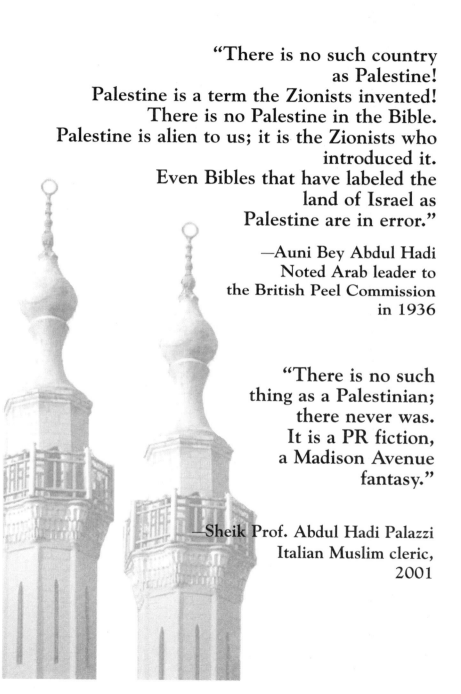

"There is no such country
as Palestine!
Palestine is a term the Zionists invented!
There is no Palestine in the Bible.
Palestine is alien to us; it is the Zionists who
introduced it.
Even Bibles that have labeled the
land of Israel as
Palestine are in error."

—Auni Bey Abdul Hadi
Noted Arab leader to
the British Peel Commission
in 1936

"There is no such
thing as a Palestinian;
there never was.
It is a PR fiction,
a Madison Avenue
fantasy."

—Sheik Prof. Abdul Hadi Palazzi
Italian Muslim cleric,
2001

Media Myths

We pulled into the Palestinian Refugee Camp, between Tyre and Sidon on the coastal road in Lebanon. I sat in the back seat, directly behind Moshe, our mandatory, armed Israeli soldier, who was appointed to serve as our guide. I was more than apprehensive, because Moshe had strongly suggested that we take an unnecessary detour for a visit to a refugee camp on our way to Beirut. All of us on the fact-finding mission burst into nervous laughter at his suggestion, thinking this soldier was kidding or had taken leave of his mind. After all, we were in south Lebanon where Israel was at war (1982) with Palestinian militia. Terrorist organizations were very present and active there. However, Moshe was serious.

"I just want you to see something," he assured us.

Our journey had started early that morning in Metulla, the Israeli-Lebanese border town. There we had waited for Moshe to arrive from the interior of Lebanon to escort us north to Beirut. The wait was long and tedious. Apprehension made the minutes pass like hours. I was accompanying Clarence H. Wagner, Jr., International Director of Bridges for Peace, one of our U.S. Bridges for Peace representatives, Norma Nation, and Gordon Young, the son of G. Douglas Young, founder of Bridges for Peace. Each of us had come to observe and file our own report on what was happening. Major media had taken every opportunity to distort the facts.

Finally, all smiles and confidence, Moshe arrived at the hotel we had been instructed to wait at by the IDF liaison. He greeted us warmly and began to brief us about where we would be going. Taking off and heading north into Lebanon, we were confronted by the range of mountains that held the ancient Crusader fortress, Montfort Castle, which Hizballah had occupied and used to fire rockets into northern Israeli towns. Israel had decided to send IDF Army Commander Ariel Sharon into South Lebanon to drive the Islamic fundamentalist forces back twenty-five miles in order to create a buffer zone.

The roads were atrocious. Before starting out, we had agreed to place a tape recorder on the console in the middle of the car and simply let it run. We knew Moshe would be briefing us all the way, and we had agreed that we would transcribe the information later. The few minutes of play time before unanimously deciding it was not going to work, sounded like a bad party joke. It finally ended

19

with four people screaming, and the recorder flying into the air as we hit a huge pothole in the road.

When we finally arrived at the Palestinian refugee camp, our car came to a halt, and Moshe confidently got out, motioning for us all to follow. Fear made the next few minutes seem to happen in slow motion for me. A United Nations truck sat in the middle of a large crowd of Palestinian men, its huge black U.N. letters like a billboard. The attention of the group was riveted on several men standing in front of the truck, engaged in an intense conversation.

I opened my car door and tried to exit as slowly as I could without appearing terrified. As I stood up, remaining behind my door, three men spotted us and broke away from the crowd and moved toward our vehicle. Their faces did not seem friendly. Horrible scenes from violent movies flashed through my mind. The men were now within earshot of Moshe, who had moved out from the circle of safety of our automobile.

"Moshe," the men called, "please tell the U.N. not to come here anymore. They are stealing what we have, let alone bringing anything to help us!"

Moshe put his arm around the man's shoulder, and I heard the man say, "You are like a brother to us. You know you are welcome here anytime, but the U.N. is robbing us blind." Moshe comforted him and moved off in the direction of the trouble.

I could not believe what I was hearing. Obviously, in a sea of trouble, kept at a froth by a handful of Islamic militants, real life was still going on that could be considered sane, except for the fact that these people were in a Palestinian refugee camp. This is what Moshe had wanted us to see. These were the people who were being harmed the most by a few militants who held them hostage, both mentally and physically by their Islamist plans.

Our fact-finding mission into Lebanon was a lesson to me in the power of the media. Television coverage, magazine reports, and newspaper stories I had seen convinced me that Israel had wiped out huge sections of Lebanese cities.

However, the truth was that in Tyre and Sidon, we had to be guided to war-damaged areas, because they were so small we might never have found them on our own. They were only a few square blocks. I recognized areas that had been under the artistic hand of master media propagandists—lies that made me stand in horror, shock, and anger at what we could be made to believe.

20

Hostage to Islamist Propaganda

I had seen it before in Jerusalem and Bethlehem. Thugs from the Palestinian Authority coming to shut down shop owners' stores for nationwide strikes for some contrived political issue, so often that the populace were being kept poor, hungry, and angry. The street leading from Jerusalem's southern neighborhoods into Bethlehem was once lined with tourist shops. No longer. The strikes and mafia-like activity of Islamic militants had killed tourism, and remaining business had been purposefully rerouted to larger stores belonging to men who had connections. Now only a few shops were still in business on Bethlehem Road.

The situation was reminiscent of Jerusalem's Old City before the 1967 Six Day War. Jordan was in control of the West Bank and all of the Old City before the war, and only a dozen souvenir shops were allowed to operate. Now there must be a thousand, or so it seems, on a shopping trip there.

But, it is the big picture that is more important than that, and the media is there to help out. Islamic fundamentalists are delighted that the world believes the Middle East to have been a pastoral, peace-filled scene prior to the modern wave of Jewish immigration. This myth is the foundation of their supposed struggle for Islamic rights.

The undercurrent in most media coverage is that the Jewish presence in Israel has upset the Palestinian's apple cart. The Jews are blamed for the unrest that could draw the world into another world war. The fact of the matter is, the Middle East was a boiling cauldron long before Jewish people in the Diaspora began their homecoming.

Modern immigration began in the late 1800s and continued through the declaration of the modern Jewish state in 1948, gathering steam right up until today.

The Islamic fundamentalists, aided by the media, purposefully steer clear of the facts on the ground. There were ninety thousand Jewish residents in Israel's cities and towns at that time. Per capita, compared to the population of the United States, the above number would make Israel's Jewish population stand at sixty million people. Furthermore, dating back to the first century, there has never been a time when Israel was without a continuous Jewish population.

21

How Did We Make Them so Mad?

The nagging question the West keeps asking themselves is: "How did we manage to make Islam so angry at us?" It is the same question Israel has asked for all the years of her modern existence. There is no answer because it is not the right question. The question should be: "What, in Islamic writings, would inspire Muslims to act in violent ways towards those who do not see eye-to-eye with them?" The answer is found in their own religious material: the Koran, Islam's Scriptures, and the Hadith, the recorded sayings of the Prophet Muhammed.

According to Islam worldwide, Palestine is the pivotal issue. Key Islamic leaders continue to champion the Palestinian cause. Osama bin Laden used the issue to justify his world-changing reign of terror. Muslim demonstrations, as far away as Indonesia, hold up the problem as the key issue. This myth presupposes an ethnic majority ruling over a preexisting state whose existence has been ended by "occupation" forces. The truth is Palestine never existed as a nation. Yes, the name was used to describe a region, but statehood was never a fact.

In 1947, the United Nations solved the problem of a Palestinian state by offering to partition the Jewish homeland into two states: Israel and Palestine. The vote passed in the United Nations session, but surprisingly Egypt voted "no," as well as Jordan, Syria, and Lebanon. Also surprisingly, the Arabs (who are now known as Palestinians) rejected the U.N. plan out of hand. This lit the fuse to the powder keg, and it led to a regional war.

The reality is that the Palestinian issue is a pawn in a much larger game. History tells the story.

The Need to Reset the Stage

We need to step back in time to get a clear perspective. The Islamic Ottoman Empire was the most significant demographic altering factor in the Middle East. That world-conquering empire swallowed nations, erased borders, and changed demographics. The Ottoman Empire ruled the Middle East from Turkey between 1517 and 1917. In World War I, they lost the land. One of the most notable results on the other side was the treaty drawn up to create a Jewish homeland.

Over the years, Arabists have rallied around different banners, heralding major obstacles to peace. Between 1917-1948, the issue was Jewish immigration. From 1948-1967, it was the "Arab refugee" problem. The surprising factor in this argument is that 900,000 Jewish refugees were driven from Islamic nations when Israel declared statehood. They are never mentioned, but they outnumber Arab refugees almost by double. Most were made to leave their homes and businesses with no remuneration from the nations from which they fled.

From 1967 to the present, the major obstacle to peace has been "occupied territory." Israel was forced into war with neighboring Arab nations. From this territory came numerous terrorist attacks upon Israeli citizens. Making this territory secure became of utmost importance to Israel's security as a nation.

It is never acknowledged by the media, but the bone in the throat of Muslims is that, according to Islam, territory once belonging to Allah (having been under the banner of Islam) always belongs to Allah and must be taken back by force if occupied by non-Muslims.

This would be true of land occupied by the Jewish nation. Arabs do not consider Israel, or the Jews, either a legitimate nation or neighbor. Therefore, militant Islamic leaders proclaim that Israelis must be driven from Allah's land. In fact, Arabs claim all of the territory of Israel as theirs. This fact is obvious from their own organizational logos, which show all of Israel as Palestine. A simple trip to a PLO watchdog website has just such a logo on the homepage.[1]

Noteworthy is the fact that Jordan never, at any time, recognized a Palestinian state. In fact, the late King Hussein was building his western palace just three miles north of Jerusalem, when the 1967 Six Day War took the territory out of his hands. The West Bank at that time was "occupied" by Jordan with no consideration of a Palestinian state. Not once in nineteen years, between 1948 and 1967, was any international pressure placed upon Jordan over occupying Palestinian land.

Weather maps, used by Jordanian television up until the signing of the peace treaty between Israel and Jordan in 1996, showed the Hashemite Kingdom of Jordan extending to the Mediterranean Sea. Jerusalem was simply referred to as "The Western Heights." Neither did the name "Palestine" nor "Israel" appear on their maps.

The wave of immigration that began as a trickle from Yemen in 1880 soon turned into a global issue, which continued until today. The first Yemenite Jews to return to Israel looked so Arab that the Jewish population already resident in Israel would not accept the fact that they were indeed Jewish immigrants. The family of Horatio Spafford, the Christian man who wrote the famed hymn, "It Is Well With My Soul," and who also founded the American Colony in Jerusalem, helped as a go-between, instructing the Jewish population that these Yemenite Jews were returning to the land as God had indeed foretold in the book of Isaiah.

What was the nature of the Middle East before these waves of Jewish immigration? Who were the players, and how did they change over time? Answering these questions will lead to a more factual view of the Middle East, and that is the aim of this book.

An "Innocent" Looks at Israel

As an important initial backdrop, a famous and well-loved American author described his journey to the Middle East in 1867, just before the first wave of modern Jewish immigration in 1882. In his book, *Innocents Abroad*, Mark Twain described his personal trip from Damascus to Tiberias:

> . . .[a] desolate country whose soil is rich enough, but is given over wholly to weeds—a silent mournful expanse . . . A desolation is here that not even imagination can grace with the pomp of life and action. . . We never saw a human being on the whole route . . . There was hardly a tree or a shrub anywhere. Even the olive and the cactus, those fast friends of a worthless soil, had almost deserted the country.

He concluded that Israel would probably never play an important role in history again.

How wrong he was. As the Jews began returning from the four corners of the earth, from where they had been scattered, the land began to flourish. In less than 150 years, the land of Israel has become lush and abundant in agriculture of all varieties.

But you, O mountains of Israel, will produce branches and fruit for My people Israel, for they will soon come home. I am concerned for you and will look on you with favor; you will be

24

*ploughed and sown, and I will multiply the number of people
upon you, even the whole house of Israel. The towns will be
inhabited and the ruins rebuilt.
I will increase the number of men and animals upon you, and
they will be fruitful and become numerous. I will settle people
on you as in the past and will make you prosper more than
before. Then you will know that I am the LORD. I will cause
people, My people Israel, to walk upon you. They will possess
you, and you will be their inheritance; you will never again
deprive them of their children.*

Ezekiel 36:8-12

Islamic Heroism?

What the West considers terrorism, Islamists consider heroism.
There is great Islamic support internationally at the grass roots
level for Osama bin Laden. Anti-American and anti-Israeli terror is
an expected norm. Spurred on by calls to *jihad*, Islamic "holy war,"
the Islamic masses can be very quickly roused to uncontrollable
riots and frightening displays of pro-terrorist violence. The almost
constantly televised Islamic confrontations in Pakistan, Kashmir,
Indonesia, Gaza, and the West Bank are current, frightening
examples. Hardly a day goes by without a militant Islamist
confrontation somewhere in the world.

Controversial debates have been heard in many circles as to
exactly what *jihad* means. Moderate Muslims, fearful of a backlash
because of the activity of militants, have been redefining terms.
Islam is the only religion in history to incorporate such a tenet in
its holy writings. There are as many Islamic scholars on the side of
violence as there are those who are trying to save face by
rationalizing away the violent demand for *jihad*.

Islamists versus Muslims

Israel, the only democracy in the Middle East, is surrounded by
Islamic states that have been in turmoil for hundreds of years.

The Ottoman Empire was not a peaceful place, and the regimes
preceding it were not peaceful. That is to say that violence has
occurred on a regular and an ongoing basis in the Islamic world.
Muslims fighting Muslims is not rare or unusual. Islamic military
dictatorships with a more secular world view often attempt to crush
Muslim fundamentalist organizations. Contrary to this, radical

25

Unholy War for An Islamic Empire

Islamic groups try to destabilize and overthrow Muslim military regimes, which they deem soft on non-Muslim infidels.

There   is a significant difference between Islamists and Muslims. Islamists are those bent on world domination through violence, by which they envision establishing an Islamic empire dominated by Koranic law. They even view existing Islamic regimes as "infidels," because they do not observe the strictest measure of the law of the Koran. Those, too, are considered "unbelievers" who must be brought into the "light of truth" as they see it.

There are Muslims, however, who follow the religion of Muhammed, who are more moderate. It was these who strongly denounced the attacks against the Trade Towers on September 11. A drawback is that it is easy for a moderate Muslim to take an extreme position for an Islamic political cause.

Moderates may not be Islamists in the strictest sense of the word, but their stance is borderline. The extreme pressure (such as that following the September 11 disaster) may cause them to lean toward hard-line Islamist thought. Under that kind of pressure, it is more likely that a Muslim would not take a hard stance against an Islamist act of terrorism or statements inciting violence by an Islamic group preaching *jihad* against the "enemies" of Islam.

September 11 drew the curtain back on Islam for the world to see. The Islamic tidal wave, which swept the world once before, stopping just short of Vienna, Austria, is on the horizon again.

This current within Islam is foundational. The Caliph Umar, (reign 634-644) the second Caliph, who fought against the Byzantines shortly after Muhammed's death, despised all infidels, but especially Christians. It is written of him:

> Umar—may he ever have peace—coveted nothing in the flesh save the undoing of Christian arrogance; for Jews are impotent and pagans are powerless; but in Christians, he saw challenge. Therefore, his meat was their humiliation; his drink was their shame; his humor was their downfall; his very breathing was their destruction. To see the whole earth bow in submission to Allah was his sure desire; but to see Christendom fall was his great delight.[3]

Islamists do not view history as a chronological time-line as do Europeans and Americans. Rather, history in their eyes resembles a wheel. Islam is flourishing when it sits atop the wheel, as in a world dominating empire like the Ottoman Empire. However, all know that the wheel continues to turn, and at different periods, Islam appears to sit at the bottom of the wheel. In that cycle, to regain the top, the position on the wheel, where Islam sits, may even appear to travel backwards for a short time. Nevertheless, Islamic hope is that, with patience and perseverance Islam will again arrive at the top of the wheel of history, and then a worldwide Islamic Empire will once again flourish.

That flourishing, astride the top of the wheel, is the very goal to which Islamist militants are now aspiring. It behooves us to understand their worldwide revolution and be acquainted with the myths and deceptions which fuel the fires of their terror campaigns. The truth, in the face of so many lies, is the beginning of stopping the militant activities of Islamists.

Jenin, Ramallah, and the West Bank

Recently, short periods of media favor toward Israel are surfacing. Major media players know it is becoming more and more obvious to the world, the kind of terror Israel has been facing. To go on making them look like "aggressors" and "war criminals" is not an accurate assessment of the facts on the ground. The media often reports incidents through their particular political filter. The facts are often very different.

Israel was inspected by the West through a microscope concerning the IDF's Operation Defensive Shield of 2002. Accusations centered specifically around the operations in the refugee camp in the Palestinian city of Jenin. Before a group of international journalists in Jerusalem, Colonel Miri Eisen, IDF spokeswoman, related finds from their operation.

Colonel Eisen covered four foundations upon which terrorism is built; ideology, people, weapons, and funding. Each of these points was detailed for journalists. The emphasis was on incriminating evidence pointing to the Palestinian Authority's direct links to terrorism, with special emphasis on Yasser Arafat's involvement in ordering and funding terrorist operations.

27

Unholy War for An Islamic Empire

PA Ideology

Not all of the Palestinian Authority are terrorists, but their ideology comes from the top. Ideology is the kingpin of the terrorist infrastructure. The ideology can be gleaned from the documents found during the operation in the offices of the PA in several different cities. Filing cabinets, computer hard-drives, and other sources provided Israel with volumes of incriminating material.

Every school that Israel entered, be it in Jenin, Ramallah, Bethlehem, Kalkilya, or Tulkarem, had posters plastered on the walls, glorifying the *shaheedeen* (suicide bombers). This includes first graders through eighth graders. Because of this, Israel looked more closely at the schoolbooks. Canadians, who funded the educational system, may be surprised what the "educational" books from which the children are being taught contain. Many of these books were printed in 1999 and in 2000. There is no recognition of the State of Israel and it does not exist on any school map. Brainwashing begins early. The glorification of suicide martyrs is very real. In contrast, one can look at any Israeli school curriculum and find none of that ideology present.

An example of what was found at the PA's Ramallah Headquarters, in the office of the personal bodyguard of Arafat, is a book in Arabic called *Nazi-Zionism*. It claims to document that there was no Holocaust. It is actually a compendium of every possible horrific anti-Semitic thing you can think of from the last one hundred years. The book was printed by the Palestinian Authority at the end of 2001 in Bethlehem.

The culmination of all this ideology exhibits itself in scenes like the recent mob trial of four Palestinians accused of collaboration with Israel in the streets of Hebron and Ramallah. This is their ideology and education. Palestinian TV, Abu Dhabi TV, Al Jazeera TV and what they say in Arabic to their own people results in lynchings, where collaborators bodies are tied behind cars and dragged through the streets by their feet until dead.

A few years ago, on PA television, Arafat issued a call for Palestinian women to give birth to many sons and dedicate at least one to him for his *jihad* against Israel. Whereas we may have considered this empty rhetoric, the program to train these dedicated sons is now evident from confiscated documents in Arafat's offices. Summer training camps for youth, school books, and training manuals for terror are now in Israeli officials' possession.

The People

In the course of the IDF military operation, 4,564 Palestinians were held for questioning. Out of that number, 1,450 have admitted to being participants in terrorist acts against Israel. This comes to an astounding twenty-five percent, a ratio high enough to cause consternation to any government. These arrests were only in six out of eight major cities in the West Bank.

Three major terrorist organizations, which are in operation, can be tied to the Palestinian Authority. Fatah's leader, Marwan Barghouti, and his nephew, Ahmed Barghouti, who served as his operations officer, were arrested. He also headed the Tanzim, the military arm of the Fatah organization. The al-Aqsa Martyrs' Brigade can now be tied to both Fatah and the Tanzim. They operate in concert one with the other. Posters on the walls of those cities glorifying recent suicide bombers had logos of all three organizations on them.

From the documentation, it is now known that Marwan Barghouti not only knew about the terrorist activity, but he directly approved many terror attacks. The IDF supplied the U.S. with a report, with Arafat's signature, documenting his ordering of these operations along with appropriate funding.

Israel feels that they have crippled the terrorist organizations but have not destroyed them. That means the arrested terrorists are talking and incriminating other guilty parties. There are many lower ranking radicals who may rise up in place of those they have arrested.

All this does not take into consideration Islamic Jihad and Hamas who are in opposition to Palestinian-run organizations. Hamas operates mainly from Gaza, and Israel did not enter Gaza during this operation. No doubt these terrorist organizations are regrouping themselves inside the Gaza Strip now.

Three major players within Hamas were Kais Adwan, who was killed by Israeli troops in Tubas, and Said Alwad, who was killed with him. Kais was the explosives manufacturer. He was the man who created explosive suicide belts and sent the young men and women out to detonate themselves and was the main terrorist in the Samaria area. He knew how to sneak his living bombs into Israel proper. Said Alwad knew how to make Kassam II rockets and was operating in Samaria as well. He imported this knowledge from the Gaza Strip. The third person is Salim Haja in Nablus in

29

the Samaria area. He plans and directs operations with the people from the Nablus area.

It is now known that these men planned to use Kassam II rockets from the edges of the West Bank, firing them into Israel from Tulkarem and Kalkilya.

The refugee camp in Jenin was the hotbed of suicide bombers. Islamic Jihad operated from Jenin, but during the Israeli military operation, Israel killed an important terror leader, and four surrendered. Two top heads are Ali Zafouri and Tabaat Mardawi. Of the suicide bombers that originated in Jenin, twenty-three found their targets.

Weapons

"We have no guns!"—was the PA rhetoric at the start of the *intifada.* In Nablus alone, Israel found eighteen explosives laboratories. Every lab was housed in a civil building, including one in the basement of an official PA building. They were carefully exploded from afar because of the danger to soldiers from secondary explosions. In one of the labs, IDF troops found twenty-four suicide belts, equipped with explosives and ready to go. Bethlehem, too, housed explosive labs and bomb-making factories.

Ninety-five percent of the explosives are being created by terrorist organizations themselves. Chemical labs were found in the most unsuspecting of places. In Bethlehem University, it was discovered that they were making chemical components for explosives. An Israeli spokesman said, "It is the sort of place you don't think of looking into at the beginning. You don't think of going into a university and looking for ingredients being made into explosives for suicide bombers." Five percent of what we call "standard explosives" are smuggled in from different areas.

There are 14,400 Kalashnikov rifles in Judea and Samaria alone, as part of the Oslo agreement for the policemen and the different security functions. During this present operation, a little over 4,000 were confiscated, which means there are still 10,000 rifles still out there ready to fire on Israeli citizens.

Then there are staggering numbers of improvised weapons. Warehouses of homemade weapons were discovered. Not those allowed as part of the Oslo agreement, but ones Palestinians have been making by hand. A bit of iron pipe and some explosives can be turned into a pipe bomb that will kill many people.

Funding

The computer of Marwan Barghouti (leader of Arafat's Tanzim Militia, a faction of Fatah), as well as the computer of Fuad Shubaki (PA Finance Minister), detailed the money trail.

All the discovered documentation reveals monies coming directly from Damascus to Jenin to fund suicide missions.

Funding for Islamic Jihad from Damascus caused problems within Jenin. The terrorist organization, Islamic Jihad, had money and could pay their terrorists for education and weapons, but the Fatah/Tanzim and the al-Aqsa Martyrs' Brigade in Jenin were being passed over in Syrian funding. One had abundant money the other didn't, and this caused great contention amongst the terrorist organizations. Saddam Hussein is another generous donor to families of suicide bombers.

Deposits of monies can be traced, because the Palestinian Authority has its own international telephone code, different from the State of Israel. Transfers of money can come either by courier in cash, or they can come through bank transfers. Although Israel was aware of it in terms of intelligence, they could not reveal it until it was clearly documented. The documents are all in IDF possession now.

In a question-and-answer period at the end of the press briefing, a vital question was asked, which played an important role in light of the U.N.'s insistence on a fact-finding mission to Jenin.

A reporter in attendance asked, "Is it true that the Israelis filmed the fighting in Jenin, and will you present it?"

Colonel Miri responded, "The films are to open up areas and pinpoint where the enemy is. These are things that we have on hand. All the information within the IDF for the Jenin committee is being prepared. As you know, a committee within the IDF has been appointed to prepare all of the information for the U.N. We are being guided by the Minister of Defense. This information will be useful in absolving Israel of accusations of a massacre in Jenin, when presented to the U.N. committee."

The Accusations

The world thought they had finally caught Israel, showing her true colors in Jenin. In actuality, they did show their true colors, but it just wasn't what the world wanted. Night after night, news broadcasts juggled the numbers. Wild guesstimates began at one thousand men, women, and children dead in the Jenin massacre. Stories of buried families and interviews with residents, telling staggering stories, were nightly fare.

One man interviewed on camera told how he had lost his whole family of eight in the intense fighting. Months later, a reporter looked him up for a follow-up to find that he was with his whole family. No one was lost, and the story was simply a fabrication.

The world viewed an abundance of Palestinian funeral processions. With flag burning, shooting into the air, armies of young men strapped with ammunition and large guns, they were riotously demonstrative, compared to Jewish funerals, so that is where the camera crews went. One particular funeral procession, following the alleged Jenin massacre, epitomized the entire debacle. All was proceeding as usual until the dead body fell off the funeral bier, which was being carried by four young men. Shockingly, the body got up, brushed itself off, and ran to jump back on the bier. It would have been laughable had it not been so infuriating to see the desperation to create numbers.

After a week, it became obvious the focus on the subject was intensifying. Israel then began to answer back with camera crews going to the scene to show how preposterous the reports were. A detailed map of the area showed how few buildings in the refugee camp had been damaged. The exaggerated numbers began to drop as news agencies could not find the bodies.

When it was embarrassingly obvious that no massacre had taken place in Jenin, and when the wild "guesstimates" of a thousand dead dropped to about fifty armed fighters, the media backed off and let the subject drop. No apologies were offered for the consumer public to hear, or more importantly, to Israel, but the "Jenin massacre" faded away, replaced by more pressing news items.

What the media wanted actually did happen, but not in 2002, nor was it at the hands of the Israelis. It happened in 1938 by the British. The British Broadcasting Company (BBC) lead the pack in the attack on Israeli Prime Minister Ariel Sharon and Israel over the alleged Jenin "massacre." They expected more of what the British had done in 1938.

Rafael Medoff filed this report exposing the "British-way" of ruling the colonies and dealing with terrorists.

How the British Fought Arab Terror in Jenin

(Jerusalem) "Demolishing the homes of Arab civilians . . . Shooting handcuffed prisoners. . . Forcing local Arabs to test areas where mines may have been planted. . ." These sound like the sort of accusations made by British and other European officials concerning Israel's recent actions in Jenin.

In fact, they are descriptions from official British documents concerning the methods used by the British authorities to combat Palestinian Arab terrorism in Jenin and elsewhere in 1938.

The documents were declassified by London in 1989. They provide details of the British Mandatory government's response to the assassination of a British district commissioner by a Palestinian Arab terrorist in Jenin in the summer of 1938.

Even after the suspected assassin was captured (and then shot dead while allegedly trying to escape), the British authorities decided that "a large portion of the town should be blown up" as punishment.

On August 25 of that year, a British convoy brought 4,200 kilos of explosives to Jenin for that purpose.

In the Jenin operation and on other occasions, local Arabs were forced to drive "mine-sweeping taxis" ahead of British vehicles in areas where Palestinian Arab terrorists were believed to have planted mines, in order "to reduce [British] land mine casualties."

The British authorities frequently used these and similar methods to combat Palestinian Arab terrorism in the late 1930s.

British forces responded to the presence of terrorists in the Arab village of Miar, north of Haifa, by blowing up house after house in October 1938.

"When the troops left, there was little else remaining of the once-busy village except a pile of mangled masonry," *The New York Times* reported.

The declassified documents refer to an incident in Jaffa in which a handcuffed prisoner was shot by the British police.

Under Emergency Regulation 19b, the British Mandate government could demolish any house located in a village where terrorists resided, even if that particular house had no direct connection to terrorist activity.

Mandate official Hugh Foot later recalled: "When we thought that a village was harboring rebels, we'd go there and mark one of the large houses.

33

Then, if an incident was traced to that village, we'd blow up the house we'd marked."

The High Commissioner for Palestine, Harold MacMichael, defended the practice: "The provision is drastic, but the situation demanded drastic powers."

MacMichael was furious over what he called the "grossly exaggerated accusations" that England's critics were circulating concerning British anti-terror tactics in Palestine.

Arab allegations that British soldiers gouged out the eyes of Arab prisoners were quoted prominently in the Nazi German press and elsewhere.

The declassified documents also record discussions among officials of the Colonial Office concerning the rightness or wrongness of the anti-terror methods used in Palestine.

Lord Dufferin remarked: "British lives are being lost and I don't think that we, from the security of Whitehall, can protest squeamishly about measures taken by the men in the frontline."

Sir John Shuckburgh defended the tactics on the grounds that the British were confronted "not with a chivalrous opponent playing the game according to the rules, but with gangsters and murderers."

There were many differences between British policy in the 1930s and Israeli policy today, but one stands out—the British faced a level of Palestinian Arab terrorism considerably less lethal than that which Israel faces.

—by Rafael Medoff [4]

So, where the British media are concerned, is it a case of residual guilt that catapulted them to the front of the line of accusers when Israel went into Jenin to root out terrorist cells?

The Israelis understand world pressure that holds them continually under the microscope. They were not stupid enough to commit criminal acts when going into Jenin. They knew what would take place immediately after the incursion.

In fact, credible stories surfaced, after the Jenin incursion, about many soldiers who cleaned up the houses they slept in, rolled up the rugs and slept on the floors, and would not even eat food from the houses where they bunked down for the night.

Strong Delusion

Almost immediately after September 11, politically-correct government spokespersons and media reporters began, in earnest, to try and convince a shaken public that Islam is a "religion of peace." It seems they cannot imagine there really are wicked people on the face of our planet. Historically, this was one of America's heaviest moments of grief, yet at the National Cathedral memorial service in Washington, DC, a teary-eyed audience, still too shaken to protest, were made to endure the opening prayer, in Arabic, of an invited Islamic Imam.

In the days following the terror attacks, attempts to soft sell the nature of Islam served as a warning of coming strong delusion:

> *And for this cause God shall send them strong delusion, that they should believe a lie . . .*

2 Thess. 2:11

The context of the chapter in which the above verse appears is the appearance of the Antichrist. What we are seeing are exercises which will lead up to major portions of our populace accepting untruth as reality. We must be on guard against what I believe to be a propensity for deception that seems to have emerged.

It is certain that there are moderate Muslims who are not a threat to those who do not believe as they do. However, it is also true that there is a large body of Islamists who are definitely a threat to the non-Islamic world. The nature of Islam and how Islamists interpret their faith is the subject of the next chapter.

Notes

1. www.netaxs.com/people/iris/plohist.htm

2. Lexington Books, 2001

3. Al Sha'ab Cairo, July 1982

4. Medoff, Rafael. *Baksheesh Diplomacy: Secret Negotiations Between American Jewish Leaders and Arab Officials on the Eve of World War II.* Medoff is a scholar in the Jewish studies program at SUNY.

"We must strive to export our revolution throughout the world, and must abandon all idea of not doing so, for not only does Islam refuse to recognize any difference between Muslim countries, it is the champion of all oppressed people.

Moreover, all the powers are intent on destroying us, and if we remain surrounded in a closed circle, we shall certainly be defeated. We must make plain our stance toward the powers and the superpowers and demonstrate to them that, despite the arduous problems that burden us, our attitude to the world is dictated by our beliefs."

—The Ayatollah Khomeini, Iran

The Nature of Islam

Our Present Quandary

A serious clash of cultures is confronting the world. Most Americans did not suspect any plot in the early seventies, when Islamic students began arriving in the U.S.A. to attend universities. In hindsight, the real objective is obvious. Recent events have created more questions regarding Islam than we have answers for. This look at the history of Islam, from the early years of its Prophet Muhammed, seeks to uncover Islam's foundations.

Is Islam really a religion of peace? How do we deal with open statements from Muslim clerics that are designed to sow seeds of fear in the West? Was the Middle East a place of peace before Jewish immigration upset some delicate balance? What are the origins of suicide bombings? And of course, what should our attitude be on the other side of September 11?

The Early Years

The early years of Islam were tumultuous, and at every crossroads on his religious path, Muhammed made violent choices.

Following the Prophet's death, Islam split into two camps. These two camps have, at best, been at odds with one another for centuries; at worst, wars have plagued Muslims, brother fighting against brother.

During the life of Ja'far al-Sadiq, the sixth *Imam* (Muslim cleric) after Ali, husband of Fatima, the daughter of Muhammed, the Fatimad Dynasty also split. Ismail, Ja'far's son, was the originator of an undercurrent within Islam that gave birth to secret societies awash in violent behavior.

As early as five years of age, Muhammed, a fatherless boy, tells of being torn apart by two white robed beings "searching for something" in his intestines. By age six, Muhammed was orphaned when his mother died. His slave girl, Baraka, took him to Abd al-Muttalib's home. His home overlooked the Ka'aba, Mecca's holy object of worship. Here Muhammed was instructed in the ceremonies of moon god worship. About the same time, he also began to accompany camel caravaneers on long journeys.

37

On these long voyages, Muhammed met and talked with Christian priests as well as Jewish rabbis. Some said that they sensed in him a predilection for spiritual matters beyond normal.

Muhammed takes a Wife

In his twenties, Muhammed fell in love with a wealthy woman almost twice his age. Khadijah was forty years old when Muhammed married her.

Muhammed's visionary, idealistic character turned out to be a detriment financially. Rather than being an asset to her, over the years, he dwindled away much of her estate. Earlier in his life, on his long camel caravan quests, Muhammed made a friend by the name of Abu Bakr. Later Abu Bakr became a very successful cloth merchant. This self-made man of means remained friends with Muhammed, and because he believed what Muhammed taught, he financed much of his spiritual quest throughout his life.

The Storm

Perhaps influenced by *hanifs* (desert nomads), who had turned away from idol worship to the worship of one, main god, Muhammed had his first life-changing vision in a mountain cave outside Mecca.

He describes a raging voice with terrible force that demanded he do something he had never learned to do—read. A silk scroll with letters of fire appeared with the message:

Read in the name of your lord, the creator,
    who created man from a clot of blood!
Read, your lord is most merciful,
    for he has taught men by the pen
And revealed the mysteries to them.

Who is Allah Among the Gods?

Multiple gods were worshiped throughout the fertile crescent and Arabia. In fact, 360 gods were worshiped in Mecca in Muhammed's time. Muhammed had one thing in common with Abraham: he began to search for the one true God. In the silence of the desert, it is easy to misinterpret the wonders of creation.

Meteorites are much more visible and remains of fallen asteroids much easier to locate in such desolation. All the circumstances gave natural rise to a cult that worshiped heavenly bodies.

After the flaming shows of falling fire, desert dwellers would find the fallen asteroids and name them as if gods from the sun or moon had come down to earth. Some of those were:

Orotal: Allah Ta'alah, meaning "Almighty."

Al-il-Lat: The goddess Allat, symbolized by a square stone at Taif, east of Mecca.

Al-Uzza: Morning star, a goddess cult that was located at Nakhalah, and the symbol was a gray granite stone in the shape of a thigh bone.

Manah: The goddess of destiny, was a black stone that resided in the village of Qudayd.

These three goddesses were known as daughters of Allah (Sura 53:21-22).

Hubal: A Moabite/Nabatean/North Arabian demon moon god. This reddish brown stone still resides in the Ka'aba at Mecca.

Allah, the spirit who for centuries had seemed content with his place in the Ka'aba, along with 359 other demon gods[1] was suddenly revealing himself to Muhammed as "the only true god." Muhammed complied by rejecting all other gods. Allah was now dictating strict monotheism to his Prophet. Interestingly, Allah's accommodation to polytheism up to this point distinctly differentiates Allah from Jehovah (יהוה Yahweh). Allah tolerated idolatry for centuries, yet Jehovah's response in a polytheistic context was swift and decisive (e.g., when the Ark of the Covenant was brought into the Philistine shrine of Dagon. Without the hands of man, the idol toppled onto his face and broke! 1 Sam. 5:1-12).

Khadijah Tries the Spirits for Muhammed

Muhammed was alarmed by his visions. He was in a state of fearful confusion by what he had seen in the mountain cave. Khadijah sought to console him by working it out logically. Soon thereafter, he sensed the presence of what he described as angelic beings in their bedroom. Khadijah disrobed as if to embrace him sexually. The white robed beings left the room speedily, which helped her convince Muhammed that the beings were angels and not demons who would have stayed to watch them.

Unholy War for An Islamic Empire

Convinced it was a valid visitation of Allah, and greatly relieved, Muhammed began to take on the character of the raging voice from the mountain cave. With great harshness, he relayed the story that all must turn from idolatry to worship one god. He was utterly rejected except for Khadija, Abu Bakr, and Waraqa, Khadija's cousin, who had been an idolater, but was in the practice of worshiping with Christians and Jews as well.

The Smarting of Rejection Hardens Muhammed

Muhammed's message was so utterly rejected in Taif, the town of his childhood, that he escaped, bleeding and being chased by slaves and children. He returned to Mecca, where he encountered a group of Arabs from Yathrib, a town founded by Jewish people some two hundred miles north of Mecca. The Arabs there, having often heard the Jews declare the message of the coming of the Messiah, mistook Muhammed for the Promised One.

A Terrifying Night Vision

In a dream, Muhammed mounted a winged horse with a man's face. The majestic steed rose from Mecca flying north. He touched down on Mt. Sinai, then again in Bethlehem before coming to rest in a place called al-Aqsa, meaning "the furthest mosque."[2] Here, he met Jesus, Abraham, and Moses, who were praying. Next, a ladder descended, and he mounted the ladder to the seventh heaven leaving the others behind. He entered God's house and reported that he was embraced by blinding light. The celestial ladder then brought him back to Mecca with the speed of thought. His new nine-year-old second wife, daughter of Abu Bakr, said his sleeping body never left her side that night.

Glory be to He who carried His servant by night,
from the Holy Mosque to the Furthest Mosque,
the precincts of which we have blessed.
So that we might show him some of our signs.
Surely He is the All-Hearing, the All-Seeing.
—Sura al-Isra' Koran 17:1

The Unsheathing of the Sword

Over time, Muhammed's rage against those who did not accept his new revelations turned the inhabitants of Yathrib against him.

40

They saw that it clearly distinguished the character of Allah from that of Jehovah. Muhammed then decreed that Allah's followers would not face Jerusalem to pray as the Jews did, but that they would face the Ka'aba in Mecca.

His sights then became set on Mecca. He gave orders to his men to attack camel caravans that were traveling to the city. For the first time, some of his men killed caravaneers, and it was during the holy month of pilgrimage. At first, Muhammad was enraged, but soon He received a holy revelation that killing in the holy month was an offense, but to deny Allah was a greater offense, which justified the act.[3]

Muhammed then became convinced that ultimate victory would depend upon the sword. The revelations from this time period are filled with maledictions against his enemies: idolaters, Jews, and Christians. A long list of bloody battles followed, including a Nazi-like massacre at Bani Quraiza. The Jewish inhabitants of the village were marched to a trench with their hands tied behind their backs, then they were beheaded and their bodies toppled into the mass grave.

A Truce for all Time

Muhammed's quest to conquer Mecca proved harder than he expected. Already en route to war, he heard that Mecca expected him and was well armed. He and his men had to camp on a seldom used route at the Oasis of Hudaibiyah, some miles from Mecca, to plot their strategy. He sent emissaries to the heads of the Quraysh tribe, the leaders of Mecca, to strike a deal. The peace treaty was a truce of ten years. The elders agreed that Mecca would be cleared of other pilgrims for three days per year so that Muhammed and his followers could worship at the Ka'aba unhindered in return for not attacking Mecca. The leaders of the Quarysh tribe also stipulated that any converts to Islam from their tribe be returned to their own religion, and that no more converts would be admitted to Islam from their ranks. To ratify the treaty, Muhammed shaved his head and sacrificed seventy camels as was traditional.

With Mecca out of his reach, Muhammed turned his rage against the rest of the world. In Khaybar, a Jewish village north of Medina, the residents who rejected his message were massacred, as well as other Jewish areas: Fadak, Wadi al-Qura, Tayma. Then he attacked the south: Yemen (at that time a Christian nation), the

41

Arabian Peninsula, and Egypt (Cyrus was the Christian Byzantine governor).

He met his match at Mutah, a Christian village at the southern tip of the Dead Sea. For the first time, Muhammed came up against the strength of a Christian army. In a bloody battle, Muhammed's troops lost Zayd and Ja'far (Ali's brother). They then retreated to nurse their wounds. Blinded by his anger, Muhammed turned his rage back on Mecca after only two years of the treaty.

In A.D. 630, Mecca fell to Muhammed like a ripe plum. The treaty had weakened their state of alertness, and the Muslims were able to step onto the scene with ease. Muhammed entered the Ka'aba and destroyed 365 idols, including Hubal the moon god, statues of Abraham and Ishmael, Jesus and the Virgin Mary, along with some angels.

"One Messenger, One Faith, for All the World"

Within two years, Islam had spread under this banner, taking foothold in many places in the world. In A.D. 632, Muhammed died, possibly of malaria. In spite of his death, the conquering continued. In 634, Jerusalem fell to requite the losses from the Christian victory at Mutah. Jerusalem's ruler, the Byzantine Emperor Heraclius, fled to Antioch of Syria, also a Christian nation at the time. In 637, Persia fell to Islam. In 639, Alexandria fell and never fully recovered. After Constantinople, it was considered the greatest city in the world. The Greek Cathedral of St. Marks overlooked the two harbors. Like an expensive watch in the hands of a child, it was destroyed. Alexandria did not function again for a thousand years. Amr ibn al-'As, general of Umar III, was the conqueror. He described the conquest of Alexandria:

> I have captured the city, but I shall forbear describing it. Suffice it to say that I have taken therein four thousand villas, four thousand baths, forty thousand Jews liable to poll-tax and four hundred pleasure palaces fit for kings.

In A.D. 640, Cyprus and Rhodes fell. One of the seven wonders of the world, the Colossus of Rhodes, was hewn down, cut into pieces, and carted away to Syria on the backs of over 900 camels.

The world felt the scourge of Islam.

The Split

Upon Muhammed's death in A.D. 632, Islam split into two camps almost immediately. The two could be categorized as the "friendship camp" and the "kinship camp."

The chart at the end of the chapter details the chronological line of both *Caliphs* (friendship camp) and *Imams* (kinship camp) to a time period some four hundred years later. A violent group was born, who came to be called "the Assassins." The story is intriguing, but more important than that, its residue is still with us today. It was the birth place of *shaheedeen*, "suicide bombers." Political assassination existed before, but the characteristics of those crazed men, who would suffer shame if they survived an assassination, were unique.

Hasan-i Sabah

Hasan-i Sabah, founder of the Assassins, was born in Qumm, Persia in A.D. 1050. Hasan suffered under the heavy hand of a Sunni government. This made him open for an *Ismaili* missionary from Cairo, Egypt, whose message was that the Sunni Muslims were usurpers of the rightful seat of authority. The message of a secret sect of Islam was just what Hasan was looking for.

Friends of Hasan and students of the same missionary were Nizam al-Mulk and Omar Khayyam, the scientist and famed poet, best known for his world-renowned book, *The Rubaiyat of Omar Khayyam*. Some degree of mystery has surrounded the book since it praises the delights of wine. Partaking of wine is strictly against Islamic doctrine.

As young men, the three made a pact that whoever of them became rich and famous first would help the other two. Nizam finally became Vizier to the Sultan and offered Omar and Hasan government positions. Omar declined and was offered instead a pension which allowed him to follow his desire to be a scientist and poet, but Hasan took a high office in the Sultan's court. Soon it was obvious that Hasan was a threat to Nizam. Nizam tricked Hasan, disgracing him in the eyes of the Sultan. Shamed and angry, Hasan fled to Cairo, where he plotted revenge.

School of Vengeance

In 1080, Hasan returned to Persia and sought a place to teach what he called "The New Propaganda." Dogged by Sunni agents, he found a remote fortress in Alamut in the northern mountains. Here he established a school. Alamut castle stood high on a rocky outcrop guarding a broad elevated plain 6,000 feet high and thirty miles long. Perfect for his plan, Hasan overran the castle and began recruiting for his base of operation.

With his new devotees, Hasan began winning the support of peasant villages in the area around the castle. In a small town called Sava, Hasan's missionaries tried to convert a *muezzin* (Islamic Imam who does the call to prayer from the tall minaret) to Ismaili, but he rejected their message. Fearing that he would disclose them to the Sunni authorities, they murdered him. Thus began the job description of the Assassins. The first two Assassins were caught and their bodies dragged publicly through the town until dead.

Hasan claimed a "higher" spiritual source of information that emancipated his followers from traditional Islamic doctrines, already fraught with enough violence. In effect, it was *carte blanche* to live as debauched a lifestyle as could be imagined; violence, murder and even moral lasciviousness were included. The Assassins lived above Koranic law by reason of the fact that they were initiates in the secret society. This may explain Omar Khayyam's praise of wine in *The Rubaiyat*.

Raids by the Assassins on neighboring castles netted the secret society a broad-based foundation from which to work. Europe and the Crusaders felt the blows of the Assassins later.

The idea of "paradise" for suicide bombers had its genesis in the castles of Hasan's Assassins. Young recruits would be drugged during their initiation ceremony with a potion of hashish that when consumed left them comatose for days. Carried into a beautiful garden in the confines of the castle, they awoke to erotic pleasures until they were sated. Later the experience was likened to the reward of the "martyr" should he lose his life during an assassination.[4] Hasan became known as the Old Man of the Mountain.

> The **Old Man** kept at his court such boys of twelve years old as seemed to him destined to become courageous men.
> When the **Old Man** sent them into the garden in groups of four, ten, or twenty, he gave them hashish to drink. They slept for three days, then they were carried sleeping into the garden where he had them awakened.
> When these young men awoke and found themselves in the garden with all these marvelous things, they truly believed

themselves to be in paradise.

And these damsels were always with them in songs and great entertainments; they received everything they asked for, so that they would never have left that garden of their own will.

And when the **Old Man** wished to kill someone, he would take him and say: 'Go and do this thing. I do this because I want to make you return to paradise.'

And the **assassins** go and perform the deed willingly.

— from *The Adventures of Marco Polo*

Suicide Bombers

The world is facing an old threat, not a new one. Now we have a hint at what would cause a young man to strap himself with explosives and commit suicide to murder innocent civilians. It is not as noble as "fighting the oppression and humiliation of occupation" as the Palestinian Authority claims. Three suicide bombers spring up for every one that detonates himself. Parents of these young men, and now young women, do not express regret. Instead, they convey pride in their son or daughter's act of violence to television interviewers. Israel has suffered almost alone in this phenomena, but since September 11, the world has entered a new phase. The world changed that day forever.

Are these suicide bombers half-wits recruited by wicked men? Actually, almost half of the bombers statistically have been found to have a high academic education. The ages seem to hover between 18 and 23, the age when unshakable ideals have not been tempered by the test of time. A high percentage of suicide bombers have come out of the Gaza Strip. These suicide bombers are the pride and joy of Arafat's military arm, since there is almost no defense against them. Someone who is willing to lose his life to take the lives of others is as good as the best missile.

Hamas admitted in a report on the internet website MSNBC recently that suicide bombers undergo months of indoctrination to prepare them for attacks. Some of the parents of recruits often do not know until the day of the suicide attack that their son or daughter has been involved in training. This smacks too closely of Hasan's secret society of Assassins to be comfortable. The clincher is the God connection. All suicide bombers believe in the depths of their beings that they are on a mission from Allah.

The following article documents vital information on the suicide bombers of the Aqsa Martyrs' Brigade.

'Aksa Martyrs' Brigade Bombers, "Educated, Middle-Class"

(London) The suicide bombers of the Aksa Martyrs' Brigade are educated, middle-class and led by a second-year university student in international relations, according to Lebanese Muslim writer Hala Jaber, who recently spent four days with the group. In an article published in the *London Sunday Times* on March 24, Jaber, author of a book on Hizballah, provided a unique insight into the profile, recruitment and mind-set of the killers.

She described traveling to Gaza, where she was blindfolded and driven for 20 minutes to a secret location for her meeting with brigade leader Abu Fatah and a group of brigade members, two of whom have been selected for the next suicide attacks. When she arrived and the blindfold was removed, she found herself in a room strewn with cushions and loosely covered sponge mattresses. Pictures of the Aksa Mosque adorned the walls, and heavy floral curtains blocked the windows.

Shortly afterward, a group of brigade members arrived—all masked, dressed in military fatigues, and carrying Kalashnikov rifles—and sat on the cushions around an oil lamp that illuminated the room.

Abu Fatah said the Aksa Martyrs' Brigade, which is loyal to Palestinian Authority Chairman Yasser Arafat, has no shortage of volunteers. He said a specialist unit is responsible for selecting candidates; another unit is responsible for selecting targets.

Anyone younger than 18 is disqualified, as are married men with children and anyone without a sibling who may be a family's sole breadwinner. Only those who "excel militarily and show steely composure in stressful situations" are likely to be chosen, Abu Fatah said. The young men must be reasonably religious and understand the meaning of "martyrdom and jihad." They should also be of a build and shape that will enable them to mingle with Israelis, disguised if necessary in a *kippa* and wig with *payot* (side curls), as they wait for the moment to strike.

Abu Fatah observes candidates over several days as they go about their business in public and at home. If his assessment is "positive," he informs them of their selection. This is followed by an intense 20-day period of religious study and discussion between Abu Fatah and each candidate, as verses from the Koran about a martyr's attainment of paradise are constantly recited. "The candidate," wrote Jaber, "is reminded of the good fortune that awaits him in the presence of prophets and saints, of the unimaginable beauty of the *houri*, or beautiful young woman, who will welcome him, and of the chance he

46

will have to intercede on behalf of 70 loved ones on doomsday. Not least, he is told of the service he will perform for his fellow countrymen with his sacrifice."

"Of course, I am deeply saddened when I have to use a suicide attacker," Abu Fatah said. "I am very emotional, and at times, I cry when I say good-bye to them. These are educated men who. . . would have had the potential of being constructive members of society."

When the bomber's preparations are complete, another member of the unit arrives to accompany him on the final journey to his target. While his fate has been well-established, the suicide bomber is told the precise nature of the attack only minutes before the operation— whether he will be a bomber, or whether he will attack a target with grenades and guns until he is shot dead. If he is to be a suicide bomber, he straps on a hand-tailored vest filled with about ten kilos of explosive and five kilos of nails and metal about 15 minutes before being dropped off at his target. At that stage, he is then given his final instructions about the precise point at which he should detonate himself.

"The later he knows, the better for the martyr, since he will not have much time to think of the target, nor to experience doubts," Abu Fatah said.

Jaber noted Abu Fatah's tone hardened when asked whether the recent killings of young civilians by suicide bombers in cafes and restaurants could be condoned. "Do you think when an Israeli tank shells a house, it considers whether there are children at home?" he snapped. "There are ugly consequences for both sides in a war."

Religion, wrote Jaber, was a constant topic of conversation throughout the time she spent with the cell. They also watched videos of past "martyrs," analyzing the attacks that had been carried out.

She was introduced to Yunis, 27, an arts graduate, who is next in line to conduct a suicide attack. "His face was covered by a *keffiyeh* to conceal his identity," she wrote. "Yunis spoke first about the paintings of Michelangelo, da Vinci, and Picasso, then abruptly changed the subject and described—with equal passion—his urge to become a martyr."

"We are educated strugglers," he said. "We are not terrorists, and the world should recognize that our acts are not intended to be pure, cold-blooded murder."

Until the day of his mission, Yunis said he would remain engrossed in study of the Koran. He is convinced he has no choice but to follow the path assigned to him, and nothing could sway him from it. "At the moment of executing my mission, it will not be purely to kill Israelis," he said. "The killing is not my ultimate goal, though it is part of the equation. My act will carry a message beyond to those responsible and the world at large that the ugliest thing is for a human being to be forced to live without freedom."

Ahmed, 27, the second suicide attacker she met, had no reservations about his mission. A student from the Gaza Strip, he said he carried the deeds and keys to the family house in Jaffa from which his grandmother was expelled in 1948. "My grandmother represented the history of the Palestinian people," said Ahmed, one of eight children who lives with his mother. "She spoke to us of Jaffa, its grape vines, and the seaside. She instilled in us a love for the home we did not know, and over many tears, recounted old stories of life once upon a time in Palestine."

He was 12 when the first intifada began, and he became determined to fight for "dignity." "I did not join Fatah to kill," he said. "My aim was to try to provide security, if only to my immediate family. Were it not for the occupation, I would not have become a Fatah member in the first place. I let go of my dreams of Jaffa and of ever reclaiming my grandmother's house. I was never a person who sought to annihilate the Israelis. I gave them the land that originally belonged to me, but instead of accepting it graciously, I found them still seeking to deprive me of the right to live freely and peacefully in my tiny few square meters. . . How can I live in a state without sovereignty, where I am forced to show an identity card at an Israeli checkpoint for permission to move? They control our electricity and water supply and our lives, and people still ask why we are rising up."

A band of fighters gathering around him as he spoke nodded in agreement. "I am committed to carry out a martyr's mission to show my rejection of being forced to live under this oppression," he said. "I and many others like me are now prepared and waiting to carry out spectacular attacks against the enemy. We are not afraid and will not cease until they withdraw totally from our areas. You can call us terrorists all you like, but we have faith that justice is on our side and that victory will be ours." [5]

The Myths are Clear

The arguments within the ranks of Islamic leadership itself, as to whether suicide bombers are good Muslims, are swept away with such comments as those of Sheik Yousef al Qaradawi, an Egyptian cleric considered to be "moderate." He says:

They are not suicide operations. These are heroic martyrdom operations, and the heroes who carry them out don't embark on this action out of hopelessness and despair but are driven by an overwhelming desire to cast terror and fear into the hearts of the oppressors." Splitting of hairs over where to blow one's self up simply underlines the absurdity of the issue. Muhammed Sayed Tantawi, a leading doctrinal authority in the Sunni Muslim world, wrote in Egypt's *Al Ahram* that "If a person blows himself up, as in operations that Palestinian youths carry out against those they are fighting, then he is a martyr. But if he explodes himself among babies or women or old people who are not fighting the war, then he is not considered a martyr.

Israel is not the bully on the block then, causing an underdog society to rebel against an oppressor. As in Hasan's time, the accusations of the Assassins fighting against an overwhelming oppressor did not fit. In Israel as well, the accusations of a downtrodden populace rising up against oppression does not fit. In light of the history of assassination and the philosophy thereof, Israel is only a victim of an age-old philosophy with its roots in Islam.

Suicide bombing by Islamic militants also terrorized Sudan under the umbrella of the British before it came to Israel. The wool over the eyes of viewers of major media is being lifted as we uncover the roots of the problems.

Israel has been loath to use methods that the British used in Sudan, i.e., wrapping the suicide bomber's body parts in pigskin to assure that no ceremonially proper Islamic burial could take place. This assured the assassin that he would miss his trip to paradise. It also was credited with bringing suicide terrorism to a halt in Sudan under the British colonial government.

With more puzzle pieces in place, it becomes easier to see the slant being placed on events in Israel.

Notes

1. This number comes from Waqqidi's biography of Muhammed, written 120 years after Muhammed's death.
2. Note: Jerusalem is never mentioned in the Koran.
3. Koran Sura ii.
4. Yule, Henry. *The Book of Sir Marco Polo, the Venetian*, 1875.
5. Article by Douglas Davis, *The Jerusalem Post*, Mar. 25, 2002.

Unholy War for An Islamic Empire

Time Line of Successive Islamic Dynasties after Muhammed

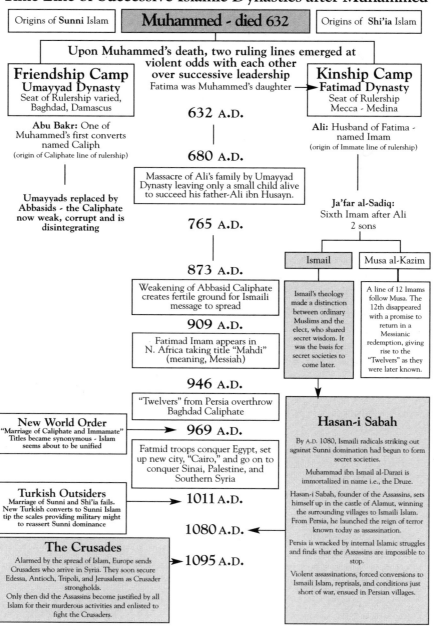

| Origins of **Sunni** Islam | **Muhammed - died 632** | Origins of **Shi'ia** Islam |

Upon Muhammed's death, two ruling lines emerged at violent odds with each other over successive leadership
Fatima was Muhammed's daughter

Friendship Camp
Umayyad Dynasty
Seat of Rulership varied,
Baghdad, Damascus

Kinship Camp
Fatimad Dynasty
Seat of Rulership
Mecca - Medina

632 A.D.

Abu Bakr: One of Muhammed's first converts named Caliph
(origin of Caliphate line of rulership)

Ali: Husband of Fatima - named Imam
(origin of Immate line of rulership)

680 A.D.

Massacre of Ali's family by Umayyad Dynasty leaving only a small child alive to succeed his father-Ali ibn Husayn.

Umayyads replaced by Abbasids - the Caliphate now weak, corrupt and is disintegrating

Ja'far al-Sadiq:
Sixth Imam after Ali
2 sons

765 A.D.

| Ismail | Musa al-Kazim |

873 A.D.

Weakening of Abbasid Caliphate creates fertile ground for Ismaili message to spread

Ismail's theology made a distinction between ordinary Muslims and the elect, who shared secret wisdom. It was the basis for secret societies to come later.

A line of 12 Imams follow Musa. The 12th disappeared with a promise to return in a Messianic redemption, giving rise to the "Twelvers" as they were later known.

909 A.D.

Fatimad Imam appears in N. Africa taking title "Mahdi" (meaning, Messiah)

946 A.D.

"Twelvers" from Persia overthrow Baghdad Caliphate

New World Order
"Marriage of Caliphate and Immamate"
Titles became synonymous - Islam seems about to be unified

969 A.D.

Fatmid troops conquer Egypt, set up new city, "Cairo," and go on to conquer Sinai, Palestine, and Southern Syria

Hasan-i Sabah

By A.D. 1080, Ismaili radicals striking out against Sunni domination had begun to form secret societies.

Muhammad ibn Ismail al-Darazi is immortalized in name i.e., the Druze.

Turkish Outsiders
Marriage of Sunni and Shi'ia fails. New Turkish converts to Sunni Islam tip the scales providing military might to reassert Sunni dominance

1011 A.D.

Hasan-i Sabah, founder of the Assassins, sets himself up in the castle of Alamut, winning the surrounding villages to Ismaili Islam. From Persia, he launched the reign of terror known today as assassination.

1080 A.D.

Persia is wracked by internal Islamic struggles and finds that the Assassins are impossible to stop.

The Crusades
Alarmed by the spread of Islam, Europe sends Crusaders who arrive in Syria. They soon secure Edessa, Antioch, Tripoli, and Jerusalem as Crusader strongholds.
Only then did the Assassins become justified by all Islam for their murderous activities and enlisted to fight the Crusaders.

1095 A.D.

Violent assassinations, forced conversions to Ismaili Islam, reprisals, and conditions just short of war, ensued in Persian villages.

The Flow Chart of Islam

The facing flow chart shows the split, just after Muhammed's death, into the "friendship" camp and the "kinship" camp.

The left hand column denotes the *Caliphate* line of rulership, known later as the Umayyad Dynasty. The right hand column, the *Imamate*, known later as the Fatimad Dynasty (*Caliphate* and *Imamate* are derivatives of the titles of the respective leadership' *Caliph* and *Imam*). The two are also known as Sunni Islam (Umayyad) and Shi'ia Islam (Fatimad).

Ali, the husband of Mohammed's daughter, Fatima, was named Imam and contested for rulership of the growing spiritual kingdom of Islam. In A.D. 680, members of the Umayyad Dynasty, massacred Ali's entire family. The killers missed one son, Ali Ibn Husayn, the youngest son of Ali. He succeeded his father in the Imamate of the Fatimad Dynasty.

The sixth Imam after Ali, Ja'far al-Sadiq, fathered two sons wherein the Fatimad Dynasty also underwent a split. Ismail, and Musa al-Kazim, the sons born to Ja'far, birthed yet another faction within an already fractured religion.

Musa's line became known as "The Twelvers" from a line of twelve Imams, of which the twelfth disappeared mysteriously. Legends grew up around the incident, cloaked in promise that the Imam would return in some degree of messianic redemption.

Ismail's brand of Islam birthed secret societies, in that it taught that there was an "elect" who were free from the laws that governed regular Muslims. With Islamic law suspended, Ismailis were free to do what their appetites dictated.

An existing community of the Middle East, the Druze, also had their genesis here from Muhammed ibn Ismail al-Darazi (from whom the title "Druze" is a derivative).

This brings us to the time of Hasan-i Sabah.

Hasan's inability to cope with rejection drove him bitterly to form the sect preaching Ismaili Islam with missionary zeal in Persia. From bitterness to bitterness, Hasan took his followers on a lawless path, nourishing their minds on being "the elect" and promises of paradise for obedience to his wishes.

From Hasan's lofty hideaway, came one of the world's great evils—the Assassins. Our own suicide bombers hearken back to Hasan's wicked teachings of exclusivity and superiority.

51

"Oh brothers! Let us not regard this holy and sacrificial war as a war between Arabs and Israel. Let us regard it as a war of all Moslems together against Jews and their leaders. It is the responsibility of all the Islamic governments with their peoples, with all their forces, and potential, to aid and support fedayeen [guerrillas] on the lines of fire."

—The Ayatollah Khomeini, from his book, *Confronting Israel*

Basic Tenets of Islam

We should understand that Allah is not just another name for Jehovah, the God that Jews and Christians worship. The two differ significantly, and these characteristic differences are evident in the tenets of their respective faiths.

Islam - means "submission" or "surrendering all to Allah." A Muslim practices Islam, submitting to the will of Allah. The Muslim clergy cannot talk or write about his faith to non-Muslims, nor question the teaching of the Prophet Muhammed.

Superiority - Islam teaches that it is superior to all other religions, and a Muslim is superior to all others. Islam cannot be influenced by outside sources. Allah is the "all-powerful," whose will is supreme and determines man's fate.

Muhammed taught that Allah first gave the revelation of truth to the Jews, who perverted it. Then he gave the revelation to the Christians, who also perverted it, so he gave it to Muhammed, the last of the prophets, who supersedes all others.

Muhammed stated that Allah had spoken before to Abraham, Moses, Jesus, and other prophets, known in the biblical record of Judaism and Christianity, but that Allah had given him the one, true, and superior revelation unto which all others must submit. Christianity and Judaism are considered altered forms of Islam, and while Christians and Jews are called "People of the Book," they are inferior and therefore second-class citizens (*dhimmis*) in an Islamic state and must submit to Islamic law.

To the Muslim, all that is relevant in life is Islamic. All Old and New Testament Bible characters and events are a part of Muslim history. Adam, Noah, Abraham, Moses, and even Jesus were all good Muslims, hence mosques (Islamic places of prayer) were placed at all Jewish and Christian holy places in the Holy Land. For example, during the Jordanian occupation of the West Bank from 1948-1967, a mosque was built in Manger Square in Bethlehem, which is predominately a Christian town. In a statement of superiority, the minaret was built higher than the church bell towers.

Scripture - The bases of the Islamic faith are the Koran (recitations) regarded as the uncreated, eternal word of Allah, and *Hadith* (traditions), containing the Sunna (the Way or Path) exemplified in the sayings and deeds of the Prophet. The Koran is

53

a mixture of desert folklore and customs, revelations of Muhammed, and elements of teaching from Judaism and Christianity.

The most important unit in Islam is the *umma*. It is the "community" of faith, sustained by faithful adherence and practice of the words written in the Koran and the Sunna. This can be very disconcerting to the non-Muslim, when we consider the exclusiveness and militancy of many of these teachings. Here are a few examples of what Muhammed said:

- Swords are the keys of paradise.
- A sword is sufficient witness.
- Expel the Jews and the Christians from the Arabian Peninsula.
- The unbeliever and the one who kills him will never meet in Hell.
- A day and a night of fighting on the frontier is better than a month of fasting and prayer.

Islamic Practice of Faith: "The Five Pillars"

1) Witness, which is proclaiming, "There is no god but Allah and Muhammed is his prophet."

2) Prayer, to be performed five times a day, facing Mecca and the sacred Ka'aba.

3) *Zakat* (almsgiving) to the poor and the mosque (house of worship).

4) *Sawm* (fasting) during daylight hours in the month of Ramadan.

5) *Haj* (Pilgrimage) to Mecca at least once in one's lifetime.

Most sources add a Sixth Pillar, which is *jihad* (meaning "exertion" in the way of God or holy war). *Jihad* has a personal connotation in the continuing inner "exertion" against the straying tendencies of individual Muslims from the tenets of Islam and also a more global connotation, where *jihad* is an ongoing warfare against evil and the enemies of Islam and the struggle in the world to spread Islamic truth. With *jihad*, Islam is to spread the *Dar al-Islam*, "The Household of Submission," meaning the territories governed by Muslims under *Shari'a* law (Islamic law), in place of the *Dar al-Harb*, the "Household of Warfare," those lands lacking the security and guidance of Allah. Any Muslim killed in *jihad* ascends to paradise immediately.

Predestination - Everything that happens is the predestined will of Allah, which leads to fatalism. *Inshallah,* "God wills it," is the byword in the Arab world. Submission is demanded. Prayer is submission, and a Muslim must pray five times a day. Prayer is not created by the individual, but is rote memory from the Koran with preset physical gestures.

Sin Concept - There is no sin concept in Islam, but the concept of shame, honor versus dishonor to the *umma* (community). Sin, according to Islam, does not change man's inner nature, nor does it effect God. God is not Savior in Islam, because man is not a sinner. There is no absolute right or wrong, but situation ethics, and, therefore, no need for divine forgiveness and no doctrine or need of salvation or redemption. The situation determines the action, not a standard of absolute right and wrong. Al-Ghazzali, a Muslim theologian wrote: "Know that a lie is not wrong in itself. If a lie is the only way of obtaining a good result, it is permissible. We must lie when truth leads to unpleasant results."

Islam believes that all humans have a *fitra* (conscience). They believe that Allah and the Koran will bring men back to truth, and that man, even non-Muslims, inherently thirst for justice and balance. Islam teaches that Allah sends prophets to guide man, and if he follows, he will end in heaven. If he does not, his end is the final judgment of hell fire. The major theme of the Koran is not love, but Allah's strict justice, according to the teachings of Muhammed.

Non-Progressive - Christianity and Judaism are progressive, always moving forward to express and encourage that which is good. Islam is circular, always seeking to return to the "pure Islam" practiced by Muhammed. There is a resistance to anything progressive, called *bid'a* (heresy), particularly if it is perceived as detracting from pure Islamic practice. This was the perception which led to the ousting of the Shah of Iran, who introduced Iran to the twentieth century, as well as the brutal murder of Anwar Sadat, who dared to make peace with Israel.

No Individualism - The good of the *umma* is the main interest of Islam, not the individual. There is no true individualism, and the individual is unimportant. Personal initiative is not good. A non-Muslim can live in a Muslim country as a *dhimmi,* a second or third class citizen, and must submit and not offend Islam or a Muslim. Nothing can be superior to Islam. A church steeple cannot be higher than a mosque minaret, a Christian cannot rise in overall rank above a Muslim, e.g., the principal of a school, head of state, etc.

History - In Islam, all truth is measured by the Koran, the Prophet, and his Sunna. The average Muslim believes the Bible has been corrupted to hide the predictions of the coming of Muhammed. The Koran mentions the names of some of the Bible prophets and gives an interpretation of some Bible events. But, most Muslims do not know the historical context of Bible events or pre-Islamic history in general. All history and truth for the Muslim is placed in an Islamic "time warp." History is unimportant for the Muslim, because Muhammed is the seal of the prophets, and the Koran contains all the revelation that he needs to satisfy Allah.

Basis of Government Policy and Law - The Koran is the constitution of a Muslim nation. The government and theology are the same. There can be no true democracy, nor the idea of separation of Church and State. Governments become dictatorial and theocratic as expressed by the leader, the servant of Muhammed. For example, even though Iraq is called a "democratic republic," Iraq is pure despotism. Its current President-for-Life, Saddam Hussein, gained power by personally shooting his predecessor in the head and rules by the bullet, not the ballot.

Islam seeks to have *Shari'a* (Muslim law), based on the Koran and Sunna, enforced in every Islamic nation. It has not been revised since the Dark Ages, when it was written. It is meant to keep the people in fear and subjection by including punishments still practiced in many Islamic countries, such as public beheadings, chopping off hands, and whippings in the town square. Slavery is legal in Muslim law. Even non-Muslims in Islamic lands must abide by Muslim law.

Territory - The spreading of Islam is through territorial conquest. Once Islam has controlled a territory or area, it is always regarded as Islamic. If the territory is lost to non-Muslims, then the nature of Allah has been diminished, and the territory must be retaken.

In relations between nations, there is the concept of *Dar al-Salaam* "House of Peace"—Muslim nation to Muslim nation, and *Dar al-Harb* "House of War"—Muslim nation to non-Muslim nation. You can never get out of the "House of War" unless you become a

Muslim nation. A nation is Muslim when its leader is a Muslim.

Peace - True peace cannot be achieved between Muslim and non-Muslim nations. The concept of *jihad* is always in force to spread Islam through territorial conquest or to reclaim "Islamic" territory that has been lost to Islam, thus not diminishing the kingdom of Allah (e.g., Israel and Lebanon). Judaism and Christianity both hold the view that "Vengeance is Mine, says the LORD." In Islam, it is the duty of the Muslim community to avenge Allah. Therefore, there can be no peace with non-Muslims, as the West understands peace i.e., as coexistence between societies or pluralism within society. All else is inferior to Islam, never equal.

Israel - Islam can never accept Israel! First and foremost, Israel is governed by Jews, making it a Jewish state, thus non-Muslim. This places Israel into the House of War. Muslims conquered this area as far back as A.D. 634. Therefore, Allah was diminished when his territory was "taken" by non-Muslims, and it must be reclaimed for Allah by the Muslim community. It is immaterial that the Land of Israel was given to the Jews in covenant with God, or that the Jews have prior historical or religious claims. Remember, according to Islamic teaching, Jews and Christians perverted Allah's word, and therefore hold no authority over the Muslim.

Did Egypt Make Peace?

In four wars, Egypt joined attempts to eradicate Israel: in the 1948 War of Independence, in 1956, again in 1967, and also in 1973. Finally, the late Egyptian President Anwar Saddat signed a peace agreement with Israel in 1973. It is a shaky peace. Terrorists still enter Gaza from Egyptian soil, seemingly undeterred by Egypt. Denouncements of Israel's activities still come from Egypt in U.N. sessions.

Why, then, did the late Anwar Sadat of Egypt sign a peace treaty with Israel? Under Islam, you can make an armistice while your enemy is stronger than you, if an armistice is good for the *umma*. However, when the enemy is perceived to be weaker, war is imperative and demanded by the Koran.

Islamists seem free to travel at will throughout these Middle East desert lands. It is nothing new; it is the way of the desert. Lawrence of Arabia was in love with the desert and its people. His colorful accounts describe the volatile region to which the Jewish people returned.

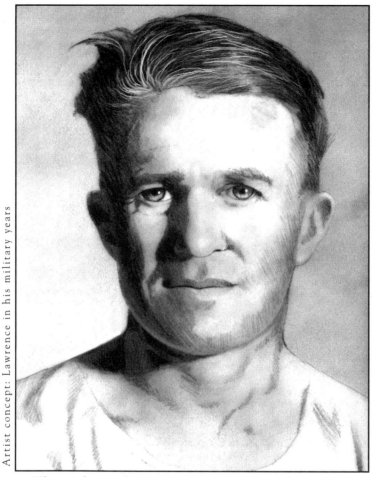

"Throughout the campaign, they had been
bothered with these same blood feuds, barely
suspended by Faisal's authority. It was a constant
strain keeping enemies apart, trying to keep
the hostile clans in friendly rivalry on
separate ventures, making them camp
always with a neutral clan between, and
avoiding any suspicion of favoritism."
—Robert Graves,
Lawrence and the Arabs

Lessons from Lawrence

The British soldier, T.E. Shaw, A.K.A. Lawrence of Arabia, is a controversial figure, some say was given to exaggeration. His stories are certainly embellished with a romantic aura, but he provides us an excellent window into the panorama of the Middle East in the early twentieth century. An excellent biography is *Lawrence of the Arabs,* written by Robert Graves. For those who appreciate a chronological story line, it is the best reading. Lawrence's own reports of incidents have come under scrutiny by some. Most of the questions center themselves around distances, time to travel those distances, and other exaggerations that analysts question. Graves offers a level-headed biography of the man.

But, Lawrence offered us a flavor of the Middle East that is easily lost in a dry historical account. It is a given that he is controversial in some areas, but there has never been a question about the character of the tribes that Lawrence joined himself to between 1910 and 1920.

Lawrence's final mandate was to play an important role in the overthrow of the Ottoman Empire and deliver the land into the hands of the Arabs after driving out the Turks. He did not accept the mission out of duty alone, for Lawrence had a love affair with the desert, its architecture, and its people, since early in his life.

For final exams in Jesus College at Cambridge University, he presented a paper to supplement his regular work entitled, *The Influence of the Crusades on the Medieval Military Architecture of Europe.* He was acquainted with most of the castles and fortifications of England and France. The castles of Syria and Palestine were calling him to examine them.

His first trip happened in the summer of 1909. Armed with rudimentary Arabic and little else, he went "walking" across Syria and the Middle East. He was thought to have taken leave of his mind in using his own two feet to make such a trip, but Lawrence proved to live outside the parenthesis of normal life most of his days.

Early on, Lawrence became enamored with the Bedouin and their love for the vast emptiness of the desert, the dry, hot empty desert air, unencumbered with the perfumes of civilization, imprinted itself upon him. He was changed for many years to come.

The interesting thing about Lawrence's time and ours is that the facts on the ground have changed little. Tribes, clans, peasant villagers, and Druze, along with simple desert brigands, who were then at deadly odds with each other, have only changed titles. Presently, they are called "terror" cells, "freedom fighters," and "liberation" organizations, but the temperature between them has not changed. The same play is being acted out on the same stage. Blood feuds still abound and unity is simply a necessity to fight a larger enemy—now "the Zionist entity."

Lawrence's battles centered themselves around the Turkish-built railway from Damascus to Mecca. It was the artery of life for the Turkish Empire and was built in order that the Turks could unify the Arab lands under the Turkish banner. The rail line had to be targeted over and over again for destruction by Lawrence's rag-tag bands. The rail line ran south from Damascus to Arar and Deraa, which were Druze-held territory. These towns are straight east inland from the Sea of Galilee. The line then traveled south from Nisib to Minifer and present day Amman, Jordan.

From Amman, the rails ran between an area known as the Desolate Desert to the east and the mountains of Jordan on the west. The longest stretch was to the town of Maan, which is halfway between the Dead Sea and the Red Sea. This is a two-hour journey by modern automobile today. Each of these areas were peopled by tribes mostly at odds with each other. Lawrence had secured the son of Hussein, the Emir Feisal, the Sherif of Mecca, into his allegiance. Hussein, had been taken hostage by the last Sultan of Turkey, Abdul Hamid. Feisal and Nuri, another Arab of importance, were Lawrence's constant companions in the drama that took almost a decade to play out. An excerpt from Graves' biographical account is quite enlightening about the strife present between the clans.

There was nearly a serious accident here, for they were invited to guest at the tent of one of the Emir Nuri's blood-enemies. Fortunately, the man himself was absent, so Lawrence's party accepted: Nuri, when he arrived, would find himself temporary host of his enemy's family and have to obey the rules. (Desert law required three days of hospitality under the protection of the host.) It was a great relief. Throughout the campaign they had

been bothered with these same blood-feuds, barely
suspended by Feisal's authority. It was a constant strain
keeping enemies apart, trying to keep the hostile clans in
friendly rivalry on separate ventures, making them camp
always with a neutral clan between them, and avoiding
any suspicion of favoritism. As Lawrence comments, the
campaign in France (WWI going on at the same time)
would have been harder to control if each division,
almost each brigade, of the British Army had hated every
other one with a deadly hatred and had fought at every
chance meeting. However, Feisal, Nasir and he had
managed successfully for two years and the end was only
a few days off. [1]

Lawrence's choice of warriors was colorful but limited. The
Arabic word for desert is *badiya*, from which comes the term
Bedouin. Arab Bedouin are the nomads of the desert. Tied to
nothing but the desert and its starkness, their mental processes
differ refreshingly to the outside casual observer—they are
indeed romantic in their rustic attack of life and stark lack of
needs. How different when you are dependent upon them. They
can be sorely disappointing and irritating. Lawrence found that
out many times over.

Blood feuds were not rare. Long standing hatreds between Arab
clans and tribes made Lawrence's job a tedious, and at times,
dangerous one. The volatility of the Bedouin is hard to understand
in light of the silent desert from which they come.

Lawrence acted, in some ways, as the barometer of British
attitude toward Arabs. The British were particularly taken with
the charm of Bedouin customs and were overly apt to protect
them like some kind of museum piece to be viewed and enjoyed at
whim.

These nomads do not refer to themselves as Bedouin, but more
often as Arabs. The term originally referred to the wandering
nomadic tribes of the Arabian Peninsula. Most Bedouin claim
descent from the early tribes of the peninsula.

Throughout history, Bedouin tribes raided lands neighboring
their vast areas of wandering. Classically, the nomadic Bedouin
lived in tents, raised sheep and camels, and often raided trade
caravans for a living. In their raids over hundreds of years, some
portions of the clans settled in villages that had been conquered

61

and looted and left the nomadic way of life, but are still considered Bedouin. Many villages in Iraq, Syria, Jordan, and Palestine are fully or partly of Bedouin descent.

From Where Did The Nomads Descend?

Predating Islam and its influence on the nomads by twelve hundred years, Jeremiah had an experience with the Recabites, a Bedouin tribe that became the audio visual tool which God used to teach an important lesson of obedience to His people. The Recabites obeyed a simple word of good advice from an ancestor, and it became tradition to them—transcending generations. God used this lesson to warn the Israelites, who were in possession of much more authoritative   advice, i.e., the "Holy Word" from heaven, but would not obey it.

The instance offers us a look into nomadic Bedouin tribes before Islamic influence:

This is the word of the LORD that came to Jeremiah from the LORD during the reign of Jehoiakim son of Josiah king of Judah:

"Go to the Recabite family and invite them to come to one of the side rooms of the house of the LORD and give them wine to drink."

So I went to get Jaazaniah the son of Jeremiah, the son of Habazziniah, and his brothers and his sons—the whole family of the Recabites. I brought them into the house of the LORD, into the room of the sons of Hanan son of Igdaliah the man of God. It was next to the room of the officials that was over that of Ma'aseiah son of Shallum the doorkeeper. Then I set bowls full of wine and some cups before the men of the Recabite family and said to them, "Drink some wine."

But they replied, "We do not drink wine, because our forefather Jonadab son of Recab gave us this command: 'Neither you nor your descendants must ever drink wine. Also you must never build houses, sow seed, or plant vineyards; you must never have any of these things, but must always live in tents. Then you will live a long time in the land where you are nomads.' We have obeyed everything that our forefather Jonadab son of Recab commanded us. Neither we nor our wives nor our sons and daughters have ever drunk wine or built houses to live in or had vineyards, fields or crops. We have lived in tents and have fully obeyed everything our forefather Jonadab commanded us.

"But when Nebuchadnezzar king of Babylon invaded this land, we said, 'Come, we must go to Jerusalem to escape the Babylonian and Aramean armies.' So we have remained in Jerusalem."

Then the word of the LORD came to Jeremiah, saying: "This is what the LORD Almighty, the God of Israel, says: Go and tell the men of Judah and the people of Jerusalem, 'Will you not learn a lesson and obey My words?' declares the LORD. 'Jonadab son of Recab ordered his sons not to drink wine and this command has been kept. To this day they do not drink wine, because they obey their forefather's command. But I have spoken to you again and again, yet you have not obeyed Me. Again and again I sent all My servants and prophets to you. They said, "Each of you must turn from your wicked ways and reform your actions; do not follow other gods to serve them. Then you will live in the land I have given you and your fathers." But you have not paid attention or listened to Me. The descendants of Jonadab the son of Recab have carried out the command their forefathers gave them, but these people have not obeyed Me.' "Therefore, this is what the LORD God Almighty, the God of Israel, says: 'Listen! I am going to bring on Judah and on everyone living in Jerusalem every disaster I pronounced against them. I spoke to them, but they did not listen; I called to them, but they did not answer.'"

Then Jeremiah said to the family of the Recabites, "This is what the LORD Almighty, the God of Israel, says: 'You have obeyed the command of your forefather Jonadab and have followed all his instructions and have done everything he ordered. Therefore, this is what the LORD Almighty, the God of Israel, says: "Jonadab the son of Recab will never fail to have a man to serve Me."'"

Jeremiah 35:1-19

It is amazing, but Bedouins—the descendants of these nomadic people—still follow the advice of their ancestor about wine and living in tents. Their attitudes, though, toward their neighbors has been altered by conversion to Islam and its teachings about the doomed fate of infidels.

Bedouin Customs

Things have changed somewhat, and today few fully nomadic tribes remain as in Lawrence's day in the desert. The convenience of acquiring food from markets and water from dependable sources has taken its toll on the nomadic lifestyle. Raising feed for their flocks is easier as well than trying to graze over vast stretches of land to find enough food to satisfy large quantities of livestock.

The government system of the Bedouin is still intact. In fact, when butting up against civilization, rough edges in Bedouin lifestyle are trying situations for civilized leaders.

The most basic element of the Bedouin is the family unit. It is sometimes quite large. Families are tied together in a tribe, and when the tribe becomes large enough, a large tribal federation forms. Over this federation, a sheik is elected who wields wide authority over his tribe members. Bedouin customs, at times, come crashing head to head with modern governmental methodology.

The curious customs of the Bedouin include a degree of hospitality unknown anywhere in the world and is only rivaled in curiosity by their tribal law. Strict regulations govern everything from how to treat a guest to what to do with a wayward girl. The court and criminal justice lie in the hands of the sheik and his advisors. Honor killing and blood feuds are practiced to this day and cause great consternation to civil governments that rub shoulders with Bedouin.

A most curious institution, called *sulha* (table), is the court of law. Over a meal, transgressors will be set before mediating tribal judges and elders. Negotiations will be arrived at over a course of many hours of deliberations, and food, of course. Once a judgment is passed, whether it be the honor killing of a girl for disgracing her family, or a blood-feud, or a payment of compensation for someone injured by another, the subject is forbidden to be brought up in public again.

Threads of this ancient custom can be found in our own Bible. King David recorded in his most famous Psalm 23, "You prepare a table before me in the presence of my enemies" (v. 5). This is not a picnic where your enemies can see you and be envious of your provision from the Lord, but rather, it is a table of reconciliation.

The Bedouin are being modernized, perhaps against their

will. Ancient trade routes are being replaced by modern highways, rendering raiding parties a thing of the past. But, just as archaeologists can find a modern blender in an Israeli home and not five miles away find a bowl from 1000 B.C., the modernization of the Bedouin does not always do away with the nomadic desert mind-set. They can be found in operation in a modern looking people who understand the world through the filter of desert life.

A Word from Wadi Rumm

The harshness of the desert and the matching harshness of the desert tribes, with which Lawrence traipsed across the burning sands, was challenged by an incident that happened deep in the desert at Wadi Rumm.

Some miles east of the Red Sea port city of Akaba, a *wadi* (canyon), walled in by red stone mountains that rise like skyscrapers, penetrates the desert and leads to a narrow gully equipped with springs. A spring is a very rare and precious find in the desert. Rocks the size of small houses have fallen from the towering mountains, giving the *wadi* a surrealistic feeling.

The luxury of bathing in the desert is just that, a rare luxury. The springs at Rumm refresh a man's soul. According to Graves' account, Lawrence had removed all his clothing, laid them on a rock in the sun with the hope that the heat would drive the lice from them, and was enjoying the cool water. Lying on his back in a small waterfall, he let the water wash away weeks of filth and dirt.

Suddenly Lawrence noticed that an old ragged man with a wizened face, tired and haggard but noble, had sat down on his clothing on the rock. He was talking to himself. Lawrence overheard him say, "The love is from God, and of God, and towards God." It was the most startling thing Lawrence had ever heard while in the desert of Arabia.

The Islamic concept of God—and any connection with divine love—was foreign to the country. Allah was powerful, Allah was judge of all, one was expected to fear Allah, and most of all, one submitted all to Allah, but never love. Love was a foreign, Hellenistic concept when uttered in the same breath with Allah.

The incident deeply impressed Lawrence and remained with him ever after.

Inquiring later about the man, the other tribesmen claimed he was a lunatic. They claimed that he followed their clans but constantly remained on the periphery. He never troubled himself about food or shelter and accepted what anyone would offer him out of pity for his extreme poverty.

Is Allah's Character Love?

Why should Lawrence have been so surprised? Is love in the Koran? Does Allah exhibit love? The word love does appear in the Koran eighty-three times. Interestingly though, very few of those instances come close to our biblical concept of love. I have taken those few times and placed them in the context of the chapters to show you that the concept which we understand of love does not exist in the Koran.

Out of eighty-three instances where the word "love" is found in the Koran, twenty-three times it is listing who Allah does not love. All the rest have to do with various other things that are loved, i.e., money, treasures, etc. Thirteen other instances I have listed below, I have tried to keep the context of their setting so that you might see the difference between the concept of love in the Koran and the Bible.

Whom Does Allah Love?

One who participates in ritual cleansing

2.222 And they ask you about menstruation. Say: It is a discomfort; therefore keep aloof from the women during the menstrual discharge and do not go near them until they have become clean; then when they have cleansed themselves, go in to them as Allah has commanded you; surely Allah loves those who turn much [to him], and he loves those who purify themselves.

One who hates Jews and Christians

The instance in 3:31 is couched in hatred for people of the Book. Abandoning the errors of the Christian faith and the Jewish faith are the subject. The faults speak of our theological errors:

3:4: Before this as guidance for men, and has sent the criterion (of falsehood and truth).

3.31 Say: If you love Allah, then follow me, Allah will love you and forgive you your faults, and Allah is Forgiving, Merciful.

One who shows superiority over Christians and Jews

3:119 Lo! You are they who will love them while they do not love you, and you believe in the Book (in) the whole of it; and when they meet you they say: We believe, and when they are alone, they bite the ends of their fingers in rage against you. Say: Die in your rage; surely Allah knows what is in the breasts.

One who shows bravery in Jihad

The context is that during *jihad*, some Muslims were fearful to go fight "to the death" against those mentioned in verse 151. Allah loves the brave who wage *jihad* against "infidels" (unbelievers), most likely Christians and Jews who were living near Mecca in Muhammed's time.

Three verses lead up to the conclusion:

3:146 - 148 Many a seeker after God has fought in the way of God by the side of many an apostle, undaunted by disaster, and did not disgrace themselves;—verily God loves those who are steadfast. Nor did they say ought but: "O our Lord forgive us our sins and excesses in our acts, and steady our steps, and help us against unbelieving people. So, God rewarded them in this world, and a better reward awaits them in the next; for God loves those who do good."

3:151 We shall strike terror into the hearts of unbelievers for ascribing compeers to God for which He has sent down on sanction. Hell is their residence, the evil abode of the unjust: ["compeers" i.e., the fact that we call Jesus, God's Son and the Jewish people who looked for Ezra—a type of Messianic figure in that time period].

3.159 Thus it is due to mercy from Allah that you deal with them gently, and had you been rough, hardhearted, they would certainly have dispersed from around you; pardon them therefore and ask pardon for them, and take counsel with them in the affair; so when you have decided, then place your trust in Allah; surely Allah loves those who trust.

Jews and Christians who convert to Islam

Love is offered to those who "do good." The good here is in context of pressuring first Jews, then Christians, to accept the "right way" presented by Allah through the Prophet Muhammed.

5:13 When they dishonored their pledge [forced acceptance of Islam] we condemned them, and hardened their hearts. So they distort the words of the Scripture out of context, and have forgotten some of what they were warned against. You will always hear of treachery on their part, except that of a few. But forbear and forgive them [the few] for God loves those who do good.

Other instances in this chapter, called "The Dinner Table," follow the same theme of Jews and Christians who do not believe. The directive is not to befriend Jews and Christians at all:

5:51 O believers, do not hold Jews and Christians as your allies. They are allies of one another; and anyone who makes them his friends is surely one of them; and God does not guide the unjust.

One who takes heed for himself

Sometimes the chapter is called "Repentance" and sometimes "The Immunity." The opening of the chapter says that God is not bound by any contract with an idolater:

9:3 . . . God is not bound (by any contract) to idolaters, nor is his apostle.

9:4 Except those idolaters with whom you have a treaty, who have not failed you in the least, nor helped anyone against you. Fulfill your obligations to them during the term (of the treaty). God loves those who take heed for themselves.

One who chooses the right Mosque

Mosques built by desert Arabs, classified as hypocrites, were not to be entered:

9:108 Never set foot in that place. Only a mosque whose foundations have been laid from the very first on godliness is worthy of your visiting it. There you will find men who wish to be purified; and God loves those who are pure.

One who denies that Allah has a Son

This chapter is dedicated to Mary, but the story is a composite of many biblical characters plus some additions unfamiliar to students of the Bible. The mention of love here is to those who realize that God cannot have a Son:

> 19:35 It does not behoove God to have a son. Too immaculate is He! When He decrees a thing He has only to say: "Be", and it is.
>
> 19:91-96 For they [Christians] have attributed a son to Ar-Rahman, [a name for Allah] when it does not behoove the Merciful to have a son. There is no one in the heavens and the earth but comes before Ar-Rahman in all obedience. He has counted them and calculated their number. Everyone of them will come before Him all alone on the Day of Resurrection. Surely Ar-Rahman will show love for those who believe and do the right.

Moses

This instance comes closest to any semblance of real love in a story about Moses:

> 20:39 Put him [Moses] in a wooden box and cast it in the river . . . We bestowed Our love on you that you may be reared under Our eyes.

One who fights against an erring brother

Here, war of Muslim brother against Muslim brother is addressed:

> 49.9 And if two parties of the believers quarrel, make peace between them; but if one of them acts wrongfully towards the other, fight that which acts wrongfully until it returns to Allah's command; then if it returns, make peace between them with justice and act equitably; surely Allah loves those who act equitably.

One who is just to only those who are just

This instance stands to justify holy war against Israel or any nation that has conquered a land once considered to belong to Allah:

> 60:8 God does not forbid you from being kind and acting justly toward those who did not fight over faith with you, nor expelled you from your homes. God indeed loves those who are just.

One who fights Christians valiantly

> 61.4 Surely Allah loves those who fight in His way in ranks as if they were a firm and compact wall.

> 61:6 [clarifies against who] And when Jesus, son of Mary, said: "O children of Israel, I am sent to you by God to confirm the Torah (sent) before me, and to give you good tidings of an apostle who will come after me, whose name is Ahmad. Yet, when he has come to them with clear proofs, they say: This is only magic." Who is more unjust than he who invents a lie against God when he is called to submit? God does not show the evildoers the way.

Studying the above verses from the Koran helps us to understand the nature of Muhammed and the character of Allah. The followers of Allah demonstrate the characteristics of the god they worship and serve.

Five times per day, Muslims bow on their faces towards Mecca, making proclamations exalting Allah.

Muslims attempting to please Allah will also demonstrate hatred for Allah's enemies. From these verses, it is clear that Jews, Christians, and people of other faiths are enemies of Allah.

Rejection of the Spirit of Rage

In weighing the differing characters of Islam and Christianity, Allah and Yahweh, the story of Ali and Samir, Muslim friends of mine from Jerusalem, bears repeating. I have changed their names.

Our first meeting was during a tour of the Old City of Jerusalem in 1981. From that meeting, a friendship developed. Ali was one of many children of a Muslim man, who had four wives. Islam allows multiple wives if the husband can provide for them. Ali's father was not one of those men. He was almost nonexistent as far as the family was concerned, and poverty was a nice word for how they lived.

I lost contact with them when we returned to the U.S. I thought of them often, but could never seem to locate their address or phone number.

Returning to Israel to work with Bridges for Peace in 1991, I thought of trying to relocate Ali. One of his friends told me he had moved to Canada and gotten married. I meant to stop by his house, but could not remember exactly where it was. I might have pursued it further, but, on top of that, I remembered that he was the only family member who spoke English.

Then, recently, I had cause to go to East Jerusalem for some business. When I arrived, I discovered that I would have about a hour's wait, so I headed back to where I had parked my car. In amazement, I realized I was standing across a small valley from the backside of Ali's home. I decided to try to locate him. Walking across the valley, I saw a man come out into the backyard of the home and look over a low back wall. He spotted me and watched my progress intently.

I was fairly sure it was Ali's youngest brother, Samir, now a grown man.

As I approached, I called out in the little Arabic I knew, "*Madhubba! Ana Ron. Wen Ali?*" (How are you! I am Ron. Where is Ali?)

His eyes grew large and he shouted, "*Tal hon!*" (Come here!)

As I made my way to the opening in his garden wall, he was handing sandwich bags, filled with food scraps, to two Arab children who were feeding cats in the field behind his home.

My Arabic was limited, but Samir spoke Hebrew and broken English, and we were able to communicate. He brought me into their simple living quarters. Laying on a bed in the corner was their mother, tubes in her nose and a bottle of oxygen by her bedside. I remembered her as a strong woman, raising her children virtually alone. Her condition was sobering.

Samir announced who I was, and she rose from the bed, pulling herself free of the tubes. She held my face and kissed me on both cheeks—I was pleasantly surprised that she even remembered me.

In three languages—at a very fast pace—Samir caught me up on the family. We sat, sipping fruit juice, under a small grape arbor that looked out over the valley I had just crossed. It was the heat of summer, and the shade felt refreshing. I commented about how cute the children were who were feeding the cats.

"Faugh!" Samir exclaimed. "I give them food so they don't kill the cats," he informed me. "Their father bought a donkey several months ago, and they cut its ears off. Then they cut its tail off, and finally they killed it," he related. "I was so angry, I went to the father to complain, and he told me they were only playing."

I could see Samir's anger. He was quiet for a moment, then said, "I am no longer a Muslim. The world is in great danger from Islam," he added.

In way of further explanation, he went on, "Many years ago, I chose not to be Islamic anymore. I was beaten severely at my school." He showed me a place behind his left ear that was visibly damaged. "They kicked my skull in with their shoes, and I had to be operated on."

He then showed me a poster on his wall of an Israeli rabbi. The message in Hebrew warned of dire consequences if Israel relinquished any land to Syria on the Golan Heights. The poster was popular on the Jewish side of town, but glaringly out of place here in a West Bank village.

"I was arrested because of that poster," he said. "The man who brings my mother's oxygen tanks called the police and they took me in. The Palestinian police were sure I was crazy and had me admitted to the psychiatric ward of Hadassah Hospital. It took them days to get around to questioning me, and when they finally realized what it was all about, they were very angry that I had been troubled with such nonsense," he related.

"I cannot stand the hatred and rage of Islam."

In amazement, I took it all in. Samir and I finished our visit, and I went home, pondering all I had seen and heard.

Weeks later, both Samir and his older brother phoned me to say they were going to an anti-terrorist rally in the center of Jerusalem, and would I accompany them?

I was pleased to be with them in their protest of the violence of Islamists. There is no doubt in their minds of the characteristics of the religion. They gathered every bumper sticker that was being handed out at the rally and made sure I had one of each.

These young men experienced the sinister side of Islam. I still see them from time to time, and they are determined to fight the establishment of a Palestinian state due to what they see as a rage just under the surface of Islam that infects its followers—and they reject it.

The Demonstration of Real Love

Christianity and Judaism exhibit unique qualities. Both have intimate worship music declaring their love for God. One of the most astounding elements of the Islamist government of the Afghanistan Taliban was that they banned music altogether.

Muslims do not speak of the love of Allah. Undoubtedly, this is why Lawrence was puzzled by the old man's remarks in Wadi Rumm. In stark contrast, Yahweh, the God of Christians and Jews, is a God of great love. The pages of the Bible demonstrate, from Genesis to Revelation, His great love—Jesus becoming man in the flesh, suffering, and dying on a cross, and atoning for our sins as the final demonstration of the Father's love for the peoples of the earth:

> *For God so loved the world that He gave His one and only Son, that whoever believes in Him shall not perish but have eternal life.*
>
> John 3:16

The commandment of Jesus to His disciples is that by God's love manifested through us and our love for each other, the world will know His love. The challenge for us as Christians is to live among those who hate us and demonstrate God's incredible love.

Truly, this is our mandate.

Notes

1. Graves, Robert. *Lawrence and the Arabs.*

The Mufti of Jerusalem, Haj Amin al-Husseini, visits Nazi troops in Germany and the Balkans to procure favor in his crusade against the Jews of Palestine.

"See how Your enemies are astir, how Your foes rear their heads.
With cunning they conspire against Your people; they plot against those You cherish.
'Come', they say, 'let us destroy them as a nation, that the name of Israel be remembered no more.'
With one mind they plot together; they form an alliance against You, the tents of Edom and the Ishmaelites, of Moab and the Hagrites, Gebal, Ammon and Amalek, Philistia, with the people of Tyre.
Even Assyria has joined them to lend strength to the descendants of Lot. Selah."

—Psalm 83:2-6

How the Nations Rage

The modern Jewish return to a national homeland was into a hostile environment. Jewish immigrants coming home to Israel had to fight for their very lives and their national existence. That battle has never stopped. The cycle repeats itself predictably. To ignore the lessons of the past is to blindly repeat history.

Arab nations have always clung to a transnational concept called Pan-Arabism. They accuse the West of drawing the lines making up the Middle East's present borders. Some, affected by the League of Nations' decisions after World War I, consider it a contrived solution that ignored their best interests.

Pan-Arabism is the idea that all Arabs constitute one people and should be unified without the hindrance of the West's borders. The fly in the ointment is, the question of who should lead that group of people. Arab one-upmanship holds visions of unity at bay.

To understand the Middle East political climate, a brief look at the nations involved gives a proper perspective.

An Area Called Palestine

The Early Story

The name Palestine was given by Romans in hatred for the Jews in A.D. 150. The name, derived from Israel's enemies, the Philistines, was never a recognized national entity. Palestine was always a small part of some larger empire, whether it was Rome, Byzantium, the Ottoman Empire, or the British Mandate.

Palestine was not much more than a bothersome territory with little to offer world-class empires during several successive Islamic empires between A.D. 638 and A.D. 1917.

The first Arab rulers in Israel were the Caliphs, who chose Ramle, a small village on the coastal plain from which to administer the territory. They soon changed their center of rule to Damascus and, finally, to Baghdad. Those cities were in the mainstream of Islamic culture and thought. Anything in the territory of Palestine was considered a provincial outstation. The succession of rulership over the territory was Omayyad Caliphs, the Fatimids, Turkish Seljuks, the Mamelukes, and, finally, the Ottoman Empire, which ruled for four hundred years from Istanbul.

75

Unholy War for An Islamic Empire

In that entire time, Palestine as a recognized nation never existed. Neither was Jerusalem ever their capital city.

The largest of the Islamic ruling empires, the Ottoman Empire A.D. 1517-1917, dealt the final blow to the beauty of Palestine by taxing trees. Therefore, trees existing on private property that did not feed a family were cut down. The land became a denuded desert, ever progressing toward infertility and uselessness.

Even during the most governmentally advanced of the empires, the Ottoman Empire, Palestine was only a general geographic description. Even the name itself was a holdover from Roman times when the Jewish inhabitants were driven from the area and the name changed in derision. It was inhabited mostly by clans whose cohesiveness existed in religious ties, family ties, and clan ties. Except in rare instances, the population during those years did not view themselves as residents of Palestine or have a national identity unless it was as an administrative satellite of the successive Islamic regimes.

Palestine After War WWI

The Ottoman Empire came to an end on October 30, 1918. After WWI, the League of Nations granted mandates to Britain and France over large sections of the Middle East, taking in most of Syria, Iraq, Lebanon, Palestine and Jordan. A national home for the Jewish people became top billing in Britain. Dr. Chaim Weizmann, who synthesized acetone for the making of gunpowder for the British, won the reward of a homeland for his people. Those awarded mandates for the territory were responsible to see to it that the land was granted to the rightful inhabitants.

The noted Arab leader, Auni Bey Abdul-Hadi, told the British Peel Commission in 1936: "There is no such country as Palestine! Palestine is a term the Zionists invented! There is no Palestine in the Bible. Palestine is alien to us; it is the Zionists who introduced it. Even Bibles that have labeled the land of Israel as Palestine are in error."

He was right. In fact, there has never been a land known as Palestine governed by Palestinians. There is no "Palestinian" language. There is no distinct Palestinian culture. Palestinians are Arabs, as are Jordanians, Syrians, Lebanese, Iraqis, etc. Therefore, to use the word to distinguish a group of Arabs who want to be known as the rightful heirs to the land is erroneous.

76

There were indeed Arab families that have lived in this region for generations, but the were never called Palestinians.

Arab attacks on Zionism would never have materialized had it not been for British inspiration, tutelage, and guidance. The British resented France's power in Syria and Lebanon after WWI when the Ottoman Empire crumbled. They wanted to steal those areas from the French, so they contrived a bogus "Arab cause," alleging that lands in the area belonged to Arab forces. The British lies were as bold and brassy as Hilter's "big lie" but they caught on, and over time have become accepted as fact. [1]

Palestine After War WWII

Palestine was a downtrodden mixed bag of humanity between WWI and WWII. Both Jews and Arabs dwelt there, but until Theodore Herzl's dream of reclaiming the Jewish homeland in 1896, Palestine was a sure candidate for failure in most categories.

Jewish immigration began to bring the land out of its desolate slumber, and as Isaiah predicted, the desert began to bloom. With fresh blood running through the veins of ancient Israel, civilization began to flourish along with the land. Jobs became available. Arabs needing work heard and came from southern Syria to find jobs and a way to provide for their families. The demographics began to change, and those villages which had before only eked by, gave way to vibrant communities, planting the land, draining the swamps, and making their homeland come to life.

The biblical name for the West Bank is Judea and Samaria. These ancient biblical roots existed long before Muhammed was born in A.D. 570. Prior to the 1967 Arab-Israeli war, there was no serious movement for a Palestinian homeland. In 1967, Arabs attacked Israel in the area that has come to be called the West Bank. An important fact has been purposely buried: the West Bank and Old Jerusalem were captured from Jordan's King Hussein—not Yasser Arafat.

Unfortunately, the leadership of the present Palestinian Authority continues to miss opportunities. An examination of the leadership of the present day Palestinians should not focus on Yasser Arafat. In reality, leadership of the Palestinians should have followed the appointed leader from the British Mandate period. From all evidence, it would not have been much better, but the real line of authority needs examination also.

Unholy War for An Islamic Empire

In Arafat's shadow, Faisal al-Husseini before his death in 2001, stood in formidable opposition to a Jewish homeland and Zionism. Feisal was the son of Haj Amin al-Husseini and the nephew of Abd al-Qader al-Husseini, the infamous anti-Zionist fighter of 1948. Haj Amin al-Husseini's legacy as Mufti of Jerusalem should at the same time both shock and warn modern students of Middle East history. His politics reflected hard-line opposition to Zionism and finally armed opposition against all opponents of Arabism, including the British. In 1937, he was dismissed by the Mandatory government, and his Arab Higher Committee was declared outlawed.

Feisal fled to Lebanon and Syria, where he directed the Palestinian-Arab rebellion. In 1939, he went to Iraq, where he fostered close links with the anti-British army officers and assisted them in their revolt against the British Mandate over Iraq in 1941. When the British put down that revolt and reasserted their authority, Haj Amin escaped to Nazi Germany. Here he was received as a leader of anti-British Arab nationalism, accorded an honored position, and aided the Nazi war effort as a propagandist. He mobilized Muslim volunteers for the German armed forces in Croatia and from among the Bosnian-Herzogovina Muslims. That ancient fight of Christians against an insurgence of Islamic population was exacerbated by Haj Amin's presence there.

Joel Brand, a member of the Relief and Rescue Committee of Budapest, was summoned to a meeting with Adolf Eichmann, who presented him with an offer that would be known as "Blood for Trucks." Eichmann told Brand that the highest SS authorities had approved the terms, in which Eichmann would barter "a million Jews" for goods obtained outside Hungary, including 10,000 trucks for civilian use, or, as an alternative, for use on the eastern front.

The one million Jews would have to leave the country since Eichmann had promised that Hungary would be *Judenrein* (free of Jews). They might head for any destination other than Palestine, since he had promised the Mufti of Jerusalem that no Jews would be allowed to emigrate there. To negotiate the effectuation of the deal, Eichmann let Brand leave Hungary.

Although Brand was unaware at the time, the offer was evidently connected with an attempt by Himmler to drive a wedge between the Western Allies and the Soviet Union, and to conclude a separate peace with the former. Brand did go to Ankara, Jerusalem and Cairo, and he negotiated with American officials and leaders of the Jewish Agency for Palestine. However, he was arrested and imprisoned in Cairo, and the rescue scheme was never implemented.

So, "Palestine," a title that Arabs rejected as late as the 1950s, is suddenly the rallying cry of a people and a mythical homeland that never existed.

Returning Jewish immigrants gladly adopted the name Palestine, and in fact, the first English Jewish newspaper was called *The Palestine Post*. It has now become *The Jerusalem Post*, read internationally.

Modern Palestine

In their struggle to become a nation, Arafat and his followers have played pivotal roles in today's crisis.

It is important to say that when the United Nations General Assembly voted for the creation of a Palestinian state in 1947, Jordan voted "no," Egypt voted "no," Syria voted "no," Lebanon voted "no," Finally and most amazingly, the Arabs of the area rejected the idea out of hand. Undoubtedly, the rejection came because it would divide the land they considered theirs alone.

However, for this, the Arabs began a war of terror with Israel which continues to this day. Of the hundreds of Jewish terror victims from 1999, over half of them were killed or maimed by terrorist attacks committed by members of the Palestinian Authority security forces. Calls for *jihad* against the Jewish people and for the destruction of the State of Israel are regularly broadcast on PA-controlled radio and television.

On September 11, the day of the World Trade Center attack, the PA-controlled newspaper *al-Hayat al-Jadida* declared: "The suicide bombers of today are the noble successors of the Lebanese bombers, who taught the U.S. Marines a tough lesson. These suicide bombers are the salt of the earth, the engines of history. They are among the most honorable people among us." The PA-appointed Mufti Ekrima Sabri gave a sermon at the al-Aqsa Mosque in Jerusalem in late August 2001, in which he called on Allah to "destroy the United States and Great Britain, as well as those who help the two countries."

The revolution is not run by grass roots citizenry though. Islamists seek a bloody war that will upset the balance of the Middle East, providing the chance to take back all land once under the umbrella of Allah.

A detailed, chronological list of PLO and other terror attacks, from the inception of the PLO to the present, can be found in Appendix B at the end of the book.

The next section documents the unsettled past of the nations that surround Israel on every side.

Jordan

The Early Story

In antiquity, the area now known as Jordan was Moabite, Ammonite, and in later periods, the southern sector was inhabited by Nabateans, a resourceful people that made a living by providing potable water, and goods for passing camel caravaneers. Smarter yet, the bulk of their revenue was from taxation to pass through the land. Jordan and Israel combined are, in fact, the hub of all trade routes, silk, spice, as well as consumer goods. Some camel caravans, traveling the spice route, were as large as two thousand camels loaded with as much as a modern equivalent of $12 million worth of frankincense and myrrh, originating in Yemen, and traveling to Europe and Asia.

The region of Jordan was never more than a desolate territory and was never a homogenous group of people. Peasants, Bedouin tribesmen (most of whom were not settled), and some village dwellers inhabited the area.

Jordan was largely Christian under Byzantine rule between A.D. 300 and A.D. 636, when it was conquered by Muslims moving north from Mecca from the Arabian Peninsula.

Command of the area flip-flopped when Crusaders took Jerusalem and surrounding areas in A.D. 1187, then lost it again shortly thereafter. After a short period of rule by the Mamluks, the Ottoman period began. Four hundred years of stagnation marked the existence of the area now known as Jordan.

Jordan after WWI

Modern Jordan falls on the heels of the First World War. The League of Nations was formed after the war to administer mandates for fledgling nations too weak to hold their own ground.

Jordan's present kingdom came about from post-war favors to

be doled out to those who helped Britain bring about the downfall of the Ottoman Empire.

The Emir Faisal, who was briefly King of Syria and whose family ruled Iraq for some forty years, signed an agreement with Chaim Weizmann over the reinstated Jewish State of Palestine. Faisal even went on record as saying that the Zionist proposals were "moderate and proper."

This was before France took a look at the League of Nations' pencil marks on the map. The dispute transpired when France let it be known that they had indisputable influence over Syria and Lebanon, leaving Faisal out in the cold. Faisal was then offered the throne of Iraq, which had been promised to his younger brother, Abdullah ibn-Huessin, leaving him without a throne. In short time Abdullah massed fifteen hundred fighting men to settle the score. They entered eastern Palestine headed for Syria to drive the French out. War weary, and fearful that the French might use the situation to grab eastern Palestine, the British suggested that Abdullah remain there and rule a new entity called Transjordan.

The area was basically a desolate 100,000 square kilometers that held only about 300,000 inhabitants. Abdullah resigned himself to the idea, and the Hashemite Kingdom of Jordan was born. The British ignored that they had promised that land to Dr. Chaim Weizmann as part of the Jewish homeland. Jordan was three-quarters of the promised area. Nevertheless, the British came up with a loophole. The treaty had not been ratified and could be changed. Change they did, and the land was granted to Abdullah; the Arabs were happy, the Jewish homecomers were happy just to have a homeland at all, and all met together in a back-slapping, hand-shaking party to congratulate one another at Jaffa Gate in Jerusalem's Old City.

Jordan after WWII

The population of Jordan swelled first in 1948, when Arab news broadcasts urged Arabs to flee from Israel to avoid being harmed in the great war they planned. They fled again in 1967, when Israel was attacked by Syria, Egypt, and Jordan, with Jordan losing the West Bank area to Israel.

Yasser Arafat was headquartered in Jordan in 1968 and held the leadership of the now well-known terrorist organization, Fatah, a branch of the PLO. An Israeli operation launched against

81

Arafat and his organizations lasted a year and a half. The end of that campaign was a bloody battle, in which the Jordanians massacred and expelled the Palestinians from their territory.

Jordan had become a base of PLO terror operations against Israel between 1964 and 1970 from where they repeatedly launched attacks. Israel confronted the Palestinians in March 1968 by entering the village of Karameh, just east of the Jordan River. Levi Eshkol, Israeli Prime Minister at the time, declared that the attack was to prevent a new wave of terror overwhelming Israel. The United Nations condemned the Israeli offensive.

This military action against the PLO, unfortunately, afforded then unknown Yasser Arafat with world attention. He gained the limelight as the "savior" of Arab dignity. Fatah grew by leaps and bounds from then on. King Hussein then faced a more bold and aggressive Palestinian contingency within his borders. Fatah began to act as police, donning uniforms and treating Jordanian citizens as subjects of a state within a state. They collected monies from the citizenry under their direct control and refused to abide by Jordan's laws. The surprising angle is that two-thirds of King Hussein's citizens were Palestinian. These supported the political aspirations of Yasser Arafat. Egypt, too, supported Arafat and his quest for recognition.

Hussein attempted to reason with the Palestinians and facilitate a peace agreement with them, whereby they would relinquish their self-appointed power structure. King Hussein detailed several items that Arafat's supporters would have to abide by. Much like today, the Palestinians agreed verbally, but the facts on the ground did not change.

They intensified their struggle against Israel from Jordanian soil. Actually, 3,170 terrorist strikes were conducted from King Hussein's territory. Counter attacks against the Palestinians by Israelis were causing problems for Jordan.

Jordan has never really been interested in a Palestinian state. Arafat knew this, and during former U.S. President Richard Nixon's term in office, Arafat feared that Jordan and Israel might become more understanding toward one another and endanger the possibility of the creation of a Palestinian state. Therefore, Arafat stepped up efforts against Israel to force another conflict between Jordan and Israel.

King Hussein, in panic, secretly met with Egyptian President Gamal Abdel Nasser to curry favor for a strike against Arafat and the PLO. Surprisingly, Nasser, who had been pro-Palestinian up until this point, agreed.

Hussein returned to Jordan February 10, 1970, with one more card up his sleeve in an attempt to negotiate the situation. Never missing an opportunity to miss an opportunity, the Palestinians were not going to play ball. In fact, they fought back by strengthening their positions and dug in for a Jordanian attack. In the negotiation battle, Arafat came out the winner. Sterner measures would have to be taken to affect Hussein's plan of action.

The PLO and Fatah wanted to overthrow King Hussein. Arafat thought it to be an unworkable idea, since the Jordanian army was three times as large as his fighting force of 15,000. Arafat kept his finger in the hole of the dike until the beginning of September, 1970. Whereupon, open defiance of Hussein emerged. An assassination attempt on the king's life on September 1 failed. On September 6, airplane hijacking was born, when three planes were hijacked: one Swiss airline and two American airlines. Three days later, a British plane was added to that number. The Popular Front for the Liberation of Palestine (PFLP) issued a statement saying that the hijackings were to teach the Americans a lesson for supporting Israel.

Arafat did not condemn the hijackings. Two things happened simultaneously. Arafat's refusal to make a statement created an international protest against him and the Palestinians. At the same time, the Palestinians declared a state within a state in the north of Jordan. They were now ready for war.

The king responded by unleashing his Bedouin Legionnaires against the PLO. On September 16, Hussein declared martial law. On the next day, the attack began. Exactly like Israel's 2002 Defensive Shield, Jordan's Patton tanks rolled into Zarqa, Sweileh, Salt, and Irbid, Palestinian-controlled areas. House to house fighting took place. Hussein felt he had to do a quick job to keep Arab and international pressure from calling for a ceasefire.

At the same time, Syria decided to take advantage of the civil war and attack. They entered the northern region with an armored force. Their vision of a "Greater Syria" was within reach.

Israel became concerned that Syria would, in fact, extend her reach in that opportune time. The U.S.A. sided with Israel, and Israel Air Force reconnaissance flights over the Syrian positions made them withdraw for fear that they would, once again, be defeated in a war with Israel.

Unholy War for An Islamic Empire

Palestinian hopes rose with the Syrian engagement but were dashed shortly after by their retreat. Soon a cease fire was implemented. Talks in Cairo concluded that Palestinian organizations would be allowed to operate. Jordan was humiliated. Estimates that several thousand Palestinians died were thought to be high. Though there was a period of quiet, tempers seethed under the surface. Hussein was smoldering, and the Palestinians had time to prepare for their next moves.

Fate did not smile on Arafat this time. Two more things took place simultaneously. Egpyt's President Nasser died of a heart attack at the age of fifty-two. Arafat's protector was gone. On top of that, Syria underwent a major change. Hafez al-Assad, then merely Syrian Defense Minister, staged a coup and seized control in Damascus. Neither of Arafat's friends were available to bail him out of his tight spot.

Arafat lost control of his ability to negotiate, when the PFLP and the Democratic Front for the Liberation of Palestine (DFLP) refused to cooperate with him. They had their own agendas. They openly voted that Jordan would be included in their struggle against Israel and would be added to their Palestinian state when it was established.

By early the next year, the senior Palestinian organizations were calling for the overthrow of King Hussein from Radio Baghdad. They insisted that Jordan was on the verge of signing a peace agreement with Israel which fueled the fires in their favor.

It was the straw that broke the camel's back. In June 1971, Jordan launched the final campaign against the PLO. Large forces expelled them from the cities of Jerash and Ajloun. Many Fatah members declared martyrdom and chose to die rather than to run. Some of them, in most humiliating circumstances, fled into the arms of the Israeli Defense Forces and surrendered.

Fatah, beaten and in a rage, formed a new terrorist force called, "Black September." Four of its members assassinated Wasfi al-Tal, Jordan's Prime Minister, at the Sheraton Hotel in Cairo.

Arafat's tactics are the same. Today he keeps playing the same game again and again. As in Israel today, when asked to honor agreements, he repeatedly violated them; he was asked to rein in terror, and he could not do that either; he was asked to formulate reasonable agreements that could be kept, and he could not do it. From Jordan, Arafat and his PLO fighters fled to Lebanon. The delicate coalition government of Lebanon was thrown off balance, and Lebanon has never recovered. From Lebanon, Arafat was expelled to Tunis and from Tunis to Gaza and Ramallah. He is the father of airplane hijacking; he is the father of modern terrorism. His hands drip with the blood of innocent victims to this day.

The Hasemite Kingdom of Jordan issued a warning to Israel not to attempt to deport Yasser Arafat back to their nation.

Lebanon

The Early Story

The name "Lebanon" is derived from the Hebrew word for "white." Snow on the mountains of Lebanon undoubtedly gave the area its name. In biblical times, Lebanon included ancient Phoenicia. Tyre and Sidon were port cities of a thriving seagoing people.

Early Christianity grew strongly in the area of Lebanon and Western Syria from the first century onward. The Kings Highway (through the Jordan Valley) and the Via Maris (the coastal road) were the highways that took the first bearers of the Good News into Macedonia, now Turkey, and on through Greece to Rome.

The area served as a bridge to the north. On that route lay a unique kingdom. Since Lebanon was not a separate state until late, the following is when the area was a territory of Greater Syria.

Christianity put its roots down in Mount Lebanon early. There are several sects of Christianity there, which are still strong today. They trace their roots back to the early church, which came from Jerusalem.

Several hundred years after Islam conquered the area, the Druze sect settled there. The Druze are an offshoot of Shi'ia Islam, known as Ismaili Islam, as mentioned earlier. By about A.D. 900, secret societies had begun to form, and the Druze are one of these.

Post War History

Lately, Lebanon has been viewed by Syria as part and parcel of "Greater Syria." The implications of this political philosophy is that Lebanon has become the launching pad for Syrian and Iranian terror organizations against Israel. The Lebanese government is a puppet of both Syria and Iran in their goal to internationalize the Islamic Revolution.

85

Unholy War for An Islamic Empire

The Bekaa Valley that runs from south to north in the eastern sector of Lebanon has, as of 1982, been a military base camp for Syrian troops, offering the "protection" of Lebanon from Israel as excuse. In fact, Syria has used the area as a training ground for the terror groups, Hizballah and Islamic Jihad.

The Sacrifice of Lebanon

The death knoll began to toll for Lebanon first in 1970, when Palestinians fled from King Hussein of Jordan into that small but beautiful nation once known as the Monte Carlo of the Middle East. The delicate balance of Lebanon's coalition government was affected by the pressure of the added Muslim population over the following twenty-five years.

The second ringing of the funerary bells for Lebanon was Ayatollah Khomeini's homecoming to the welcoming arms of millions of Iranians, who saw him as the Islamic messiah. Khomeini came back from France with a fresh new fire for Islam. He ignited the ready minds of hundreds of thousands of Muslim young men with the idea of catapulting the Islamic Revolution from beyond their borders to the rest of the world. "The umma (the worldwide Islamic body) must be drawn into unity; not just pan-Arab, but a pan-Islamic entity to fight the West." That concept made pan-Arabism, the unity of all Arab peoples, pale in comparison.

The laboratory for experimentation was Lebanon. All the circumstances were right. Israel, the "antagonist," was already in place. In collusion with Yasser Arafat, who was already waging a war against Israel, the Revolution could actually test their might by joining the fray. Lebanon was expendable. Syria was willing, and they viewed Lebanon as a slice of Greater Syria, which could be treated as they wished.

In 1979, Teheran established "The Department for Islamic Liberation Organizations," dedicated to exporting their worldwide Islamic Revolution under the direction of Ayatollah Muhammed Montazeri. He traveled to Damascus and Beirut in December 1979 to meet with Syrian intelligence and military commanders as well as Palestinian leader Yasser Arafat to discuss and plan future terrorist operations. In January of the following year, Montazeri called a press conference in Beirut to announce Iran's intention of sending "volunteers" to fight Israel from Lebanon and of launching a world liberation struggle. On June 28, 1981, Montazeri died in an explosion in Teheran; however, his vision didn't. Lebanon was on the altar of sacrifice to the god, Jihad.

The entrance into Lebanon of the United States military peace-keeping force in1983 ended in disaster. They had little recourse to understand that the north was against the south, the east against the west, and the northwest against the southeast, etc. The U.S. Marines stepped into a quagmire in Lebanon. Confident they could bring logic and peace to any situation, they settled down to the job at hand. Neglecting the extra high level of security that is necessary in the Middle East, they were taken by surprise when a suicide bomber drove a truck packed with explosives into the U.S. Marine military barracks, taking 249 lives. America stood aghast at what terrorism had cost in innocent lives.

Syria

The Early Story

Ancient Syria has existed since the fifth century B.C. The nation has one of the most patchwork quilt histories of the region. A landbridge between east and west, and north and south, Syria was traversed time after time by conquering armies and heroes of military might.

The water resources which ran through Syria were the drawing card for travelers from Europe to Asia and Europe and Asia to Africa. The life-giving water resources made Syria center stage in world history.

The Assyrian Kingdom, that existed there almost two thousand years before Christ, was overthrown by Hammurabi of Babylon in 1759 B.C. Next on the long list, the growing Persian Empire reached out to swallow Syria and the Canaanite area that would later become Israel.

Alexander the Great conquered the area in 333 B.C. Hellenization of the area continued on until Rome came on the scene in 64 B.C. The Silk Route and Spice Route flourished under Roman rule, as did the spread of Christianity. Antioch of Syria is the place believers in the Messiah Yeshua were first called Christians.

. . . The disciples were called Christians first at Antioch.

Acts 11:26

87

Unholy War for An Islamic Empire

At the end of the sixth century, the Persian and Byzantine Empires fought over the area. The Christians lost to the Persians and the land was in turmoil until the Muslim hordes came conquering out of the Hijaz. The area was quickly subjugated and placed under Islamic rule until 1917, when the Ottoman Empire fell to British rule, and modern Syria was born.

Syria After WWI

In the modern era, Syria existed as part of the Ottoman Empire from 1517 until the end of WWI, when the League of Nations began to carve the whole of Mesopotamia into states.

When the Ottoman Empire collapsed in 1918, Syria was conquered by Allied forces. These forces included Arab troops commanded by Emir Feisal, son of Sharif Hussein of Mecca. He entered Damascus in October 1918, setting up an Arabic government in the interior of the country.

However, other nations had interests in Syria, and the Sykes-Picot Agreement of 1916 between Britain, France, and Russia designated the interior "an area of French influence," while the coastal areas (i.e., Lebanon) were to be directly administered by France.

The decision was more than unpopular among the Muslims of Syria, and by 1925, a serious national uprising took place. Clashes between Arab and French nationalists intensified.

Political differences continued to deteriorate, and a General Syrian Congress finally declared Syria's independence. The Congress proclaimed the Emir Faysal of Mecca, King of Syria. No borders were defined at this time—rather a loose Greater Syria emerged that would include Lebanon and Palestine. France was offered some influence, as well as allowing French troops to remain in the country.

Syria After WWII

Syria desired to be free of French domination. In 1944, Syria annulled the article in their constitution giving special privileges to France. The same year, both the U.S.S.R. and the United States recognized Syria, and Britain followed suit shortly thereafter. In 1945, Syria established a national army and was welcomed into the United Nations. By 1946, Syria had completely ousted all French troops.

Outside the bonds of the French Mandate, Syria emerged as an independent state with a very weak political structure. The problem raised questions that might seem absurd now, but Syria was faced with a possibility of merging with other Arab states in the region, namely Jordan or Iraq. After Transjordan became an independent state, King Abdullah announced a policy of unifying Greater Syria under his leadership. Though it had been considered, when the words took shape and form, Syria balked. Several factional groups in Syria were in support of Abdullah's plan: the Alawites, the Druze, and tribes of the Jazira. This firmed the resolve of Damascus "not" to become one with Jordan.

This very event may have set the stage for Syria's future attitude toward Palestine. Britain was touting a false Arab cause to stir trouble in the region to their own benefit, making Syria suspect that they were behind Abdullah's plan as well. Jordan also had plans for Palestine. It did not involve the creation of a Palestinian state, but rather, to annex the area to Abdullah's grand plan of Greater Syria under his leadership.[2]

Syria then took on the cause of Palestine as their own. Once again, it was not for the sake of the Palestinian people; it was to keep the British from realizing their plans in the region.

Fawzi al-Kaoukji, heading the Arab Liberation Army for Syria, became the predecessor of Yasser Arafat. Fawzi was a colorful character, and his life a political labyrinth. Born in Lebanon, he served as a Turkish officer in WWI against the French, but he joined special French services in 1920 against Syria. He also joined the Druze revolt against France in 1926. In 1928, he became a military instructor in Baghdad. Fawzi also joined the Mufti of Jerusalem in his collaboration with the Nazis. A confused character to say the least, Fawzi was also a ruthless anti-Semite.

Succeeding rulers in Syria continued the party line of not unifying with either Iraq or Jordan. Several coups later and much of the same riotous water under the bridge, an Alawite general of the Syrian Army, Hafez al-Assad, took partial control in a semi-coup. This was January 1969. By November of the same year, Assad took total control.

Under the reign of the late Hafez al-Assad, Syria became one of the world's centers of terrorism.

Unholy War for An Islamic Empire

In the wake of Egypt's peace treaty with Israel, Assad embarked on a militant inter-Arab policy to isolate Egypt and prevent other Arab states from following Sadat's peace strategy. Assad joined Libya, Algeria, South Yemen, and the PLO in establishing the "Front of Steadfastness and Confrontation," aimed at keeping the situation at a boiling point.

Between 1975 and 1982, over 100,000 Lebanese were killed in the Lebanese civil war between the PLO, the Shi'ite and Sunni Muslims, the Druze, and the Maronite Christians. In the Syrian-controlled Bekaa Valley, the Hizballah terrorist groups trained and send out forces to attack Israel. According to the U.S. State Department's Office of the Coordinator for Counter-Terrorism's 2000 Report, Syria oversees the following terrorist networks operating and training in Lebanon's Bekaa Valley: Hizballah, Osama bin Laden's al-Qaeda (meaning "The Base" in Arabic) Network, Hamas, the Palestine Islamic Jihad, George Habash's PFLP, Asbat al-Ansar, and several local Sunni extremist organizations. Other sources would add the names of the Japanese Red Army and the Egyptian Islamic Jihad. Syria not only controls Lebanon's terrorist training camps, but allows Islamic terrorists to base out of Damascus. In February 1982, the Syrian city of Hama was subject to a 27-day siege. The Syrian Army, under the command of Rifa al-Assad, surrounded the city and trapped nearly one hundred members of the Muslim Brotherhood who were opposed to President Assad's regime. Artillery shelling of that city caused between 10,000 and 38,000 civilian casualties. Fifteen thousand people turned up missing as a result of the massacre.

In September 2001, two PFLP terrorists were arrested crossing into Israel from Jordan, having been trained in Syria to blow up the two towers of Tel Aviv's Azrieli Center.

Saudi Arabia

The Early Story

The Saudi Arabia we know today is not more than eighty years old. Before the Sa'ud family came to power as a national entity, the area was tribal. Some seventeen tribal groups inhabited the peninsula. The present Al-Sa'ud family date back six generations to the early leaders, called *emirs* (princes), of the area known as the Najd, the eastern sector which were Bedouin lands. In the extreme east of present day Saudi Arabia, the Najd is harsh terrain with a harsh climate. Early conquests were against neighboring clans. In one of those disputes in 1891, the Al-Sa'ud clan was defeated and forced to leave the Najd. They fled, wandering the deserts, finally, to settle temporarily in Kuwait. Abdul Aziz, then but a small child, was spirited out of the area, dangling from a camel saddle in a large bag where his father was hiding him. He would later rule Saudi Arabia.

Refugee life was so distasteful to Abdul, that he vowed to take revenge on the Rashid tribe, who had made his family flee their homes, and take back the land they had lived in. Finally in 1902, Aziz returned to the Najd, amassed his men, and defeated the interlopers, driving them from the area.

Abdul Aziz planned to keep the area for himself, so he married three hundred women who produced for his kingdom fifty sons and eighty daughters. Fahd, now King of Saudi Arabia, is one of these sons, the son of Abdul's favorite wife, Hass Sudairi. Today, the extended family of the Al-Sa'ud's numbers over twenty thousand members. More than six thousand of those are princes and princesses or members of the immediate royal family who are directly descended from that first king, Abdul Aziz.

This piece of Middle East turmoil could not possibly blame its troubles on Zionism, as do so many today. Israel was not yet rebirthed.

The Arabs of the Arabian Peninsula embraced a puritanical and radical brand of Islam called Wahhabism, an offshoot of Salafi Islam, started by Muhammed bin Adbul-Wahhab in the mid-1700s. Even Muslim leaders today say that his brand of Islam was cultish and could be likened to Jim Jones and Jonestown. It is an austere belief, based more on fanatic intensity than scholarly pursuits. They accuse Muslims who are not Wahhabis of being "polytheists" who should be killed if they are unwilling to convert to Wahhabism. They insist that Shi'ia Muslims are not true believers and should have no right in Saudi Arabia. Wahhabism is decidedly an aberrant form of Islam.

The Saudis, in their zeal for fundamentalism, burned rival mosques and terrorized pilgrims traveling to Mecca on the *Haj* (the Muslim annual pilgrimage). Their raiding moves to the south and west were interpreted as an attempt to consolidate conquests and become "guardians of the two shrines," Mecca and Medina.

Brother in religion, Muhammed Ali of Egypt, attacked them in 1818 and ruled Mecca and Medina until 1843. In a table-turning attack of vengeance, Feisal ibn Turki (Sa'udi) reconquered and ruled until 1865. Then the Turkish Ottoman Empire asserted its power, and with the help of the Saudi's most hated rivals, the House of Rashid, took back the West of the Arabian Peninsula, pushing the Saudis back to Riyadh.

Saudia Arabia after WWI

The next rising of the Saudis came between 1915 and 1924 with the stamp of approval of the British monarchy. The war of 1924 between Ibn Saud and Hussein of Jordan settled the issue for all time. This time they drew their lines deeply in the sand of the Arabian Peninsula. In 1929, a rebellion of tribal chieftains was put down. In 1932, Ibn Saud unified the Najd and Hijaz (southwest), combining them into the unified Kingdom of Saudi Arabia.

Saudia Arabia after WWII

In 1953, Abd al-Aziz died and was succeeded by Sa'ud, his eldest son. Under Sa'ud's kingship, the kingdom suffered severe financial decline. His desert nomad mentality of budgeting did not fit a national scope. Then his brother, Faysal, stepped in to save the day.

The kingdom tottered between these two brothers for some years but finally, Sa'ud was forced into exile and died in Athens in 1969, leaving Faysal on the throne.

Modern Saudia Arabia

The Saudi totalitarian monarchy rules all without rival and without question. Saudi Arabia continues to bankroll many terrorist groups, though the funding mostly comes through private individuals. Many terrorist organizations receive substantial chunks of their funding through the government-tolerated generosity of the Saudis. Jews are forbidden to set foot in Saudi Arabia, and anti-Jewish literature is readily available. Unlike Western host countries that allow mosques to be built for Muslim worship, Christian houses of worship are illegal anywhere on the Saudi Peninsula. Christians who are discovered practicing their faith are often arrested, tortured, and sometimes beheaded. United States soldiers who put their lives on the line to save the Saudis from Saddam Hussein were told not to pray in a demonstrative manner, lest they offend the Muslims. Most other Muslim nations have Christian populations as a minority, but Saudi Arabia has driven all Christians out of their nation. The only Christians there are foreign workers, and only allowed to congregate quietly in their own homes.

Imagine for a moment that Saudi Arabia was an international club. Such rules would not be tolerated for a moment without human rights groups causing a major storm. Why is the world quiet about an entire nation which exists on bigotry at every level of its society from the top to the bottom? Yet they are treated as if they had something valid and constructive to add to the worldwide community.

Saudi's recent gestures are case in point. Saudi Arabia is proposing an Israeli-Palestinian peace plan to both the U.S. and Europe with such bravado that one might imagine the Al-Sa'ud clan to have a reputation that could back it up.

Oceans of oil have played the major role in how the Al-Sa'uds have kept hold of the desert sands of the Arabian Peninsula over the years.

Oil was discovered in the 1930s in Saudi Arabia. The first abundant oil field was the Dammam No. 7 well. Then in the next decade, the Abqayq oil field, bigger than any ever found in the U.S.A. brought America to the realization that she would become an oil importer rather than an oil exporter. In 1933, the technology came from the U.S. through Standard Oil of California, now known as Chevron, Exxon, and Mobil. These merged in 1948 to become ARAMCO, the Arabian American Oil Company.

Unlike the West where money might allow one to influence government, in Saudi Arabia, money allows one to wrest power and keep a firm grip on it.

Saudi Arabia is guilty of oppression of women, perhaps more than most Islamic nations. Just as in Iran and Afghanistan, Saudi Arabia has ethics police that beat women on the street if their dress is not up to code.

Saudi money has also been funding Islamic evangelistic outreaches to Muslims around the world. Even in America, young Muslims are being introduced to this fanatical undercurrent of Islam, which is now the fastest growing religion in America.

Fifteen of the nineteen men who hijacked airplanes on September 11 were of Saudi Arabian origin. Mastermind, Osama bin Laden is from a wealthy Saudi family.

Egypt

The Early Story

The early history of Egypt is voluminous. There is not room to detail the thousands of years and many dynasties of early Egyptian history, except to highlight where our subject comes into contact with its history.

Egypt has been ruled by foreigners since the last dynasty of Pharaohs came to an end under Alexander the Great. The Greeks, Romans, Byzantines, and, finally, the Arabs all took turns ruling Egypt. The majority of Egyptians are now Muslim.

Alexandria was considered the second most beautiful city in the world after Constantinople. The beautiful Greek Orthodox Cathedral of St. Marks overlooked the two harbors. Alexandria fell to Islamic invasion as early as A.D. 639. Christianity had begun to spread in Egypt since A.D. 190 and by A.D. 415, was declared to be the religion of the empire.

The Ottomans ruled Egypt from Istanbul for three hundred years until the French invasion led by Napoleon Bonaparte. That conquest lasted only three years, but Egypt was introduced to modern technology under the short French occupation.

Egypt fell back into the hands of the Ottoman Empire for some time, until huge debts to Europe granted Britain and France a degree of control over the nation.

Egypt gained independence around 1936 when Britain agreed to withdraw all troops except those stationed at the Suez Canal.

Egypt after WWII

In 1950, Egypt entered a time of crisis. Egypt's Wafd government declared that all foreign influence over the Suez Canal was at an end. Gamal Abd al-Nasser, later Egypt's President Nasser, was leader of a group called "free officers," who were convinced that they could solve Egypt's problems by taking things into their own hands. On July 23, 1952, they launched a coup, and the government fell into their hands like a ripe fig.

In 1956, Nasser shocked the West by proclaiming the nationalization of the Suez Canal after being sorely disappointed by U.S. withdrawal of finances for building the Aswan Dam. Britain, France, and the U.S. joined forces in 1956 to end the canal crisis. In the fray that followed, the U.N. finally oversaw a cease fire on November 6, and the attacking forces withdrew in late '56 and early '57. Egypt guaranteed open shipping to everyone—except Israel.

The following years, Nasser worked to unite the Arab world. Those attempts failed, and all his efforts to do so fell apart.

After signing a peace treaty with Israel, Egypt's President Anwar Sadat was assassinated in October 1981 by terrorists associated with Egyptian Islamic Jihad. This same group was later co-planner in the World Trade Center bomb attack in 1993 and seems to have been involved in the September 11, attack as well. Its top leader was Ayman al-Zawahiri (one of the planners of Sadat's assassination), who functioned as Osama bin Laden's top deputy. Egypt was also the first Islamic country to use poison gas against fellow Muslims in the North Yemen war of 1962-67. The Christian Copts of the Egyptian Nile Valley have been subject to decades of torture, murder, rape and destruction of property on a regular basis, with a blind eye being turned by Muslim authorities, and surprisingly, by other Christians in the world.

Iraq

The Early Story

Historically and geographically, Iraq is one of the most important areas of the world. In fact, it is known as the Cradle of Civilization. Iraq needs a more thorough examination than other nations we have looked at. If we want to know what the future holds, the past will tell us. This area is now bearing fruit that has been in process of maturation for close to six thousand years.

Known in antiquity as Mesopotamia, or "the land between the rivers," it is indeed the Cradle of Civilization. Present day Iraq covers a major portion of the area also known as the Fertile Crescent. Around 4000 B.C., long before her surrounding neighbors were heard of, the Sumerian culture was flourishing. Urbanization, the harnessing of the two rivers, and the control of flooding by building intricate canals created perfect conditions for the flowering of civilization.

It was here that writing evolved. This paved the way for each succeeding generation to learn from their predecessors. It also allowed agriculture to rise from haphazard desperation to become a science. By 3000 B.C., pictographic writing evolved into a full syllabic alphabet. Double entry accounting practices, still used today, have their genesis in Mesopotamia. Sumerians also developed a sixty-base math system, which may seem confusingly cumbersome unless you take into consideration our modern clocks and time pieces.

The first code of ethics, known as Hammurabi's Law, came out of the Fertile Crescent. It spelled out in detail how to conduct oneself, and it protected the weak and poor from the rich and powerful.

Unlike her neighbor Egypt, Sumerians believed in private ownership of property. The Egyptians served Pharaoh, their god-king, who owned all things including they themselves, but in Mesopotamia, the king was subject to his people. The seeds of totalitarianism in Egypt and democracy in Sumeria were already sprouting side by side.

We can thank the Sumerians for the wheel and the plow, calendars, poetry, epic literature, and writing instruments. All these came from the obscure recesses of the Fertile Crescent. The Epic of Gilgamesh, one of the greatest stories of all time, was birthed here. A story of friendship, escape from a great flood by building an ark, the search for immortality, and other timeless themes were recorded for succeeding generations. These historical accounts of man and his God are familiar to us from the Bible. They are the biblical stories told by a people slowly moving away from the worship of one God into the quagmire of multiple gods and local deities. They allowed time to steer them toward great empires, where simple ideas evolved into erroneous and rigid dogma.

Other seeds were germinating as well. War reared its head through the Akkadians, a people who migrated from the Arabian Peninsula in the south. They were a Semitic people (descendants of Shem, son of Noah). Their language, Aramaic, is the mother of Hebrew, Arabic, Assyrian, and Babylonian. When they arrived on the scene, the Sumerians lost control over their empire and fell under the yoke of the Akkadians, based far south near the Persian Gulf in Agade. The greatest capital of human empires would be set up in this land between the rivers, that of Babylon. Unlike our modern nations, whose duration spans from 250 years of the Americas to hundreds of years of European rule, Babylon was the commercial and cultural center of the Middle East for almost two thousand years.

Sargon, king of Akkad, conquered the area in 2340 B.C. His

world-class empire stretched from Akkad as far as Lebanon. Only 215 years later, Ur, the Sumerian city, rose up in revolt, and the Akkadian empire fell to a renewal of Sumerian rule. Ur, known biblically as "Ur of the Chaldees," is where our well-known biblical character, Abram, later known as Abraham, comes into the picture.

Jewish sources tell us that Abraham was in search of the one true God, and that God led him out of Ur to a place that He would show him. His great desire led him out of the pantheon of multiple gods, that was to continue in its deterioration, while Abraham and his family would arrive at the hinge of the world of that time. His new home was the intersection of all trade routes, both east and west, and north and south, and would stand as advertisement for the worship of the One True God in a sea of idolatry.

While Israel, Abraham's new spot in the sun, became the crossroads of monotheism, Mesopotamia became the crossroads of war. First the Akkadians, then the Assyrians, known for their horrors in war, the Hittite invaders from the eastern reaches of what is now Turkey, the Persians, the Medes, and the Kassites waged war after war. It seemed to become the major export of the area.

This was followed by an era that we are more familiar with from biblical and extrabiblical sources. Nebuchadnezzar and his father, Nabopolasar, ruled Babylonia from 612 B.C., to 562 B.C. They brought Assyria to its knees, never to rise again. Cyrus the Mede conquered the land in 539 B.C. Alexander the Great, the Greek, took his turn in 331 B.C. The Greeks founded the capital of Seleucia which became part of the Persian Empire and remained so until the Arab Muslim invasion of the seventh century A.D.

The Arab invasion marks the beginning of the steady decline of Mesopotamia. The demands of the new Islamic invaders to the inhabitants of the area of that time is chillingly familiar:

> Accept Islam and you are safe; otherwise pay tribute. If you refuse to do either, you have only yourself to blame. A people is already upon you, who love death as you love life.

The West has been warned by bin Laden's al-Qaeda that thousands of warriors for the faith are loose in the earth, who love death as much as we love life. In this declaration both then and now, a spirit of violence and death was loosed upon that area of the earth.

97

Unholy War for An Islamic Empire

Many Caliphates ruled from Baghdad over a period of three hundred years before the center of Islamic thought and culture shifted to Cairo, the city Islam created to replace Alexandria. By this time, Baghdad had grown in population to almost one million people.

Then a new scourge confronted Islam from the east in A.D. 1219. A powerful Mongol leader, named Temujin, better known as Genghis Kahn, meaning "world conqueror," swept through China, and with a force of 700,000 men, he headed west. He devastated Bukhara, Uzbekistan, Afghanistan, Turkmenistan, and present day Iran.

He was not like Alexander the Great, who used only the amount of force that was absolutely necessary. Genghis Kahn slaughtered every living thing in his path. Genghis' death afforded only a short respite before his grandson Hulagu continued his sweep. He marched on Baghdad in A.D. 1258 with 200,000 warring Tartars. Baghdad was not able to resist, and after forty days of bloody massacre, Baghdad ceased being the center of Islam. Blood flowed in the streets; bodies littered the alleyways. Hundreds of thousands of people were murdered, including the last Abbasid Caliph, who was trampled to death. The soldiers of Hulagu destroyed the canal system of Iraq and, in the ensuing years, Iraq became a provincial backwater, ruled from Hulagu's capital of Tabriz in Iran.

Political chaos, severe economic depression, and the disintegration of social structure soon became the ruling power in Iraq.

The next four hundred years of Iraqi history was punctuated by conflicts and, finally, the rising of the Ottoman Empire on the horizon. Iraq was viewed by the Ottomans as a buffer zone to keep Shi'a Islam from spreading to their area. Not caring to improve Iraq's conditions, they simply sought to maintain a Sunni area on their border. Sporadic uprisings, by the almost broken Safavid Empire in Iran finally moved the Ottomans to conquer Iraq, and in A.D. 1638, the area was under the full yoke of Murad IV, Sultan of the Ottomans.

By the early 1700s, the Mamelukes, a group of slaves turned soldiers, had taken control of the rivers and canals from the Persian Gulf marshes in the south to the extreme north where the Kurds dwelt. The Mamluk period ended in 1831 when a plague decimated Baghdad. The Ottomans reestablished rule, but it was weak, and at least ten governors ruled between 1831 and 1869.

By the turn of the century, the Ottoman Empire was struggling to enter the modern world. Western models of government and culture were being pushed by a group known as the "Young Turks," who took power in Istanbul. They stressed secular politics and patriotism, leaving the idea of pan-Arabism in the dust. The Young Turks were seeking to "Turkify" the whole of the Ottoman Empire, which faced a backlash of rebellion from an Arab nationalist movement as well as Iraqi nationalists. Cairo was far enough removed to be used by the Arab nationalists as a base from which to plot the downfall of the Ottoman Empire. The city of Basrah on the Euphrates River, as well, became the headquarters, from which Iraqi nationalists also began to plot against Istanbul. These conflicts beset Iraq early on in the twentieth century and kept it from progressing toward modern statehood.

Iraq after WWI

Modern Iraq, as we know it, existed as three separate provinces of the Ottoman Empire before WWI. Mosul in the north, Baghdad in the central section, and Basra in the south on the Persian Gulf became what we now know as Iraq.

The League of Nations awarded the British the mandate for Iraq in 1920 (Treaty of San Remo). Britain imported King Faisal, the son of the Sherif of Mecca, and set up a quasi-democratic government in the area.[3]

Powerful clan leaders resented Faisal's presence, and only with British backing did he ever succeed in ruling Iraq.

In 1932, Iraq, a quasi-democracy, became quasi-independent. Britain was still pulling the strings behind the curtain. Britain was loathe to really give up Iraq, since it was a major position on the route to India, where they had strategic interests. The second reason being Iraq's rich oil fields.

In 1941, there was an attempted coup, which Britain squelched, taking back full control again. This situation lasted until 1945, when the British Mandate began to fall apart finally, and Iraq seriously took control of the helm.

Iraq after WWII

Turkey simply joined the wrong side in the First World War. Sided with Germany and Austria, Turkey faced off against Britain,

France, and the United States. At the same time, Turkey was being stabbed in the back by her Arab constituency. The Hashemite family of Hussein ibn-Ali joined Britain by revolting against Istanbul. The plot worked and the Ottoman Empire collapsed; British forces entered Baghdad in 1917, and Arab rule began.

The Arabs expected to be handed their empire in full. The newly formed League of Nations had other ideas in mind and ascertained that Iraq was not in a position to manage independence successfully. Therefore, a mandate was offered to the British to administer large sections of the Middle East, Iraq being one of them. The Iraqi oil fields were, of course, among the appetizers on the tray. The other was the right to build a transcontinental railroad from Europe, across Turkey, down through Iraq to Kuwait on the Persian Gulf. This would mean the long trip around the Cape of Africa, en route to India, would no longer be necessary.

The Iraqis did not appreciate being a pawn on Britain's chessboard. Uprisings in 1920 made Britain rethink its plan, and they drew up a new plan for Iraq. With little consultation, Britain imposed a Hashemite Monarchy and drew their own lines in the sand of the desert. No ethnic considerations were entertained. The area of Iraq was to become a kingdom ruled by Emir Faisal ibn Hussein, brother of Jordan's newly instated King Abdullah Hussein of the Hashemite family.

In 1932, huge new oil fields were discovered in Iraq. The British still had their fingers in the Iraqi situation, and oil rights went to a British-dominated company.

Faisal died in 1933 and was succeeded by his son, Ghazi I. A non-aggression pact, known as the Pan-Arab Movement, was signed by King Ghazi I in 1936. Ghazi's declared ambition was to see Syria, Palestine, and Kuwait united under the umbrella of Greater Iraq. The Kuwait question was not solely the brainstorm of Saddam Hussein; even Ghazi, in 1938, moved to annex Kuwait into his kingdom. Ghazi's death in an automobile accident averted Kuwait's annexation at the last minute.

Further modernization milestones include Iraq's becoming a founding member of the Arab League in 1945, as well as a member of the United Nations.

Further decline in Iraq is marked by Rashid Ali al-Gaylani, who became Iraq's Prime Minister. A strong hatred for the British moved him to establish close ties with Nazi Germany, with the hope of moving Iraq out from under the umbrella of the United Kingdom. As part-and-parcel of that unsavory marriage of leadership, the German Embassy in Baghdad supplied anti-Semitic material in the form of books and films, as well as money to fuel hatred against the Jews of Baghdad, specifically, and Iraq, in general.

The British did not take kindly to the move and hit back hard. British troops marched on Baghdad and, in less than a month, drove al-Gaylani from the country. Nevertheless, the hatred fomented against the Jewish population had already taken hold. Between 1941 and the 1948 war in Israel, Jews escaped Iraq by every means possible and were driven out of Iraq finally, in the hope that the large number of new immigrants would topple the economy of the fledgling nation of Israel to the point of collapse. The Jewish people view that final exodus from Iraq as the last curtain call on the Babylonian exile of the Jews. Actually the anti-Jewish sentiment backfired and had a negative impact on the Iraqi economy. An oil pipeline to the Haifa Port in Israel was cut off, and funding for the army and donations for Palestinian refugees, who fled at the request of Arab governments, sapped Iraq seriously.

A move by the monarchy to join a British supported defense pact with Iran, Pakistan, and Turkey inflamed anti-Iraqi sentiment in Egyptian President Gamal Abdel Nasser. Nasser retaliated with a media campaign, challenging the legitimacy of the Iraqi monarchy, calling on the military to overthrow it. The military, inspired by Nasser's rhetoric, succeeded on July 14, 1958, in a short coup to overthrow the monarchy. Bloody public massacres of the royal family followed. Iraq was proclaimed a republic, the Arab Union was dissolved, and Iraq's participation in the Baghdad Pact ceased.

Only one year later, the nation was dissatisfied with the government. In a 1959 assassination attempt on Iraq's leader, young Saddam Hussein makes his appearance as a soldier in the assassination squad for the first time. He would not come fully into the picture until 1979. In the following twenty years, many power struggles and attempted coups rocked Iraq. Growing instability with its neighbor, Iran, by the early 1970s, coupled with Kurdish rebellion, plagued Iraq. Iran and Iraq were squabbling over a border dispute on the Persian Gulf in an area called the Shatt el-Arab. Border crossings by Iraqi terrorists into Iran continued to bring the dispute into focus. Iraq's final slide into maniacal dictatorship was just around the corner.

In July 1979, Saddam Hussein took Ahmed Hasan al-Bakr's

place as ruler of Iraq. Immediately, he purged his nation of political rivals. Almost without skipping a beat, Saddam declared the Iraqi-Iranian border agreement null and void. Five days later, the Iran-Iraq war broke out, lasting eight years and taking the lives of one million soldiers, some of whom were mere children of the ages of eleven and twelve.

Iraq is perhaps the country most well-known for both exporting terrorism and murdering its own citizens. In March 1988, Saddam Hussein launched a chemical warfare attack against the town of Halabja in northern Iraq. Mustard and nerve gases were deployed. Between 5,000 and 12,000 Iraqi Kurds were killed immediately, and an estimated minimum of 40,000 were injured. His brutality against the Kurds, the Iranians, and the Kuwaitis have earned him the Arabic title, "The butcher of Baghdad."

The Iran-Iraq war ended in 1988. Saddam's demons could only be quieted for a short time. In 1990, Iraq invaded Kuwait. Oil fueled Saddam's march into the tiny nation. He accused Kuwait and the United Arab Emirates of cornering the world market. He accused Kuwait of infringing on Iraq's rights in the Rumaila oil field. Negotiations quickly failed. The United States pledged to stay out of what they saw as an internal dispute. That was all Saddam needed to hear. An attempt at negotiations in Jidda, Saudi Arabia ended in a shouting match. Iraq invaded Kuwait the next day. Saudi Arabia feared for their own safety against Saddam, and the United States reneged on its pledge to stay aloof. Amidst U.N. resolutions against him, as well as economic embargoes, prohibiting trade and condemnation from all sides, Saddam launched a confrontational move and annexed Kuwait as a province of Iraq. Over the next several months, after many attempts, through various venues, to persuade Saddam to pull back from Kuwait—which were of no avail—twenty-eight countries launched a concerted aerial bombardment of Baghdad.

Saddam stirred up mob celebrations across the Muslim world when he declared that he was leading a *jihad,* the "Mother of all Wars," against the forces of the "godless West" and Israel. His drive to obtain non-conventional weapons (atomic, biological, and chemical), coupled with his cruel invasion of Kuwait, triggered the Gulf War of 1991.

Saddam was one of the world leaders who publicly applauded the terrorist attacks on the World Trade Center and the Pentagon.

Iran

The Early Story

Being next door to the "Cradle of Civilization," although physically separated from the "land between the rivers" by the Zagros Mountains, Persian history is intertwined with Mesopotamia.

Persia was conquered by the first Assyrian Empire in the year 2050 B.C. Persia resurfaces independently in 1936 B.C. under Chedorlaomer, whom we hear of in the Genesis chapter fourteen biblical account of the slaughter of the kings. Persia loses its identity again in 1661 B.C., swallowed once again by Assyria.

Cyrus, King of Babylon, finally gave Persia a permanent place on the map in 559 B.C. as the Medo-Persian Empire, administered from Babylon, which lasted 229 years. Alexander the Great added Persia to his string of conquered Middle East jewels in 331 B.C.

Alexander's reign was sweeping, but short-lived. His four generals split his empire after his death, but Rome was on the horizon already, swallowing kingdoms regularly.

Persia resurfaces as part of the Parthian Empire and remains there through the Sassanide Empire. Rome's yoke was thrown off by the Parthians several times during its climb to a world empire. The Sassanide Empire was finally defeated by Muslim Arabs in A.D. 637. Still yet, Persia asserted its influences strongly against total Islamization. Persia evolved through the Abbasid Empire, then the Seljuks, followed by the Safavids, and, finally, the Qajars, who moved the capital from Isfahan to Tehran, where it still stands today under a renamed nation, Iran.

Iran after WWI

Iran chose to support the Turkish Ottomans during WWI, though their stance was not active enough to be considered anything but neutral. The serious economic depression following WWI paved the way for Britain to receive a mandate to reorganize the economy.

In a coup in 1921, a military officer in the Russian-modeled Cossack Brigade, Riza Khan, overthrew the existing Qajar regime. He crowned himself the first Pahlavi Shah and served as the Shah of Iran until the militant Muslim uprising in 1979, which ushered in the dictatorial reign of the Ayatollah Khomeini and resulted in the Shah's expulsion from the nation.

Unholy War for An Islamic Empire

Following Turkey's leader, Kemal Ataturk, the Shah of Iran began a determined modernization that moved away from traditional Islamic values. Dress was westernized: women were not allowed to wear the *chador* (head to toe covering) in public, and men were forbidden to wear cloaks and turbans.

Iran after WWII

Relationships with Western nations from the mid-1960s until Iran's crisis, which began in 1978, were warm and friendly. Perhaps too warm and friendly. Like a child in a candy store, the Shah was busy ruining his economy purchasing weapons, offered him under the U.S. Presidency of Richard Nixon. Food shortages and demographic shifts of farmers moving to the cities to get rich quick, turned grass roots opinions against him.

Armed with the brewing troubles, Ruhallah Khomeini was fomenting trouble among the religious of the country who were ripe for a retreat from the modernization of the Shah to a calmer more religious time. Women began to rebel by donning the *chador* once again.

The U.S. change of Presidency from Nixon to Carter (Carter having been more of a human-rights activist) heralded a shift in policy of the U.S. toward the Shah's heavy handedness in Iran. The final blow came on September 8, 1978, when the Shah's troops opened fire on peaceful demonstrators in Jaleh Square, massacring close to a thousand people. By the end of the year, it was clear that the Shah would leave Iran. He did so on January 16, 1979, paving the way for Khomeini to return and launch his Islamic Revolution.

The Iranian Revolution was one of histories most violent revolutions, with the population marching in the streets daily, offering themselves as human sacrifices, if need be, to see the remnants of the Shah's government and military dismantled.

By November of 1979, the West got its first taste of what the Islamic Revolution meant, when fifty members of the U.S. Embassy staff were taken hostage. The United States decision to admit the Shah for medical treatment turned the dark gaze of Khomeini upon us, and the backlash lasted for 444 days, as the world watched on television.

The formal declaration of the Islamic Republic of Iran followed. Khomeini's theologic politic is that in the absence of the Twelfth

Imam (from Twelver Shi'a theology), it is the right of the clergy, as trustees of the Prophet himself, to establish a just social system that will implement Sharia Law.

The four divisions of Sharia government are the Council of Leadership, the Legislature, the Executive, and the Judiciary. They are ultimately headed by the Ayatollah in charge at the time.

Iran is now perhaps the most virulent hotbed of anti-Western hatred. They are not just angry and frustrated, they have been busy making serious strategic plans to avenge their imagined grievances against the West—"The Great Satan."

A terror training camp in northern Iran was opened by Khomeini himself. One of its first commanders was a Palestinian by the name of Sheik Abbas Golru, who had been a member of a Syrian-hosted terrorist organization al-Saiqa in the early 1970s.

Many mistakes were made in the beginning, but unprofessionalism was attacked stringently. The training camp was initially weak in military skills, but strong in ideological indoctrination. The Iranians soon realized they needed help from expert terrorists.

Soon Golru was replaced by another Palestinian, Nasser Kohladuz, a graduate of the Palestinian training camps in Lebanon, administered by Arafat. Kohladuz opened the training camp to expert trainers from North Korea, Syria, and well-trained Palestinian groups.

As I mentioned earlier, over a period of about ten years, Iran's training camp evolved into the highly technical and well-funded military installation, equipped with airplanes for practice hijackings and flying into tall structures. The growth of the program resulted in the opening of a second school of terror at the Shiraz Airport in 1983. Sabotage training and a high level of intelligence accompanied the new school. Graduates of Iran's hate training took part in all the major hijackings of the 1980s.

Iran's program could not fulfill its main objective of exporting the Islamic Revolution to the world just from its training bases inside the country. A new program was instituted as "phase two" of the strategy against the "Great Satan." Student, workers, diplomats, and employees of many companies were dispatched from Iran for the sole purpose of worming their way into the fabric of major Western cities in America, Europe, Africa, and Asian cities. They were to become citizens of the nations to which they had been dispatched. Where they had problems entering a country under the above pretenses, they applied for "refugee" status or "asylum seeker" status.

The small and easy to overrun nation of Lebanon was perfect for military games to test the students of Iran's schools of Islamic Revolution. Syria was only too glad to be part. Hizballah became the scourge with which to whip Israel. The plot seemed sensible to the Western media—they bought it hook-line-and-sinker. Major media television reporters climbed the hills of Lebanon like ants, searching in every possible nook and cranny for Israeli "war crime" activity. Meanwhile, Arafat, married to Iran and Syria, stockpiled underground tunnel systems with enough arms to start World War III. Palestine, a nation that had never existed, became a historical fact. "The Palestinian people," who never existed before 1964, were suddenly written into history as cleverly as if we all lived in George Orwell's novel, *1984*.

The world should be standing on Israel's doorstep with gifts of thanksgiving for entering Lebanon on June 6, 1982. Israel unpacked the storehouses of war, supplied by Iran, that had been stashed in man-made mountain caverns, bored out by massive Russian tunnel boring machinery. There were those there who knew the importance of Israel's presence. They were the sorely vexed Christian Maronites of southern Lebanon. They came out to welcome Israel with flowers and tears, when Israel began its offensive against terror in 1982. Later, they were threatened so severely that they ceased their very visible support for Israel, which allowed the media to report that they had turned their backs on Israel. That angle suited Western media's contrived stories much better. Lebanese that greatly appreciated Israel did not fit the mythical picture that had been painted at great cost by the media.

Turkey and The Ottoman Empire

The Early Story

Today's modern nation of Turkey began as a group of eight nations (Mysia, Phrygia, Bithynia, Pontus, Galatia, Cappadocia, Armenia, and Cilicia), which covered a larger area called Macedonia in the book of Acts.

Paul's mission trips into the area resulted in churches established in seven major cities and thousands of followers of Yeshua. Many turned from the idolatry practiced in that day to embrace a new faith, then considered an offshoot of Judaism.

Unfortunately, the churches did not follow the laws of the new faith closely. It was less than fifty years later that the Apostle John received a vision, foretelling the fall of those churches. Christianity in Turkey today has all but disappeared. Ninety-nine percent of Turks are now Muslim. Christians still living there are a silent minority. Christianity officially ended in Turkey in 1071, when the Byzantine Emperor, Romanus Diogeness, was defeated by the Seljuk Sultan Alp Arslan in the battle of Malazgirt.

At that time, Turkey was the northwestern frontier of the expanding empire of Islam. By 1345, Islam crossed the Bosphorus, a narrow waterway separating Turkey from Europe. In the following fifty years, Islam had conquered most of the Balkans. Constantinople fell to Sultan Mehmed II in 1453. The city name was changed to Istanbul, and the jewel of the city, the Hagia Sophia Church, was converted to a mosque, with minerets rising to the sky at each corner.

Thus began a four hundred year reign by the Ottoman Empire. During that time, Islam swept through Europe, stopping just at the door of Vienna, Austria.

It is a myth that Christians lived in peace and safety under Islamic rule. Incidents that took place in Albania, Bosnia, and Croatia under Ottoman rule tell the true tale.

Katerina Vukcic-Kosaca (1424-1478), the last Queen of Bosnia, an ardent Catholic and wife of the Bosnian King Stjepan Tomasevic (1461-1463), is still one of the most beloved personalities among the Croatians living in Bosnia.

When Bosnia fell under the Ottoman rule in 1463, her two children (a boy and a girl) were kidnapped and taken as slaves, and they were then educated under Islam. Her husband was murdered by decapitation. She managed to escape to Dubrovnik and then to Rome. She had been deeply involved in the humanitarian activity of the Franciscan community to help Bosnian Croatians under Turkish rule. She built the St. Katerina Church in the picturesque Bosnian city of Jajce (totally destroyed by the Serbs in 1993).

In the face of the overpowering tidal wave of Islam sweeping their homeland, Croatian women would tattoo their bodies with crosses and Christian symbols to keep their husbands from being murdered and themselves from being raped and kidnapped to be married off to a Muslim man. Even today, Bosnian Catholic Croatian women tattoo their hands and other visible parts of their

107

bodies (brow, cheeks, wrist, or below the neck), with Christian symbols (usually with a small cross). This occurs not only in middle Bosnia, but also among exiled Bosnian women living in Zagreb, Yugoslavia.

They undoubtedly knew the Islamic prohibition written in the Hadith:

> Abdullah (bin Masud) said: "Allah curses those ladies who practice tattooing and those who get themselves tattooed, and those ladies who remove the hair from their faces and those who make artificial spaces between their teeth in order to look more beautiful whereby they change Allah's creation." His saying reached a lady from Bani Asd called Um Yaqub who came (to Abdullah) and said, "I have come to know that you have cursed such-and-such (ladies)?" He replied, "Why should I not curse these whom Allah's Apostle has cursed and who are (cursed) in Allah's Book!" Um Yaqub said, "I have read the whole Koran, but I did not find in it what you say." He said, "Verily, if you have read it (i.e., the Koran), you have found it.[4]

The Ottomans also exacted the *Devshirma* (tax in blood) from the Christians. Every three or four years, three hundred to one thousand healthy boys and young men had to be taken by force to Turkey, converted to Islam and educated for a military profession or religious disciplines. Some desperate mothers even mutilated their children trying to save them.

After the arrival of the Turks, the states of Bosnia and Albania, which had been previously Catholic, became more and more Islamized. The penetration of the Ottoman Empire to Europe was stopped on Croatian soil.

The Croatians endured the greatest burden of this four century-long war against the Turks. The most tragic fact in this war was that many Islamized Croats had to fight against the Catholic Croats, brother against brother, at the behest of an occupying force.

Post WWI History

The First World War brought the Ottoman Empire to a close. The Treaty of Sevres was signed by Turkey's last reigning Sultan, in effect, dismembering the Empire. Turkish national resistance began in Anatolia, led by Mustafa Kemal Pasha, also known as Ataturk, (or father of the Turks). By 1920, the foundations of modern Turkey were laid, when the Grand National Assembly met in Ankara and proclaimed itself the *defacto* government of the country.

Under Ataturk, the defeated Islamic Empire became a humble parliamentary democracy. The government was secularized, the remnants of the Ottoman Empire were banished from the country, Western European laws were established, Islam disestablished, the Latin alphabet replaced Arabic script, European forms of dress were imposed, and Ottoman Turkish dress, including the red hat, called the *fez* and worn by most men, was outlawed. Probably one of the most remarkable and un-Islamic moves was the full emancipation of women in 1935, when they were accorded full political rights.

Though defeated by the Allies, Turkey held its own and moved productively into the modern age providing its twelve million citizens a solid footing with which to build a nation, which swelled to seventeen million in fifteen years.

Ataturk's successor, Ismet Inonu, managed to keep Turkey out of World War II and brought Turkey into the United Nations as a member in 1945.

However, not all of Turkey's moves were good. In the highlands of northwestern Turkey, the Armenians existed as a minority population within greater Turkey. Their language is an independent member of the Indo-European family and is written in a script that can be dated back to A.D. 404. Friction, between Ottoman Islam and Armenian Christianity over a two hundred year period, led to Armenian uprisings to liberate themselves from harsh Islamic rule.

Armenians began to emigrate to the New World in 1894, after the first of a series of massacres of their people. The Armenian underground movement caused friction on their northeastern border with Russia as well. Basically directed at their Ottoman oppressors, the socialist ideology of the Armenians began to alarm the Czars, who also lashed out at Armenians.

In the few years leading up to WWI, Armenians who were serving in the Turkish military were disarmed, due to rising Turkish fear of an uprising by the Armenians. They were forced into labor camps in the interior. Continued rising tensions caused Turkey to deport masses of Armenians toward Mesopotamia and Syria. Many died on the way, and many were shot on the spot.

Armenians put the numbers of murdered and dead at 1.5 million human beings. They consider this period a holocaust and an attempt at genocide of the Armenian people.

Post WWII History

Turkey worked hard to stay neutral during WWII. She has steadily built strong and healthy relations with the foreign nations surrounding her. Relations with Arab nations have been strained, due to Arab support and direct aid to the British during WWI. The fall of the Ottoman Empire would never have happened if Arab states had not made a confederate effort to oust the Ottoman government from the Middle East.

This has created friendly terms with Israel. Turkey views Israel as having fought, and held their ground against the Arabs. Turkey is now both politically and physically on the periphery of the Islamic block.

Other Nations

Other nations enter the picture in the Middle East, but in a more distant relationship. Within the context of international terrorism, they need to be mentioned, although not as detailed as the major players we have just covered. These nations make up a secondary circle, offsetting the major players listed above.

Libya

Libya is an Islamic dictatorship under Muammar al-Qaddafi. It has been one of the chief training centers for world terrorism, executing many attacks, such as the bombing of a Berlin discotheque in March 1986, where U.S. soldiers were murdered. They were also partly responsible for the terrorist bombing of Pan Am flight 103 over Lockerbie, Scotland, in December 1988. Libya has cooperated with Pakistan in the funding and development of an Islamic nuclear bomb, as well as developing chemical warfare capabilities. It has been a main supporter of such terrorist groups as the Columbian M-19, Red Brigades, IRA, Ahmed Jibril's PFLP, Arafat's PLO, etc. In the 1970s, Qaddafi awarded Yasser Arafat $5 million in recognition for his terror operation at the 1972 Munich Olympics, which led to the massacre of eleven Israeli athletes.

Algeria

Algeria has been reeling from a war between the GIA (Armed Islamic Group), who are radical Muslim terrorists and its established government (a more secular Muslim military dictatorship) since 1992. Gruesome reports are heard of entire villages having had their throats slit and heads cut off with chain saws, famous pop singers assassinated for singing Western influenced music, and government-instigated massacres of regions whose loyalties are suspect. More than 70,000 people have been murdered over the past nine years. GIA cells are believed to have cooperated in Osama bin Laden's September 11 attacks.

Sudan

Sudan is considered one of world terrorism's main centers. Osama bin Laden has a strong network in this country. According to the U.S. Grand Jury indictment against bin Laden, the bombers of the U.S. Embassies in Nairobi, Kenya, and Dar es-Salaam, Tanzania, were trained and sent out from Sudan. The Islamic dictatorship's National Islamic Front (NIF) ruling Sudan has been overseeing the massacre, enslavement, rape, and murder of the Christian and animist inhabitants of southern Sudan, forcibly converting the survivors and prisoners to Islam. Years ago, the NIF proclaimed a *jihad* against its domestic enemy, and since 1983, more than 1.9 million people have been murdered or have died as a result of the actions of the NIF in southern Sudan and the Nuba mountains.

Afghanistan

The disintegration of two mighty empires, the Safavid based in Iran and the Mughal in India, gave way in 1747 to what we now know as Afghanistan. An Afghan chieftain, Ahmad Shah Durrani, seized control of the landlocked area. Almost immediately, a split politic emerged between the royals and the Pushtun clans and warlords.

Afghanistan lay sandwiched between the empires of Russia and its interests in Central Asia and the British and its interests in India. Afghanistan struggled to retain its independence from outside pressures, while, at the same time, struggling with its own pressures from within.

By 1901, Abd al-Rahman, known as the "iron Emir," brought a

degree of civility to the region. A central government emerged, and some economic development took place.

By 1919-1929, King Amanullah tried to follow Kemal Ataturk's social changes with disastrous results. Tribesmen, clans, and the more civilized clashed repeatedly.

Afghanistan was not directly touched by WWII, but the division of India into the new nation of Pakistan did affect Afghanistan.

Afghanistan is a primary example of the difference between a Muslim and an Islamist nation. Afghanistan's non-Arab country was ruled by the hard-line Islamist Taliban dictatorship. It has been a center for training some of the most radical, and violent Islamic terrorists and one of the many bases of Osama bin Laden's al-Qaeda Network. The cruelty of this Islamic regime against its own people is now internationally known and documented.

Hopefully, the West is learning about Islamists and will keep a close watch on Afghanistan over the coming years to make sure that a Taliban-style government does not reemerge from the ashes of their dissolution in the West's "War on Terrorism."

Pakistan

Pakistan is a non-Arab Muslim country. However, it has become a critical factor in Islamist factions in Afghanistan. Pakistan came into being after a split of Muslims and Hindus that redrew the borders of India. Due to Pakistan being a very Islamist nation, Christians accused of sharing their faith in Pakistan have been jailed, tortured, and lynched. Osama bin Laden has contacts with Pakistan's intelligence community and has received active support from many sources in Pakistan. Over 30,000 Pakistanis fought as *jihad* warriors against Russian forces in Afghanistan during that war. Recent violent anti-American riots and calls for *jihad* against the West show the volatile nature of many Pakistani Muslims. Recently President Musharraf publicly accused Hindus and Jews of plotting against Pakistan. This was partially done in an effort to divert Muslim anger away from Pakistan's leaders, who are cooperating with America against fellow Muslims in Afghanistan and the *mujahid* (*jihad* fighter) Osama bin Laden.

Islamic insurgency into Kashmir has brought India to the brink of major war with Pakistan several times.

The Gulf Cooperation Council (GCC)

The GCC is an organization of six nations: Saudi Arabia, the United Arab Emirates, Kuwait, Qatar, Bahrain, and Oman. The Council's permanent secretariat is situated in Riyadh, Saudi Arabia.

The need for the Council was determined in 1981, from a growing sense of threat from Saddam Hussein, then waging war against Iran, and the Shi'ia revolution which was being exported by the returned Ayatollah Khomeni after the overthrow of the Shah.

Primary objectives of the Council are to promote cooperation of its member states in domestic and regional security. The Iraq-Iran war broke out over a border dispute in the area where the Tigris and Euphrates Rivers empty into the Persian Gulf. Therefore, one of the Council's main objectives is the resolution of border disputes.

The GCC tried to intervene in Saddam's attack against Iran with an appointed "Rapid Deployment Force," but failed. Their attempted intervention may have been the incentive for Saddam to invade Kuwait later.

Iran also caused the member states worry by pressure through sabotage, political subversion, propaganda warfare, and military attacks against oil tankers in the Persian Gulf and Kuwaiti territory.

Because Arafat supported Saddam Hussein in the Gulf War, the GCC decided to suspend all financial aid to the PLO. After the Olso Agreements between Israel and the Palestinian Authority in September 1993, the GCC members renewed their relations with the PLO, and the Saudis pledged to contribute $100 million over five years for the development of the Palestinian-governed territories of the Gaza Strip and the West Bank.

The GCC States

The true Arab homeland is Arabia, the southwestern peninsula of Asia. It covers 1,027,000 sq. miles. This peninsula embraces the nations of the GCC. These nations are stronger because of the organization of the Council, which seeks to push their influence in the world forward. The nations comprise the following:

Qatar

Qatar is an Emirate on the Arabian coast of the Persian Gulf. It lies on a peninsula of the same name, jutting north into the

113

Unholy War for An Islamic Empire

Persian Gulf. Its length is 105 miles and is 25-40 miles wide. Qatar borders Saudi Arabia and the UAE. Until the late 1960s, the population was 50,000 to 80,000, which then began rapidly growing due to the influx of foreigners attracted by the expanding oil economy. Fifty percent of the present population is made up of foreigners from Pakistan, India, Iran, and the Philippines.

Qatar's inhabitants are Sunni Moslems, as are Saudi Arabia's. The Turkish Ottoman Empire claimed a nominal sovereignty over the area, but never really controlled it. From the 1820s, when the British established a network of treaty relations with various Gulf rulers, originally to put an end to piracy, the Sheik of Qatar became part of that network. Even up to 1968, a British political officer guided the ruler of Qatar, when Britain decided to withdraw from its Gulf commitments. In April 1970, he provisionally declared independence and solidified it in September 1981, when the British protectorate lapsed. That same month, Qatar was admitted to the Arab League and to the U.N.

In 1940, oil was discovered on the west coast of Qatar. Previously, Qatar's economy was derived from animal husbandry, pearl diving, fishing, and limited cultivation. Qatar is now home to one of the world's largest gas fields. The revenues from oil and gas have allowed Qatar to develop its economy and social infrastructure (a network of health and educational institutions covering all its inhabitants, including a university which was opened in 1977).

Internal politics have been stormy in Qatar. Conflicts and rivalries among the al-Thani sheiks have left their government reeling on a regular basis. Sheik Abdallah ibn Qassem (1913-1949) was compelled to abdicate. Abdallah's son, Ali ibn Abdallah (1949-1960), suffered the same fate. His son, Hamad ibn Ali (1960-1972), was ousted by his cousin, Crown Prince and Prime Minister Khalifa ibn Hamad (1972-1995). Khalifa was ousted by his own son, Hamad ibn Khalifa, who has ruled Qatar since 1995.

Qatar's foreign relations are marked by close relations with the U.S., culminating in Qatar's participation in the coalition and war against Iraq in 1991. In a very low-profile foreign policy, Qatar managed to develop relations with Israel without attracting hostile Arab reaction. Mutual visits were held and low-level diplomatic representation was instituted. Qatar also ended its participation in the Arab boycott of Israel.

United Arab Emirates

The UAE is a seven-state federation set up in 1971, which became independent in December of the same year. These are Abu Dhabi, Dubai, Sharjak, Ras al-Khaima, Umm al-Qaiwain, Ajman, and al-Fujaira. The United Arab Emirates juts out into the Persian Gulf, creating the Straits of Hormuz directly across a narrow body of water from Iran. A census in 1992 placed the population of the UAE at 2.25 million, of which seventy-five percent are foreigners attracted by oil revenue.

The seven sheikdoms had been under British protection since 1820. Preparations for independence began in earnest in 1968 when Britain announced its plan to abolish its protectorate. The newly independent UAE was admitted to the Arab League and the U.N. in December 1971. The seven Emirates are governed by a Supreme Council, composed of representatives of the seven sheikdoms, appointed by their rulers. Each sheikdom's size determines the number of representatives it is allowed in the Supreme Council. The Supreme Council elects one of its members as President of the UAE for a five-year term. The sheikdoms retain their own identity, though the currency and customs are united.

Sheik Zayed of Abu Dhabi has been re-elected every five years since independence. He has direct impact on the policy of arms and technological procurement. There is rivalry between his sons, the Crown Prince, and a younger half-brother over a $6 million aircraft deal.

Attempts to unify a UAE army have fallen into irreconcilable differences, therefore the UAE is protected by six separate armies.

The bulk of the oil production is centered in Abu Dhabi, which began producing in 1962. Dubai exported its first oil in 1969, Sharja in 1974 and Ras al-Kharima in 1984. Oil production is not a federal matter, and the revenues belong to the producing sheikdom.

In the Arab League, the UAE takes a low-profile stance. It is considered a moderate mainstream camp, refrains from spectacular initiatives, and usually follows the lead of Saudi Arabia. The UAE was one of the founding members of the GCC in 1981. In November 1985, the UAE became the third Gulf country to establish official relations with the former U.S.S.R.

Unholy War for An Islamic Empire

Kuwait

Kuwait's population growth has been in direct proportion to its acquired oil wealth. In 1910, the population was 35,000 residents, less than a small Western city. The first official figure in 1957 was 206,000. The blossoming of Kuwait into a major oil producing country created massive growth, and by 1985, the population was topping 1.7 million people. The 1990 census saw a massive increase at 2.1 million people. Seventy-five percent of the population are non-Kuwaiti residents who have come because of the economy.

On the surface, Kuwait and Iraq's squabble centers around two islands off Kuwait's coast. The Persian Gulf contains a number of islands near the Iranian coast. The largest one is Qishn, the historically important Hormuz, and Sirri (all at its eastern end, near the straights of Hormuz), and the small islet of Kharg (at its western end). Kharg and Sirri were developed in recent years as oil loading terminals. Near the Arabina shore, are the islands of Bahrain and, farther east, the small islet of Abu Mussa and the Tanbs. Both were claimed and forcibly occupied by Iran in a dispute with the UAE. Huwar and smaller islets nearby are disputed by Bahrain and Qatar. At the northwestern end of the Persian Gulf, several Kuwaiti islands, e.g., Bubiyan and Warba, have been a matter of dispute between Kuwait and Iraq.

One of Kuwait's distinct advantages, that may have drawn the covetous eyes of Saddam Hussein, is Kuwait's deep water bay, which can easily handle oil tankers of all sizes. This is not a new problem. Until WWII and the beginning of oil production, Kuwait was a small, poor settlement of Bedouin, fishermen, pearl divers, and boat builders with a negligible population. But, situated on the Bay of Kuwait, the only deep-water bay in the Gulf, it had a natural port. It thus acquired an important strategic role as a potential gateway to Iraq and the Arabian Peninsula. For this reason, Germany intended, at the end of the nineteenth century, to extend the planned Baghdad Railway to the Bay of Kuwait. Great Britain saw these plans as a threat to its domination of the Persian Gulf and its route to India.

Beyond foiling the railway extension scheme, in 1899 it agreed with the Sheik of Kuwait to place his realm under British protection—though the Ottoman Sultan's nominal sovereignty was not formally abolished. Under this protectorate, Britain conducted Kuwait's foreign affairs, supervising its administration, law, and order. After the Ottoman Empire entered WWI in

November 1914, Britain recognized Kuwait as independent under British protection. The protectorate remained in effect until 1961 when Kuwait became fully independent under its Sheik of the House of Sabah, now styling himself Emir.

By the mid-1990s, Kuwait's crude oil reserves stood at about ten percent of world reserves. Most of Kuwait's oil is processed locally and exported as refined product.

Kuwait has become a richly developed modern urban conglomeration. Kuwait has an extensive network of roads, an international airport, and an international finance and banking center. The decline of Beirut from the 1970s onward only added to Kuwait's growth as a world banking center.

Dangers to Kuwait lie not only in the form of hostile neighbors, but internal difficulties brought about by importing a foreign labor force. Kuwait is having to face the reality that it is one of the world's top-rate welfare states, providing a variety of services to its residents free of charge or at a symbolic fee. Palestinians, Jordanians, Egyptians, Iraqis, Yemenis, Iranians, Indians, and Pakistanis have come to live off the wealth of Kuwait. The largest foreign group are Palestinians—nearly twenty percent of the total population.

Civic and voting rights became an issue as the number of foreign workers found their way into higher level positions over the years. Nearly fifty percent of the civil service and eighty percent of the teachers were foreign Arabs, mainly Palestinians and Egyptians. This vast presence of foreigners resulted in growing tension with the autocratic regime, which objected to granting any civic or voting rights to foreigners.

Foreign Arabs, and particularly Palestinians, were presumed to be the main reservoir for radical and subversive groups, as was manifested by the overwhelming support Iraq was given by this population during the 1990 invasion. Iranian Shi'ites, especially after the Iranian revolution in 1979, became a source of concern for Kuwait, since the Kuwaitis are Sunni Muslims, as are their neighbors, Saudi Arabia. In the late 1980s, the Iranian Shi'ites constituted approximately 25-30 percent of the population.

The Kuwaiti regime conducted a systematic policy of expulsion of most of the 400,000 Palestinians who resided in Kuwait until the Iraqi invasion. Only 15,000-20,000 remained as the Gulf War heated up.

The disintegration of the U.S.S.R. and the formation of the

world-coalition by the U.S. eventually made Kuwait fully identify with the U.S. in its foreign affairs. Kuwait had to maneuver a complex neutral stance between its two big brothers on the northern border, Iraq, and Iran. This became increasingly difficult as the dispute between them rose over borders very close to Kuwaiti soil.

Kuwait has calmed the spirit of Saddam Hussein by granting him large-scale financial aid. It came in the form of grants and credits, and the assurance of supplies and help in channeling Iraqi oil imports and exports, since Iraqi facilities on the Gulf were paralyzed and largely destroyed.

Terror cells were uncovered in 1983 after a series of car bombs, mainly against American targets. They were apparently linked to the Iranian inspired Lebanese Hizballah, the radical Shi'ite organizations, whose actions in Kuwait corresponded to its suicidal bombings against the multinational forces (American and French) in Beirut. More terror attacks of Iranian origin occurred in 1985.

Iran targeted Kuwait with missile attacks in 1987 on the grounds of extending support to Iraq, thus exacerbating Kuwait's resort to Western protection.

A Kuwaiti "Fund for Arab Economic Development," established in 1962, is actually a buy-off to keep radical Arab groups from tearing it to shreds. Palestinian and other subversive elements and Egyptian Nasserists took a rather radical line in their verbal, declarational postures. Over $3,500 million have been poured into this fund. It contributed over $150 million each year to Egypt and Jordan after 1967, following the Khartoum Arab Summit's decision to aid the countries confronting Israel. Four hundred million dollars per year, after 1973-74, were paid to the confronting states and Palestinian organizations, and $550 million per year after 1978.

Large additional sums of Kuwaiti money, with no details published, were given directly to Palestinian institutions in the West Bank and Gaza Strip, as well as to the PLO until 1990.

U.S. human rights reports state that political parties and private associations are still banned and that limitations on women's rights remain in place. Even after the war, reports regarding oppositional activity in Kuwait surface at times.

The Kuwaiti chapter of the "party of God" (Hizballah) is an underground Shi'ite organization linked to Iran and has been

118

active in post-Iraqi occupation of Kuwait.

The ruling powers are separated into two dynasties, whose members continue to hold key positions and ministerial posts and most of the major executive positions. The dynasty itself is made up of the Jaber-al-Sabah and the Salem-al-Sabah branches, who have, since 1915, alternated in power with a certain degree of rivalry. Since 1965, the branch not holding the Amirate (supreme power) has served as Crown Prince and Prime Minister.

The Temperature is Volatile

In light of all the above, it is safe to say that the temperature of the Middle East was volatile enough without laying a mantle of blame on the shoulders of Israel. To think that Saudi Arabia would broker a "peace plan" is ludicrous. Will they offer their blessing of emotional and financial support to terror organizations behind the scenes, but expect to be paraded before international cameras as the bright light with a Middle East peace deal? More likely it was a smoke screen in Yasser Arafat's closest brush with death as Israel's IDF had him imprisoned in Ramallah in his besieged compound.

There is a strong desire among these nations to return to an Islamic empire of world dominating power, modeled on those of the past. One leader must arise to lead the way to realization of that ambition. The saving grace is that Muslim unity is an ethereal politic, seemingly unreachable by the Islamic nations.

Notes

1. Katz, Samuel. *Battleground, Fact and Fantasy in Palestine.*

2. Ibid

3. Ibid

4. Narrated Alqama: Volume 6, Book 60, Number 408.

"Abu Huraira reported Allah's Messenger
(Muhammed) as saying:
The last hour would not come unless the Muslims
will fight against the Jews
and the Muslims would kill them until the Jews
would hide themselves behind a stone or a tree
and a stone or a tree would say:
Muslim, or the servant of Allah, there is a Jew
behind me; come and kill him; but the tree Gharqad
would not say, for it is the tree of the Jews."

—Sayings of the Prophet
From the Hadith Sahih Muslim
Book 041, Number 6985

Recognizing the Threat

Many people do not like to talk about religion or politics, but the situation following September 11 has awakened us. Shying away from talk about religion is a secular way of escaping confrontational topics. Many secular people believe themselves to be a majority, but surprisingly, secular people are in the minority.

Islam has just topped 1.3 billion people. That is almost one-sixth of the world's population. Christianity stands at two billion, which takes up another two-sixths of the world's population. Next in line are the Hindus, standing at 900 million. The secular population is 850 million. This includes non-religious, agnostics and atheists. Buddhists come in next, numbering 360 million. It is a fact that religion makes up close to eighty percent of the world's demographics. In the majority of these religions, faith *is* their politics, so, we can no longer hide our heads in the sand and glibly remark that we don't like to talk about religion and politics. We need to know their politics. For the Islamist, religion is politics.

The technical difference between a Muslim and an Islamist is the critical issue. An Islamist is an instrument of state policy, controlled by a terror-harboring state such as Libya, Saudi Arabia, Sudan, Iraq, Iran, or Syria. There are broader concerns than Israel and the Palestinians, though this is, at present, the lightening rod. The main goal of Islamist states is to make sure that America does not become the sole superpower that would impose Western democratic values on Islamic nations through varied economic pressure tactics (e.g., sanctions and withholding foreign aid).

In light of this, and realizing the fast growing religion of Islam with its universal objectives, we must understand that our present situation is not solely about Israel. The present crisis facing us is Islamist politics.

While the West worried about what type of entertainment they would enjoy next, Islamists moved into the neighborhood. Not only in the United States, but almost every nation has experienced this same quiet influx. These were not just Muslims that look like Westerners, but more observant Muslims in full dress, living near a mosque with a minaret just like what they left in Saudi Arabia, Iraq, Iran, or whatever Islamic nation they came

121

from. On shopping trips to the mall in any large Western city, women in full Islamic dress have joined mainstream Western life.

Are these Muslims dissatisfied with their own nations and looking for new places to live? They are certainly not an economically deprived people looking for a "land of opportunity," since Islamic nations now hold much of the world's oil wealth. In fact, the more radical forms of Islam encourage their people to revert backwards in lifestyle and rally against Western culture, deeming it "infidel." Therefore, Western nations that are technologically and culturally progressive are appealing for other reasons.

The National Unity Coalition for Israel, an American pro-Israel organization, doesn't think it is dissatisfaction with their nation of origin. A recent television production, called *Jihad in America,* which they produced and aired on PBS Television networks in America, makes a bold assessment of Islamist wanderings. They believe the Islamic militant organizations to be actively seeking converts, as well as securing strongholds for the growth of Islam worldwide. The establishment of a worldwide Islamic empire is the final assessment.

In 1981, Islamic militants assassinated Egyptian President Anwar Sadat in a bold vicious bloodbath that shocked the world. He was murdered in retaliation for making a peace agreement with Israel at Camp David. This gave Islamic extremists the confidence that they could strike their enemies successfully in future attempts.

The carefully planned attack on America by bin Laden has been another "success" in their schemes.

What Does America have to Fear?

Israel has had the privilege of hosting former U.S. Marine Lieutenant Colonel Oliver North (Ret.), who broadcast his radio show live from Jerusalem over several weeks. His pro-Israel stance was a refreshment to listeners here. He spoke with authority because in the late '80s, Lt. Col. North was personally threatened by terrorists himself.

The often repeated report states that Lt. Col. North warned the U.S. Congress during a senate hearing in 1987, of impending terrorist activities from Osama bin Laden, who had threatened his life. In essence, the story is true, but the facts have become confused with the retelling. Lt. Col. North, former National Security Council Staff member and United States government's

Counter-Terrorism Coordinator from 1983-1986, straightened out the story during a recent radio program:

> I don't know who saw what video "at UNC" or anywhere else, but for the record, here's what I do know:
>
> It was the committee council, John Nields, not a senator who was doing the questioning. The security system, installed at my home just before I made a very secret trip to Teheran, cost, according to the committee, $16K not $60K.
>
> The terrorist who threatened to kill me in 1986 was Abu Nidal, (who worked for the Libyans—not the Taliban and not in Afghanistan) not Osama bin Laden.
>
> I never said I was afraid of anybody. I did say that I would be glad to meet Abu Nidal on equal terms anywhere in the world but that I was unwilling to have him or his operatives meet my wife and children on his terms.
>
> I did say that the terrorists intercepted by the FBI in Feb. 1987 to kill my wife, children and me were Libyans, dispatched from the People's Committee for Libyan Students in McClean, Virginia.
>
> And I said that the Federal Government had moved my family out of our home to a military base (Camp Lejeune, NC) until they could dispatch more than 30 agents to protect my family from those terrorists (because a liberal judge had allowed the Libyan assassins to post bond and they fled).
>
> And for your information, those federal agents remained at our home until I retired from the U.S. Marines and was no longer a "government official." By then the United States government had spent more than $2 million protecting the North family. The terrorists sent to kill us were never apprehended.
>
> Semper Fidelis,
> Oliver L. North

What does the United States have to fear? Have we been sleeping while the demographics of our cities changed around us?

We have covered the early histories of Islamic nations previously, but what about those same nations now? Have they changed their ways? Some have, but it has not been for the better, rather, for the worse.

Jihad in America

In the mid-1980s, with the Soviet invasion of Afghanistan, a new type of war began. Hindsight is always best, but the cost in this instance has been enormous and promises to increase.

Abdullah Azzam set up a support network to train *jihadis* (holy warriors) to fight against the Soviets in a full-blown "holy war." It was not just the Soviets at whom Azzam aimed his network of hatred. Jews, Christians, and moderate Muslims, whom he deems "infidels" were focused in his sights. The United States CIA was giving money to help defeat the Russians in Afghanistan. Instead of properly distributing the money, it was sent to radical Afghan Muslim militants. Indirectly, the government of the United States was funding those who would later turn on them in the biggest terror attack in the history of the world.

Now, terrorism has moved a portion of its headquarters to American soil.

In English, the sign says, "The al-Kifah Refugee Center;" but in Arabic the sign reads, " The Office of Service to Holy Warriors." Brooklyn is the site of an office that serves as a recruiting office—providing money, weapons, and all that is needed—to a frightening number of fighters of Islamic Jihad within America's borders.

That's right, it is not the Middle East—it's Middle America. As far back as 1988, Islamists in the midwest state of Kansas hosted a militant by the name of Abdullah Azzam. Abdullah has been inspiring *jihadis* in various places in America for some time. "What matters is the will power that springs from our religious beliefs," Azzam preaches to his listeners.

Pride in the fact that Afghanistan had driven Russia out of what they consider to be Allah's land, Azzam encourages them that they are invincible since they "fight in the way of Allah," a euphemism for *jihad.*

Azzam was not content to limit himself to Brooklyn. There are support and recruiting centers in thirty-eight American cities.

Palestinian Sheik Tamim al-Adnani, Azzam's aide, raised funds for the Islamist cause in Lawrence, Kansas. His vision includes a worldwide liberation movement along the lines of Ayatollah Khomeini's Islamic Revolution.

The first American Jihad Conference in Brooklyn hosted Azzam as keynote speaker. The soft-sell, plausible deniability answer to *jihad* is that it is a "personal struggle," one any religious person might engage in to better himself spiritually. Azzam clarified what the term *jihad* means to him: "The word *jihad* means fighting, fighting with the sword."

Azzam was assassinated in Pakistan later in the year of 1989. His cousin did not miss a beat and took up the American crusade where Azzam left off with even more venom. "Blood must flow, there must be widows, there must be orphans. Blood must spread everywhere in order that Allah's religion will stand on its feet!"

It is eye-opening that, according to an Islamic website, there are some 1,250 Islamic centers already in operation in the United States. New York and California vie for numbers with 176 and 157 respectively. New Jersey and Illinois follow with 86 and 91 respectively. These centers range from simple information centers to full service centers for the Islamic Umma in their areas. Some advertise Islamic schools, ranging from elementary to college level. Some of the centers have websites with news sources. Most are not openly anti-American, but have stories printed as fact that have already been proven false in the Israel-Palestine struggle. Out of that number at least thirty-eight of them are actively teaching and preaching holy war against America—"The Great Satan." Few people realize how the Islamist revolution has progressed over the last fifteen to twenty years in America's heartland.

There is nothing wrong with a Muslim Community Center which serves the needs of a people, living legally in our midst. We are a democracy. But when the violent overthrow of America is the subject of conferences, something must be done, legally and swiftly.

Not long after the Azzams indoctrination campaign really got going, groups of Islamic militants began weapons training on American soil. They were sited visiting shooting ranges and other places where they could hone their skills with weapons.

One of the leaders of the Brooklyn al-Kifah Refugee Center was arrested for the assassination of Jewish activist leader, Meir Kahane, in 1990. The presiding judge, Alvin Schlessinger, commented "I have never seen such raw red hatred that existed between any groups or persons. It was hatred that went beyond doctrine—it was raw red violent hate." The police searched this leader's apartment and found forty-seven boxes of Arabic language transcripts. Not having the readily available resources to translate all the documents, they dismissed them as religious material. After the September 11 attacks, the boxes reemerged and were translated. Those forty-seven boxes were the largest amount of terrorist material ever confiscated. Their translation provided police with masses of information on terror organizations and their plans.

In 1991, a new leader emerged from Egypt, Sheik Omar Abdul Rahman. His militant movement took the helm of the *jihad* movement in America. After being accused of plotting the assassination of Egyptian President Anwar Sadat, he fled Egypt. His list of followers include:

Siddiq Ali, the *jihad* architect who was apprehended a few months before the World Trade Center attack. He had been recruiting followers.

Clement Rodney Hampton, an American who was wounded in Afghanistan, fighting in the "holy war" against Russia, and is also a follower of Sheik Rachman. He was also involved in the assassination of Rabbi Meir Kahane.

Akman Ajaj, was arrested in an airport carrying false passports, bomb making manuals, and video tapes on *jihad*.

Ramzi Yousef, now well known from so much media coverage of his trial in the United States. Yousef came to America and went to an Islamic safe house in New Jersey where he began building the bomb that was used in the first attack on the World Trade Center. He escaped hours after the blast and was not caught until after the September 11 attack. A two million dollar reward was offered for his abduction.

Four followers of Sheik Rahman were sentenced to 240 years each in prison. Sheik Rahman's group has set up networks throughout the United States to support international terrorism. Hizballah and Hamas are included in these organizations.

Former FBI Officer Oliver B. Revell says, "Hizballah and Hamas are very active in the United States. They are involved in military training, including firearms training as well as construction of bombs."

Also in 1989, a secret meeting, that did not stay secret, took place in Kansas City. It was never meant to be broadcast to the world. Hamas terrorists, hiding their identities, boasted of their successful executions of Israelis. This conference was held for Islam's most radical leaders. Sheik Muhammed Siam, a leader of Hamas from Palestine, was there. Abdullah Anas, a leader of the Algerian Islamic Front, Washi Ganushi, head of the radical

Tunisian Fundamentalists' group called Alnada, Tofik Mustafa, leader of the Muslim Liberation Party based in Jordan, and Yousef Alkar Dawi, a militant Muslim leader from Egypt were also present.

Another active group, the Islamic Association for Palestine, IAP, which publishes books, magazines, and pamphlets on Hamas, produced a video called "Aqsa Vision," which takes credit for executions, torture, and terrorist operations inside Israel. It is named for the al-Aqsa Intifada which began in 2000. They released a communique that was intercepted, urging Muslims to die in the holy war against Jews.

Some organizations that have been investigated have claimed to have nothing to hide, only to be found later fronting terror organizations and laundering monies going to fund terror, like Sami Dhafar's Islamic Charity Project.

A catchy rally song was introduced at a conference in New Jersey organized by the IAP. They sang, "We solve our problems with an automatic rifle. We buy paradise with the blood of the Jews."

Sheik Mohammad al-Asi is a frequent speaker at radical Muslim conferences. The Tampa, Florida-based Islamic Committee for Palestine, the ICP, supports Islamic Jihad. They have been responsible for some of the bloodiest terrorist attacks in Israel. Their leader, Sami al-Arian, is seen on cable television in a program called—of all things—"Peace be upon You."

Sheik Abdl Aziz Oder, spiritual leader to militant Muslims, is invited frequently to ICP conferences. He is an active member of Sheik Rahman's group in Brooklyn.

Islamic Charity Project International is a gateway for terrorists in America. They claim to be a humanitarian relief organization. Their money goes to the *jihad* activist, Ahmed Nofal, a known recruiter for Hamas terrorists in Jordan.

And how about Alabama and Missouri?

"We use the U.S.A., because whenever we go to Afghanistan, the U.S.A. labels us as terrorists. Okay, so let us go to America where you call us tourists."

The above quote is from Sheik Bakri Mohammed, a firebrand Islamist and founder of the London-based militant al-Muhajiroun organization. From them we learn how easy it is to use training camps in America. Al-Muhajiroun, by the way, advocates uniting the world's fifty-plus Muslim nations under a single *khilafah*, or Islamic state. This is certainly proof that if Iran's Islamic Revolution begins to get bogged down, there is always another one to take its place.

The American connection is sobering. Bakri reports up to two thousand British Muslims per year going abroad to get military training, because Britain's gun laws are too stringent. However, because certain states in America have very loose gun laws, militants can easily train in these camps.

Mark Yates, a British bodyguard and firearms trainer, has allegedly been making use of America's self-service training camps as well. He operates both in the U.K. and the U.S.A., and investigations are currently underway, which may link Yates to an operation called the "Ultimate Jihad Challenge," a special project of Sakina Security Services in the U.K.

Sulayman Bilal Zain-ul-abidin, founder of Sakina Security Services, who offers this specialized *jihad* training course, promises that after learning the art of bone breaking and improvising explosive devices, the trainee will be privileged to fire off up to 3,000 rounds of live ammunition in a shooting range in the United States. Zain was arrested October 1, 2001 in Britain for providing instructional training in the making and use of firearms, explosives, chemical, biological, or nuclear weapons. Zain's apartment yielded documents linking him to Osama bin Laden and al-Qaeda. Zain was allegedly trained at a camp by Yates in the southern Wales village of Yetgoch.

This all leads us to Alabama and Missouri, where the FBI has been investigating the Ground Zero training camp outside Marion, Alabama. Ground Zero advertises a two-week course on a thousand-plus acre, state-of-the-art training base. After September 11, their website was quickly retooled to describe anti-terrorist training. CNN recently reported the story and showed viewers the compound of Ground Zero, where police cars had been used as target practice, as well as school buses equipped with crash-test dummies, also used as target practice; a bullet riddled, dilapidated house with dummies inside, also filled with bullet holes. Should the FBIs investigation find that Ground Zero is not a terrorist training ground, the question begs to be asked, "What, exactly, were the students training for?"

This news video footage was shockingly similar to the al-Qaeda terrorist training videos that we all viewed on TV following September 11.

A spokesperson for Sakina Security Services told an MSNBC reporter that three or four men who signed up for the training course were sent to an unidentified shooting club in the state of Missouri to practice their marksmanship.

The rush to cover tracks is undoubtedly in full swing by those under investigation. Retooling websites is keeping someone up all night. Then there are those claiming that storming buses and shooting crash-test dummies somehow fits into any valid and legal training program. Preposterous!

In the Middle East, we have heard this rhetoric. At the beginning of the al-Aqsa Intifada in 2000, the Palestinian cry was, "We have no guns!" as television, news media, and magazines showed hundreds of Palestinian, gun-wielding young men participating in shooting marches on the streets of Gaza, Nablus, Jenin, and Ramallah, firing their "non-existent" guns into the air.

The wake-up call has come to America. What we do with it is up to us. There is no single solution. There are many avenues from which to approach the problem. How to work toward peaceful coexistence begins in the simplest exercise: checking the most suspicious suspects.

The Flap About Profiling?

Looking for the most likely suspects during security checks according to a specific set of standards is profiling. Following the September 11 attacks, Middle Eastern, Arabic-looking men in their twenties were targeted as potential terrorists. This was the beginning of heated debate.

There are two schools of thought. One says that it is always wrong to profile people; they liken it to stereotyping, which, between the 1950s and the new millennium, evolved into a political incorrectness that bordered on criminal in the United States. It was about the absurdity of searching everyone at airports. The other school of thought is that if you don't profile people and target the most likely group, you are sure to miss the most dangerous terrorists.

"Stop Frisking Crippled Nuns" is an article that suggests the FBI should wise up and tackle the most obvious suspects—young Arab men. I think the title says it all. The author of the article is in favor of profiling people and leaving innocent people alone. Since most terror acts are perpetrated by young Arab men between the ages of eighteen and thirty, he suggests it is not wrong to profile them.

The article has some good points, but there are some points that must be taken into consideration along with his warning of caution.

Living in the Middle East, under the intense pressure of suicide bombers, a word of advice is in order. First of all, Israel is a testing ground for terrorists to see how well stratagems work. When they are tried and proven, they are exported to the rest of the world.

On the subject of profiling—last year a suicide bomber disguised himself as an Ultra-Orthodox Jew, dressed in orthodox-style clothes, hat and even long earlocks. He detonated himself in front of Jerusalem's Bikkur Holim Hospital, close to the center of the city. His body disintegrated, but to the horror of high school students, who had just been dropped off by their parents for school, the blast launched his head over the wall of their school, directly across the street from the hospital.

In another incident, a female suicide bomber disguised herself as a pregnant woman. Her "baby" was, in fact, explosives packed around her mid-section. She took the lives of many innocent victims.

A few years ago, a team of suicide bombers, disguised as an elderly couple, took a stroll down Jerusalem's most populated outdoor shopping mall with many sidewalk cafes. According to plan, they separated from each other. Situating themselves in position near Cafe Atarah, one detonated himself on one side, then the other waited until a crowd gathered and detonated himself in order to kill as many people as possible.

Then Fatah, Arafat's military militia, took to packing Red Crescent ambulances (the Islamic Red Cross) with explosives and guns for running to terror cells inside Israel proper. After a female Palestinian suicide bomber was delivered to her target by a Red Crescent ambulance driver, Israel began stopping and searching ambulances. Humanitarian agencies castigated Israel for the practice, calling it cruel and unusual punishment and going as far as blaming Israel for causing some people to fail to receive proper medical treatment due to the delays. The news media overplayed this greatly.

Arab terrorists disguise themselves as Israeli soldiers, elderly people, and Orthodox Jews; men dress as women, women dress as men. There is nothing safe. As sure as you think you have figured out a pattern, they change tactics. Crossing all lines and utilizing the element of surprise is what terrorism is all about. That is why it is called "terrorism"—the purpose is to surprise and terrify the population in hopes of effecting religious/political change.

Terrorist tactics continue to change, as do disguises. So the next time you see a nun being frisked, or a suspicious-looking old lady or man, thank God that someone is being careful and probably obeying an impression to check everyone. Here in Israel security checks occur even when we go shopping at the mall, or to a grocery store, and we are all thankful for it. I must mention though, that the only place we are not checked is when shopping in Arab sections of the city. It is well known by the Arab population that Jewish people do not bomb innocent civilians. I have never heard of an Arab bus, market, or place of business being bombed.

Stop Frisking Crippled Nuns

(Chicago) When political correctness got going in the Eighties, the laconic wing of the conservative movement was inclined to be relaxed about it. To be sure, the tendency of previously pithy identity labels to become ever more polysyllabically ornate ('person of color', 'Native American') was time-consuming, but otherwise PC was surely harmless. Some distinguished persons of non-color, among them Sir Peregrine Worsthorne, even argued that conservatives should support political correctness as merely the contemporary version of old-fashioned courtliness and good manners.

Alas, after 11 September, this position seems no longer tenable. Instead, we have to ask a more basic question: does political correctness kill?

Consider the extraordinary memo sent three weeks ago by FBI agent Coleen Rowley to the agency's director Robert Mueller, and now, despite his best efforts, all over *Time Magazine*. Ms Rowley works out of the Minneapolis field office, whose agents, last 16 August, took action to jail a French citizen of Middle Eastern origin. Zacarias Moussaoui had shown up at a Minnesota flight school and shelled out 8,000 bucks in cash in order to learn how to fly 747s, except for the landing and take-off bit, which he said he'd rather skip. On investigation, he proved to have overstayed his visa and so was held on an immigration violation. Otherwise, he would have been the 20th hijacker, and, so far as one can tell, on board United Flight 93, the fourth plane, the one which crashed in a Pennsylvania field en route, as we now know, to the White House. In Mr Moussaoui's more skilled hands—Flight 93 wound up with the runt of Osama's litter—it might well have reached its target.

Ms Rowley and her colleagues established that Moussaoui was on a French intelligence watch list, had ties to radical Islamist groups, was known to have recruited young Muslims to fight in Chechnya, and had been in Afghanistan and Pakistan immediately before arriving in the U.S. They wanted to search his computer, but to do that they needed the OK from HQ. Washington was not only uncooperative, but set about, in the words of Ms Rowley's memo, 'thwarting the Minneapolis FBI agents' efforts', responding to field-office requests with ever lamer brush-offs. How could she be sure it was the same guy? There could be any number of Frenchmen called 'Zacarias Moussaoui'. She checked the Paris phone book, which listed only one. After 11 September, when the Minneapolis agents belatedly got access to Moussaoui's computer, they found among other things the phone number of Muhammed Atta's roommate.

What was the problem at HQ? According to the New York Times's William Safire, 'Intimidated by the brouhaha about supposed ethnic profiling of Wen Ho Lee, lawyers at John Ashcroft's Justice Department wanted no part of going after this Arab.' Wen Ho Lee was a Taiwan-born scientist at Los Alamos accused of leaking nuclear secrets to the Chinese and arrested in 1999. His lawyers mobilized the Asian-American lobby, his daughter embarked on a coast-to-coast speaking tour, and pretty soon the case had effectively collapsed, leaving the Feds with headlines like 'Investigator Denies Lee Was Victim of Racial Bias' (the San Francisco Chronicle).

This was during an election campaign in which Al Gore was promising that his first act as President would be to sign an executive order forbidding police from pulling over African-Americans for 'driving while black'. Dr Lee had been arrested, wrote the columnist Lars-Erik Nelson, for 'working in a nuclear weapons laboratory while Chinese'. In August 2001, invited to connect the dots on the Moussaoui file, Washington bureaucrats foresaw only scolding editorials about 'flying while Arab'.

Example number two: another memo from last summer, this time the so-called 'Phoenix memo' sent by Kenneth Williams. This is Kenneth Williams the crack FBI Arizona agent, not Kenneth Williams of Carry On Up the Khyber fame, though in the end it might just as well have been. Agent Williams filed a report on an alarming trend he'd spotted and, just to make sure you didn't have to plough through a lot of stuff to get to the meat, the Executive Summary at the top of the memo read, 'Usama bin Laden and Al-Muhjiroun supporters attending civil aviation universities/colleges in Arizona'.

Three weeks ago, FBI director Mueller was asked why the Bureau had declined to act on the memo. He said, 'There are more than 2,000 aviation academies in the United States. The latest figure I think I heard is something like 20,000 students attending them. And it was perceived that this would be a monumental undertaking without any specificity as to particular persons.'

A 'monumental undertaking'? OK, there are 20,000 students. Eliminate all the women, discount Irv Goldbloom of Queens and Gord MacDonald of Winnipeg and Stiffy Farquahar-ffarquahar of Little Blandford-on-the-Smack and just concentrate on fellows with names like ...oh, I dunno, Muhammed, and Waleed, and Ahmed. How many would that be? 150? 200? Say it's 500. Is Mueller really saying that the FBI with all its resources cannot divert ten people to go through 2,000 names apiece and pull out the ones worth running through the computer?   Well, yes, officially, he is. But what he really means is not that the Bureau lacked 'any specificity as to particular persons', but that the specificity itself was the problem. In August 2001, no FBI honcho was prepared to fire off a memo saying 'Check out the Arabs'.

On 15 September Robert Mueller said, 'The fact that there were a number of individuals that happened to have received training at flight schools here is news, quite obviously. If we had understood that to be the case, we would have—perhaps one could have averted this.' Indeed. There weren't a lot of dots to connect. Last summer, within a few weeks of each other, the Phoenix flight-school memo and Moussaoui warrant request landed on the desk of Dave Frasca, head of the FBI's radical-fundamentalist unit. He buried the first, and refused the second.

Example three: On 1 August, James Woods, the motion-picture actor, was flying from Boston to Los Angeles. With him in the first-class cabin were half-a-dozen guys, four of whom were young Middle Eastern men. Woods, like all really good actors, is a keen observer of people, and what he observed as they flew west persuaded him that they were hijackers. The FBI has asked him not to reveal all the details, but he says he asked the flight attendant if he could speak to the pilot. After landing at LAX, the crew reported Woods's observations to the Federal Aviation Administration. The FAA did . . . nothing. Two of the four were on board the 11 September planes. There are conflicting rumors about the other two. Woods turned out to be sitting in on a rehearsal for the big day.

After 9/11, the standard line was that Osama bin Laden had pulled off an ingenious plan. But he didn't have to be ingenious, just lucky. And he was luckiest of all in that the obviousness of what was happening paradoxically made investigating it all the more problematic. His men aren't that smart—not in the sense of IRA smart, or Carlos the Jackal smart. The details Woods is permitted to discuss are in themselves very revealing: the four men boarded with no hand luggage. Not a thing. That's what he noticed first. Everyone going on a long flight across a continent takes something: a briefcase, a laptop, a shopping bag with a couple of airport novels, a *Wall Street Journal* or a *Boston Globe*. But these boys had zip. They didn't use their personal headsets, they declined all food and drink, they did nothing but stare ahead to the cockpit and engage in low murmurs in Arabic. They behaved like conspirators. And Woods was struck by the way they treated the stewardess: 'They literally ignored her like she didn't exist, which is sort of a kind of Taliban, you know, idea of womanhood, as you know, not even a human being.'

So they weren't masters of disguise, adept at blending into any situation. They weren't like the Nazi spies in war movies, urbane and charming in their unaccented English. It apparently never occurred to them to act natural, read *Newsweek*, watch the movie, eat a salad, listen to lite rock favorites of the seventies, treat the infidel-whore stewardess the way a Westerner would. Everything they did stuck out. But it didn't matter. Because the more they stuck out, the more everyone who mattered was trained not to notice them. The sort of fellows willing to fly airplanes into buildings turn out, not surprisingly, to be fairly stupid. But they benefited from an even more profound institutional stupidity. In August 2001, no one at the FBI or FAA or anywhere else wanted to be seen to be noticing funny behavior by Arabs. In mid-September, I wrote that what happened was a total systemic failure. But, as the memos leak out, one reason for that failure looms ever larger. Thousands of Americans died because of ethnic squeamishness by federal agencies.

But that was before 11 September. Now we know better . . . don't we? The federal government surely wouldn't want to add to that grim body-count . . . would they?

Well, here's an easy experiment that any *Spectator* reader can perform while waiting to board at Newark or LaGuardia. Fifteen of the 19 hijackers were young Saudi males, Osama himself is (was) a youngish Saudi male, and some 80 per cent of all those folks captured in Afghanistan and carted off to Guantanamo turn out to be young Saudi males (though, out of the usual deference to our Saudi friends, the administration is keeping studiously quiet on the last point). So you're at Newark standing in line behind a young Saudi male and an 87-year-old arthritic nun from Des Moines. Who'll be asked to remove his or her shoes? Six out of ten times, it'll be the nun. Three out of ten times, you. One out of ten, Abdumb al-Dumber. Even if this is just for show, what it's showing is profound official faintheartedness.

Norm Mineta, the Transportation Secretary, is insistent that fairness demands the burden of inconvenience be spread among all ethnic and age-groups. 'Any specificity as to particular persons' is strictly forbidden. Meanwhile, his colleagues have spent the last three weeks assuring us that another catastrophe is now inevitable. 'There will be another terrorist attack,' Robert Mueller told the National Association of District Attorneys the other day: 'We will not be able to stop it.'

We must, I suppose, take him and Cheney and Rummy and all the rest at their word. They wouldn't scare us if they hadn't done all they believe they can do. So, naturally, the mind turns to all the things they haven't done: as I write, young Saudi males are still arriving at U.S. airports on routinely issued student visas. If it lessened the 'inevitability' of that second attack just ever so slightly, wouldn't it be worth declaring a temporary moratorium on Saudi visitors, or at least making their sojourns here extremely rare and highly discretionary? Oh, no. Can't be done.

Ask why the Saudis are allowed to kill thousands of Americans and still get the kid-gloves treatment, and you're told the magic word: oil. Here's my answer: blow it out your Medicine Hat. The largest source of imported energy for the United States is the Province of Alberta. Indeed, whenever I'm asked how America can lessen its dependence on foreign oil, I say it's simple: annex Alberta. The Albertans would be up for it, and, to be honest, they're the only assimilable Canadian province, at least from a Republican standpoint. In 1972, the world's total proven oil reserves added up to 550 billion barrels; today, a single deposit of Alberta's tar shales contains more than that. Yet no Albertan government minister or trade representative gets the access in Washington that the Saudis do. No premier of Alberta gets invited to Bush's Crawford ranch. No Albertan bigshot, if you'll forgive the oxymoron, gets Colin Powell kissing up to him like 'Crown' 'Prince' Abdullah and 'Prince' Bandar do. In Washington, an Albertan can't get

. . . well, I was going to say an Albertan can't get arrested, but funnily enough that's the one thing he can get. While Bush was governor of Texas, he even managed to execute an Albertan, which seems to be more than the administration is likely to do to any Saudis.

So it's not oil, but rather that even targeting so obvious an enemy as the Saudis is simply not politically possible. Cries of 'Islamophobia' and 'racism' would rend the air. The Saudis discriminate against Americans all the time: American Jews are not allowed to enter the 'Kingdom', nor are American Episcopalians who happen to have an Israeli stamp in their passports. But America cannot be seen to take any similar measures, though it has far more compelling reasons to. James Woods puts it very well: 'Nineteen of 19 killers on 11 September were Arab Muslims - not a Swede among them.' But au contraire, in a world where the EU officially chides the BBC for describing Osama as an 'Islamic fundamentalist', we must pretend that al-Qa'ida contains potentially vast numbers of Swedish agents, many female and elderly. Even after 11 September, we can't revoke the central fiction of multiculturalism—that all cultures are equally nice and so we must be equally nice to them, even if they slaughter large numbers of us and announce repeatedly their intention to slaughter more. National Review's John Derbyshire calls this 'the reductio ad absurdum of racial sensitivity: better dead than rude'.

Last October, urging Congress to get tough on the obvious suspects, the leggy blonde commentatrix Ann Coulter declared, 'Americans aren't going to die for political correctness.'

They already have.

—by Mark Steyn[1]

A Very Credible Threat

As you can see, in light of the above, there is no doubt a credible threat to non-Muslim nations exists. We are beyond the point of preventing Islamists from settling in Western nations. Besides that, democratic nations are based upon the rights of everyone to live where, and how they choose, regardless of race or religion.

Democratic societies also defend freedom of speech. Extremist Muslim organizations abuse this freedom. In some cases, the ruse has been discovered and brought to a halt, i.e., the case of Holy Land Charities, which turned out to be a broad-based money-laundering scheme for terrorist organizations in the U.S.A.

The Taliban, and al-Qaeda familiarized us with Islamist rhetoric and coded catch-phrases inciting other Muslims to "kill infidels." We are smarter now, because in a tragic way, suffering does cause one to mature quickly.

The time of burying our heads in the sand, and hoping for the best is past now. It will not solve the problems. There is a portion of the population who desire to do something about the crisis they see—to take some kind of action. It is not their aim to harm Muslims, but to bring a halt to the threatening actions of militants. Often, governments hesitated to take action because they didn't know how to approach the issue, and feared violating civil liberties.

Understanding who the enemy is, and being able to differentiate between those who are, and those who are not threatening, is the key for the future.

The need right now, is knowing how to be effective in fighting terrorism and Islamic militancy in the West. There is no lack of places to expend energy to stem the tide of hate against innocent people.

We now know what there is to fear, and with carefully weighed reactions, directed in the proper channels, we will come out victorious.

Notes

1. Associated Press, Chicago

"In three to five years, the Iranian Islamic Republic will have the ability to construct atomic weapons without the importation of materials or technology from abroad."

—Benjamin Netanyahu, *Fighting Terrorism* [1995]

How Then Do We Live

United States President George W. Bush said in a speech in June 2002, "If we wait for threats to materialize, we will have waited too long."

The real issue of how we live now is wrapped up in aggressive damage control. The patterns of the Middle East repeat themselves consistently. Between major Middle Eastern wars, there is a period of relative calm followed by renewed terror incidents. These terror incidents escalate until they capture the attention of world powers. The bombings and killings come to a critical level and war breaks out. Each of the Middle Eastern wars has followed the same pattern. We have reached a critical level again.

Arafat would like the world to believe that it is Israel's fault that he now has "no control" over terrorists. They cite Israel's bombing of civil administrative buildings for causing them to be unable to function effectively against terrorism. Such is not the case—suicide attacks are the very reason Israel bombed Arafat's structures—many of which were bomb-making factories.

Israel is the only democracy expected to tolerate suicide bombings as part of everyday life. This type of terrorism is impossible to stop and hateful to live with. In a moment of mental clarity, Ari Fleisher, the White House spokesman, coined the term, "homicide bombers" to accurately portray suicide bombers. Their intent is not suicide, but the homicide of as many innocent people as possible.

Israel is arriving at the line drawn in the sand, which, once crossed, will mean another Middle East war.

The question then is, "How then do we live in the face of such threats?" We see Scripture being fulfilled before our very eyes in this day and time. As prophesied in Isaiah, Jewish people are coming home to the land of their Patriarchs. However, it is not only the exciting prophecies that are coming to pass, but also those things which act as the barometer of our times.

Because of the increase of wickedness, the love of most will grow cold, but he who stands firm to the end will be saved.

Matthew 24:12,13

Unholy War for An Islamic Empire

Constant attitude checks can temper the anxiety that goes with the times in which we live. Staying in tune with the Lord helps our perspective as we are bombarded by one earthly crisis after another. Remembering to view earthly events from a heavenly perspective will help us keep our sanity.

However, it behooves us to know about Islam: the differences between our faith and theirs, and be ready to stand as emissaries for the Eternal Kingdom against all false doctrines leading men astray. To separate the Muslim from his dogma and pray for him effectively means we must know what he believes. At the same time, we must understand the universal objectives of Islamists.

It is certain that other terror attacks will rivet our attention in the near future. Nevertheless, with these few points in mind, it is easier to face the future with confidence—and with a sense of joy—regardless of the time of stress that is upon the world.

How Do We Win Against Islamist Terror?

The question of "How do we live?" is synonymous with "How do we win the war against terror?" Several things need to be taken into consideration in the post-September 11 world. There has been nothing in history that has drawn the nations of the world together as quickly as the attack on the World Trade Towers in New York City. For good or for bad, attention keeps being focused on how to deal with legal questions of international terror in an international venue.

There are some flies in the ointment, making it difficult to think single-mindedly about terrorism and how to defeat it.

The United Nations as Peacekeepers

For students of the Bible, it is not hard to see how the nations of the earth will view a one-world government as a necessity for the not too distant future.

The United Nations have desired to play policemen in the Middle East since their founding in 1945. The U.N. is fast becoming a world army, with multinational forces ready to go into any area of conflict. Lately, Arafat has been on the sidelines, cheering for them as well. Arafat knows intimately the magic of diplomatic immunity, which the United Nations abuses when not under watchful eyes. Talk of a U.N. peacekeeping force in the

Middle East has begun to take on the aura of a panacea for all
Middle East ills. The need is real, as Israel is expecting a
continuation of suicide bombers and terror attacks until a new
Palestinian Authority can be put into place. However, a
transitional period is needed, so that a new PA can become
equipped to take control of the violent factions that have torn at
the region until now.

As early as 1949, Kermit Roosevelt, son of Theodore Roosevelt,
wrote about the United Nations:

> Are we yet aware of the danger that in the Middle East the
> United Nations may come to be regarded and mistrusted
> and hated as the guardian of the New World Order—the New
> Age trappings for the old Humanistic conspiracy of Left and
> Right together? The danger of Russia and the United States
> is the seen danger, and a grave one it is. Seen, it must in
> time be settled by peace or war. The danger of Orient versus
> Occident—or Islamic culture versus Christian culture—
> seems as yet unseen. That could be ruinous. We may well
> succumb to it from not seeing. We must not assume in the
> days ahead that the crisis in the Middle East can be solved
> through military alliances, political connivance, or strategic
> initiative. Beware of the politicians that propose such a
> solution—they may be fairly regarded, whether from the Left
> or Right as a part of the same old entrenched interests that
> have stood against the Christian faith and have fought for a
> mechanical imposition of a New Age or a New World Order
> since the time of the Fall.[1]

The need for help in this conflict is obvious, but jumping into a
program before all things are considered is dangerous. Several
things need to be taken into consideration before forcing upon
Israel a third party to act as hall monitor. In light of recent events,
what kind of a peacekeeping force would need to be sent?

Two major issues need addressing: the de-legitimization of
such a force by Islamic terrorists, and the track record of the
agency most likely to set up such a force, the United Nations.

De-legitimization

In March 2002, a vehicle of the Temporary International
Presence in Hebron (TIPH) was attacked near Hebron. The TIPH is

an observation force of six nations appointed by a U.N. resolution in the late 1990s. The nations involved are Norway, Italy, Denmark, Sweden, Switzerland, and Turkey.

White TIPH vehicles are clearly marked with enormous black letters to make them instantly identifiable. The Turkish TIPH Capt. Huseyin Ozaslah told rescue workers that on the night of March 29, traveling on a road near Hebron, a Palestinian policeman was standing in the middle of the street, motioning them to stop. Ozaslah hailed the man who was dressed in a Palestinian police uniform, telling him in Arabic that they were TIPH workers and not to shoot at them. From a distance of five or six meters, the man shot anyway and killed the two workers in the front seat and then shot Ozaslah, who was sitting in the back seat, only wounding him. Supposing Ozaslah to be dead, the terrorist left the scene.

A Hebron spokesman said, "The murder of the TIPH observers proves that terror knows no borders."

If the people that the U.N. is sent here to protect are rising up against them, the logical conclusion is that the regional instability will render a peacekeeping force organized by the United Nations useless. This was an attempt at a soft peacekeeping force. It failed. Who then should be sent here? And who will take responsibility for peacekeeping forces that fail at their jobs?

Don't Appoint the United Nations as Overseer

The U.N. has sullied its reputation a number of times. A very important one being early in the Israel-Lebanon crisis in the 1980s. Several miles south of Sidon in Lebanon, stood a United Nations Vocational Training Center, perched atop a mountain with a commanding view of the Mediterranean. Israel, upon taking command of the area during its war against terrorist factions in southern Lebanon, discovered that the school had also served as a training camp for Fatah, Arafat's terror organization. This wasn't just a chalk board in a school hall. Hosted by United Nations Relief and Works Agency (UNRWA), the school housed a modern audio-visual language laboratory, rivaling any university campus. The amount of ammunition was stunning. Day after day, Israelis worked to defuse bombs, remove booby traps, and sort and load trucks of ammunition and weapons stored in the complex. Arafat's personal quarters were outfitted with a large flag on which was a black swastika against a red background. Unfortunately, no UNRWA staff could be found to comment on the misuse of the United Nations Vocational Training Center.

This incident spurred the *New York Times* to run a full-page advertisement entitled "Call to Conscience." The article condemned, in no uncertain terms, the assaults orchestrated by the Arab bloc, which was then married to the Soviet bloc, in their campaign to isolate and discredit Israel. Among those signing the "Call to Conscience" were thirty-four Nobel Prize winners. They stated, "Those who vow to eliminate the State of Israel and refuse to make peace are permitted to sit in the councils of the peacemakers, while Israel, a member State, created in fidelity to the principles of the United Nations, is slandered and faced with the threat of de-legitimization."

Stories of convicted U.N. gun-runners and U.N. suppliers of explosives to terror organizations exist in the archives of the *Jerusalem Post* newspaper. Diplomatic immunity freed these criminals to strike again.

More recently, Israel has been the continued target of a heavily Arabized U.N., which has welcomed Arafat, the yet-to-be president of a hoped-for state. Many feel that the United Nations prematurely appointed Palestine member nation status and would like to see it revoked. The track record of Palestine should be enough to do that if there is a governing body with any propensity toward legal protocol. The bone in the throat of Arab and Islamic leaders who pull great weight in the U.N. is that they cannot push Arafat's desired state into being, because Israel stands in their way. Therefore, with the help of the United Nations, the Arab-Islamic bloc continues to sanction Israel at every turn.

In the summer of 2000, diplomatic immunity stood in the way of calling the U.N. to criminal account. U.N. trucks and equipment were used on the Lebanon-Israel border to kidnap three Israeli soldiers. A video of the kidnapping was taken, and edited parts made their way into the news media. Israel's repeated request to view the unedited footage of the video fell on deaf ears. The U.N. was never called to question, nor was any kind of punitive action taken by their own organization.

Israel's requests for help in locating the three soldiers went ignored by the U.N. Finally, Israeli authorities and the Chief Rabbi of Israel pronounced the soldiers "dead" in order to allow the three families closure regarding their sons.

Unholy War for An Islamic Empire

New York City Council members are presenting a resolution asking President George W. Bush to declare the Palestinian Authority a "terrorist organization." and they will then demand that the U.N. remove PA offices from the precincts of the United Nations buildings.

The above evidence is incriminating enough to block the deployment of any U.N. peacekeeping force. All things considered, it is evident that the U.N. cannot successfully broker a peacekeeping force in the region.

Palestinian Refugees

The United Nations has a pick-and-choose method of operation when it comes to refugees and how they offer aid. When the U.N. Security Council voted in favor of partition in 1947, dividing the land into two states, one Jewish, one Arab, the Arabs rejected it. In the ensuing war, 600,000 Arab refugees fled to escape the battle. Panic caused them to flee when Arab radio urged them to escape the danger until the Jewish population could be annihilated by their armies. Israel urged the Arabs to ignore the sensational broadcasts and to not leave their homes, assuring them of their safety.

The fact that is less often heard is that many more Jews were forced out of Arabic nations in retaliation for the war. Most of them were forced to leave everything behind and arrived in Israel with nothing. Their homes were confiscated and goods stolen.

These statistics are baffling for several reasons. For starters, fifty-four years later, according to Arafat, there are still 400,000 Palestinian refugees wanting to come home. He is demanding the "right of return" for them in any peace treaty that will be agreed upon. Amazingly, from the same war, there are no Jewish refugees, even following the hundreds of thousands left homeless after Hitler's regime or those expelled from Arab lands. All the Jews were systematically absorbed into Jewish society by a nation scraping to make ends meet. With incredibly wealthy Arab nations surrounding the Palestinian refugee problem, why were the Arab refugees not absorbed? Why have they not been properly cared for over these past fifty plus years?

Therefore, it must be acknowledged that the U.N. chose to cooperate with Arab leaders who have kept the Palestinian refugee camps in operation through UNRWA since the 1950s. These

144

refugee camps and their squalor continue to be used as political tools.

UNRWA's operation in the Middle East leaves much to be desired, in that, even though they are the agency aiding the refugees, they are forced to deal by the rules of organizations like Hamas, Fatah, and other militias. United Nations facilities have routinely been abused by the militias. U.N. facilities have been used as storehouses for weapons and explosives and even bomb making factories.

Speaking of picking and choosing, India is a good example. More than 15 million Indian and Pakistani refugees were left homeless. There are now 100 million descendants of the original number. The U.N. did not make an international issue of India's refugee problem, nor did they urge them not to settle as has been the case with Palestinian refugees.

UNRWA and the Arab League combined use the Palestinian refugees as pawns in the chess game of Middle East politics.

Legal Action Against Terrorists

What promises to become an international problem of grave proportion is how to deal with apprehended terrorists. International terrorism constitutes an unseen army with no borders. Never in history have nations been posed such a dilemma.

Since April 2002, the arrest of Fatah-Tanzim leader Marwan Barghouti, Arafat's right-hand man, is now presenting Israel with just such decisions. Israeli Justice Minister Meir Sheetrit has warned heads of Israeli justice that Barghouti's case is fraught with snares. Sheetrit warns that Barghouti should be tried in a civil court instead of a military court. The civil trial would allow all the world access to the documented evidence of Arafat's Fatah-Tanzim militia's terror funding and participation. The rest of the world would be able to have access to documentation of his plans and the actions he took in carrying out planned terrorist attacks. If Barghouti was tried in a military court, all documentation would be classified.

There are at least two ways to approach Barghouti's trial. The first being Penal Law, and the second is a 1945 Emergency Defense Regulation. Penal Law would forbid Barghouti's execution, whereas the Emergency Defense Regulation would allow his execution, should the evidence point to the stricter measure.

Another plan that Israelis considered was the Fourth Geneva Convention. This law was drawn up to protect populations in areas of dispute considered "occupied" territory. Such is the case with Marwan Barghouti.

A military trial might draw the ire of human rights organizations as well, since evidence would not be available to public media organizations. Barghouti's guilt would be supposed instead of proven fact.

In the U.S., cautious levelheaded thinking is needed. The present trials of John Walker Lindh, the Californian who joined the Taliban in Afghanistan against his own country, and Zacarias Moussaoui, the French-born terrorist, will set precedents for future prosecution of terrorists on American soil.

Documented Proof

With the lengthy list of PLO atrocities in Appendix B, Yasser Arafat should be on the top of the agenda to be put on trial for criminal acts against humanity. It is a disgrace to ascribe to Arafat the position of leader of a people, as well as a Nobel Peace prize laureate.

The documented evidence found by the IDF during Operation Defensive Shield is enough evidence of Arafat's direct involvement in terror operations.

His track record has nothing that qualifies him to the exalted position of Chairman or President of a State. Rampant mismanagement of donated funds dogs his chairmanship. The list of his terror victims and his inability—or refusal—to bring terrorism under control in Gaza and the West Bank underscore his lack of credentials to lead any people.

Crimes Against Humanity

The total number of victims of terror before 1994 is 112—with the U.S. Marines added, it is 353. At the writing of this book, the total number from 1994, when other terror groups became involved, is 414, bringing the numbers to 767.

In a twenty-one month time period between the beginning of

146

the al-Aqsa Intifada, September 2000, and July 2002, 120 human "homicide" bombers were dispatched into Israel proper, taking the lives of 250 people. The increase in terrorism goes off the chart.

Saleh Abdal Jawwad, head of the Political Science and History Departments at Bir Zeit University in the West Bank, said, "Sharon's policies are pushing the Palestinians to this" (speaking of suicide bombings). If this is true, why does the list of victims (Appendix B) show an ongoing reign of terror from the PLO's inception? And why did they decline the offer of statehood on ninety-two percent of the West Bank, East Jerusalem, and a large portion of the Old City of Jerusalem, when former Prime Minister Barak was ready to hand it over to them in 2000? Why, instead, did Arafat launch a new wave of terror, called the al-Aqsa Intifada?

Israel has given Arafat detailed lists of wanted terrorists to place under arrest. It was an exercise in futility. When world focus is on the PA, arrests are made, prisoners are placed in comfortable quarters until the heat dies down, and then they are released.

If statehood is awarded to the Palestinians now, it will be the reward of bloody violence. How will they handle other matters, such as water rights, municipality division, electricity (now provided by Israel), gas for cooking and heating, health care, and transportation? They are not prepared to govern a state.

To fight terror properly, Arafat should be tried in an international court for the deaths of the victims of his terror organizations. He has overseen situations within his own nation that have created the present crisis, that threatens to spill over the borders of Israel into the rest of the world. Those factors that threaten stability are:

- Glorification of *shaheedeen* (suicide bombers as heros)
- Posters of martyrs in public places including schools
- Substantial financial rewards to families of martyrs
- Rage instilled in children from text books, K-University
- Television coverage of young children shouting hate slogans against Jewish people
- *Shaheedah* (martyr) videos with farewell messages that are shown to students, some even showing their parents blessing the young suicide bombers just before their missions
- Not arresting known terrorists and leaving them still active

147

- Harboring terrorist groups on the U.S. list of terrorist organizations such as, Hamas and Islamic Jihad within PA-controlled cities

After Operation Defensive Shield in 2002, Arafat was forced to restructure his Palestinian Authority. The restructuring he did was called a farce by the Israeli government, when he announced that he would add Islamic Jihad and Hamas to his governmental cabinet.

Shortly thereafter, U.S. President George W. Bush called upon the Palestinian people to oust Arafat and begin with a new government, if they ever expected to see a Palestinian state become a reality.

Within days of Bush's call to oust Arafat, over four thousand citizens in Gaza protested in the streets against Arafat and PA policies. These citizens are hungry, desperate and unemployed. Where they once worked for Israeli employers, now they cannot even feed their families, thanks to Arafat's strategies. The Palestinian people are the ones suffering under the Palestinian Authority.

The Question of Diplomatic Immunity

The harsh military strike that was perpetrated against Libya in 1986 should be considered as an option against other terrorist states, organizations, and leaders.

Mu'ammar Ghadaffi does not possess the charisma that some other Islamic leaders have. Therefore, being no one's favorite, the measures that worked against him were not contested. Libya was, for the most part, taken completely out of the terrorism exporting business.

Unfortunately, that victory in the war against terror is just about to be sorely contested.

Daniel and Susan Cohen, who lost their twenty-year-old daughter, Theodora, in the bombing of Pam Am flight 103 over Lockerbie, Scotland, are coming to the end of their fourteen-year horror ordeal. The Libyan government is going to pay punitive damages of $12.7 billion to the families of victims on that airline. The Cohens stand to collect remuneration totaling $10 million— but not all at once. The payments will come in three installments. This has the Cohens up in arms, not over money, but over a principle that is being spelled out by the circumstances.

It should be more than obvious that the punitive damage claim is as good as a guilty verdict, but not exactly. Four million dollars come to the Cohen family when the U.S. lifts governmental sanctions against Libya. Libya is supposed to take full responsibility for the terrorist act, publically, through the media. However, the Cohens report that this has not been written into the settlement agreement.

The second four million dollars will be handed over to them when all commercial sanctions are lifted against Libya. Amazingly, the West learns its lessons the hard way, as there are U.S. companies lining up to invest billions in Libya. This, unfortunately, will put Libya back on the fast track to becoming an A-1, terror-harboring nation.

The last two million dollars come to the Cohens when Libya is taken off the list of state sponsors of terrorism. This paves Libya's way to receive major finances from the West once again. It is guaranteed that Libya will be back in the news once all this has been accomplished.

The Cohens are not against relieving Ghadaffi of huge sums of money. As a matter of fact, they see it as a method of harming his abilities to continue on. However, they doubt that they will agree to the settlement, seeing it as the enrichment and rehabilitation of one of the Middle East's terror kings, placing him back in the running.

All this is to say that to win the war against terror once and for all, international conventions need to agree on suspending immunity normally extended to heads of state. Actually, just the opposite, legal regulations need to be put in place.

Immunity for other heads of state should be rescinded as stringently as with Libya if they exist on an internationally agreed upon terrorist list.

Is Genesis 12 for Here, Today?

There are several examples of what life can be like outside the parenthesis of hatred and violence. The Arab Islamic village of Abu Ghosh, on the outskirts of Jerusalem, is a prime example of proper coexistence. Abu Ghosh has not been responsible for any terror attacks in Arafat's uprisings. The village enjoys prosperity and a symbiotic relationship with Jewish people. They understand that they live in Israel under the umbrella of an Israeli government. Restaurants thrive and are always filled with Israeli restaurant goers. Other businesses thrive as well and are frequented not only by the people of the village, but by Jewish Jerusalemites as well.

Arabic areas in the north of Israel, such as Haifa and Tiberias, also enjoy the same prosperity. Terror incidents in the north are orchestrated almost 100-percent by outsiders, generally from Jenin, and other West Bank cities, which have been a hotbed of terrorist activity, since as far back as the British Mandate period.

There is an appropriate blessing—or curse:

I will bless those who bless you, and whoever curses you I will curse.

Genesis 12:3

The villages mentioned do not curse the Jewish people, engage in violent activity, or incite their people against Israel. As a result, they enjoy a good life, they are healthy, and prosperous, and enjoy proper relationships between two people groups inhabiting the same area. Creating a Palestinian state will not solve the deep-rooted problems. Almost as many Palestinians live in Israel proper as will fall within the boundaries of a newly created state.

The obvious plus of cohabitation is the social infrastructure already in operation in the State of Israel. Sick or wounded Palestinians are taken to Israeli hospitals (even suicide bombers who manage only to wound themselves), because they prefer them to Palestinian hospitals. Palestinians enjoy all the benefits of a first world nation at Israel's expense.

Do Not Relax

It is important not to be lulled into an "everything will work out" syndrome. Looking at the escalating Islamist revolution and how it has spread over the world in the last twenty years should tell us that there is a long-term job ahead.

The threat of Communism was a smoke screen covering what we have seen since the fall of the former Soviet Union. The Islamic populations in the southern provinces of Russia were hidden behind a wall of godlessness. When the restriction was removed, the rush to reassert religious tradition was astounding.

Now that the Islamic Revolution has successfully spread to the shores of America, Europe, Australia, South America, and Africa, we, as Christians, are facing new difficulties. In Western democracies, Muslims have a right to choose their living place. The fact that they live in Western nations is not the point. It is the Islamists that live among them that is the concern.

Terrorists cannot exist without supporting communities. Terrorist-harboring nations could end terrorism today if they would remove their safe havens of refuge. Likewise, in our Western societies, there are safe havens of refuge, where terrorists hide and plot terror attacks. These acts are not done in a vacuum. Those who know of them and their plots need to make decisions to end their reigns of hate by turning them in to authorities.

Friday messages from mosques that incite violence should be met with immediate legal action. The closing of Islamic community offices and centers will get the message across in record time. We cannot wait for them to commit a crime. There are laws that cover hate crimes and incitement that will quell a rising tide of *jihad* in our midst.

Weapons of Their Warfare

Why does the West agree to be held hostage? We are three decades on the other side of the Arab Oil Embargo of 1973. The Oil Embargo was only one incident in a long string of oil wars: the Suez Crisis of the 1950s, the Six Day War of 1967, the aforementioned Arab Oil Embargo of 1973, the Iranian Revolution, the Iran-Iraq War, and the Gulf War, which all used oil as part of the equation. Once again, world consumer nations are being threatened with being held hostage by oil.

Iraq has tried to use oil threats to force Israel to withdraw from Palestinian cities. Saddam Hussein said in a speech, "The oppressive Zionist and American enemy has belittled the capabilities of the [Arab] nation." In his threat of 2002, the pipeline in Turkey at Chyhan stopped receiving oil during a 30-day embargo which he imposed. Saddam tried to enlist the help of other Arab nations in his pressure tactics against Israel's "incursion" into Palestinian territory. Saddam's little black phone book included Iran and Libya, who (no surprise) expressed their support. Iranian supreme leader Ayatollah Ali Khamenei also called on Islamic countries to stop supplying oil for one month to countries who have close relations with Israel. Libya announced, shortly thereafter, that it had supported the call as well.

Unholy War for An Islamic Empire

In a world struggling to recover from the September 11 terror attack, the oil embargo added salt to an open wound. It has been reported that just a one percent increase at the pump can affect spending by $1 billion in the U.S. alone.

Many Americans look back nostalgically to the time when we pumped our own oil. Texas, Oklahoma, Alaska, and other fields were rich and adequately supplying us. In fact, in 1950, the United States provided 52 percent of the world's oil needs, compared to only 10 percent today. Americans question why we need to purchase outside oil when we have our own oil fields.

On a flight to the United States from the Middle East, I met an Iraqi Christian who worked as an oil engineer, fleeing Iraq for his life to live in the United States. I asked him why America no longer pumps their own oil. The answer was that Iraq's oil fields are artesian. When tapped, the oil gushes out of the ground of its own accord, no pumping is needed. Saddam's psychotic arson spree after the Gulf War in the Kuwaiti oil fields was so hard to extinguish, because the oil is under pressure and was blasting its way to the surface. Oil pumping raises the price of a barrel of oil substantially.

That is the bad news, but there is also good news. The saving grace of this situation is that the 1973 Oil Embargo harmed several of the Arab nations who became involved in it. Some of those nations' Gross National Product is as much as two-thirds in oil revenues, and, thus, can not afford to stop the flow of oil. Should boycotts not attain their goals, the search for oil may just begin to move out of the Middle East to other fields and bring promise to some oil producers who otherwise may not have risen above the cartel. In addition, the Strategic Oil Reserve was started after the 1973 debacle. Four billion barrels of oil stand ready to be tapped, should the Arab nations throw themselves fully into another embargo. This is equal to more than five years of Iraqi oil production.

The final bit of cushion is that in 2000 Saudi Arabia hosted a pledge by the Organization of Petroleum Exporting Countries (OPEC), indicating that oil would not be used as a political weapon.

The New Anti-Semitism

A new emerging anti-Semitism is the worst part of this tragedy. It is naive to think that anti-Semitism would resurrect with the same face it wore in Hitler's Germany.

The new anti-Semitism is pressure from the West, specifically Britain, the U.S., and Europe upon Israel to "restrain" herself from striking hard against terrorism, even as America has had to do in Afghanistan.

What this implies is that Jewish lives are expendable.

It also says that we have no plans to take our own war against terrorism where its roots really are. Even more troubling is that we see a percentage of Jewish people unconsciously buying into the West's assessment of them. A sense of worthlessness in the world arena of nations seems to hover over Israel's citizens. Any program, statement by a politician, or request from a government official which reinforces the message that Israel refrain from defending itself is anti-Semitism. The pressure reinforces Israel's suspicions that somehow she does not belong to the community of democratic nations. The United Nations has been foremost in fomenting this "new anti-Semitism" in the world arena. And this is the reason Israel is adamantly against a U.N. or E.U. peacekeeping force here.

Arafat's hands drip with the blood of Jews and his lips have never uttered a sincere word of remorse for all he has been responsible. Arafat invented airplane hijacking. He is known as the father of terrorism and continues to this day. In 1974, Yasser Arafat addressed the United Nations General Assembly. He is the first representative of a stateless organization to do so. He was wearing a pistol. At that assembly, he held up an olive branch and offered the world his olive branch or his gun. His warning was, "Do not let the olive branch fall from my hands." It is now evident which one he meant to use. His presence was highly controversial, since much of world opinion considers him a terrorist bent on Israel's annihilation. Following his historic address, the U.N. granted the PLO "observer status" and has formally supported the Palestinians' right to "sovereignty and national independence."

Europe's anti-Semitism is also on the rise. It is reportedly worse than before WWII. A high percentage of participants in rallies against Israel are made up of Arab Islamic extremists.

Recent media coverage of suicide bombings in Israel brought the Israeli government to the boiling point. Threats were made by Israel to cancel certain television news media rights when the family who lost a mother, grandmother, and baby in the same attack were given passing coverage, whereas, the family of the suicide bomber was interviewed for fifteen minutes.

America's swift retribution against Osama bin Laden in

Afghanistan is testimony to her sense of the indignity of feeling violated. Why is Israel not allowed to act against the same indignity to protect her citizens? To win this war on terrorism, we must be willing to support and assist efforts on all fronts.

"Either" "Or"

This is a book with no end! Without doubt, future editions will be amended to include the next terrorist crisis. Too many times, succeeding attacks make the previous one pale into insignificance.

There are two avenues of action. Either we mentally forfeit the battle and step back from the arena and let it all happen around us, or we step up to the fight and do all we can—in proper legal spheres, of course—to protect ourselves from a wave of Islam gone berserk.

Yeshua told the parable of a man of noble birth who went to a far country to have himself appointed king. He told the parable just prior to His triumphal entry into Jerusalem. There, people spread their cloaks in the road before Him (a practice reserved for kings).

To his servants, the man gave monetary gifts and commanded them to "occupy" until he returned.

> *And he called his ten servants, and delivered them ten pounds, and said unto them, "Occupy* [pragmateuoma] *till I come."*

> Luke 19:13 (KJV)

The Greek word, *pragmateuomai,* from which we get pragmatic, means "to carry on the business to which you have been appointed." If we see this as meaning that we should be about the business of the coming Kingdom, the only obvious answer is to "occupy" actively and busy ourselves with divine ambassadorship. It is not easy work, but it is rewarding. Fear, which is followed by just holding on to what has been given you, will cause us to lose this battle, and any battle to which we are assigned.

154

Turn the Other Cheek?

One problem for Christians is confusion about Yeshua's command to turn the other cheek.

How do we interpret His command, when slapped by those who hate us in light of our present worldwide terror dilemma?

If someone strikes you on one cheek, turn to him the other also. If someone takes your cloak, do not stop him from taking your tunic.

Luke 6:29

There must be differentiation between interpersonal relationships and national crisis. Jesus' directive must be seen in light of another directive in the book of Romans:

Everyone must submit himself to the governing authorities, for there is no authority except that which God has established. The authorities that exist have been established by God. Consequently, he who rebels against the authority is rebelling against what God has instituted, and those who do so will bring judgment on themselves. For rulers hold no terror for those who do right, but for those who do wrong. Do you want to be free from fear of the one in authority? Then do what is right and he will commend you. For he is God's servant to do you good. But if you do wrong, be afraid, for he does not bear the sword for nothing. He is God's servant, an agent of wrath to bring punishment on the wrongdoer.

Romans 13:1-4

Therefore, turning the other cheek in Luke chapter six is in the context of an interpersonal relationship. Submitting to the governing authorities is an international affair. Submission to governors, and entreating them in legal venues is the avenue with which to defeat an enemy wishing to destroy us nationally.

Notes

1. Bodanski, Yossef. *Target America.*

Artists' rendition of a soldier from WWI

"It is right that Palestine should become a Jewish state, if the Jews, being given the full opportunity, make it such. It was the cradle and home of their vital race, which has made large spiritual contributions to mankind, and is the only land in which they can hope to find a home of their own; they being in this last respect unique among significant peoples."

—American delegation to the peace conference after World War I, January 21, 1919

The Mandate

As the swirling dust of WWI settled and nations brought their soldiers home from foreign lands, almost as an after thought, a new Middle East emerged from the farthest reaches of the conflict. Far away and very different from the West, the romantic sands of the deserts of the Middle East were the stage for drama. Lawrence of Arabia and others like him were the new movie material. Classics rose from the sun-baked land. From as far away as Australia, proud horsemen, known as the "Lighthorsemen," aided the British against the German-backed Turkish forces in photogenic settings, such as the oasis of Be'er Sheva, which sits astride the southern Negev Desert in the Holy Land.

The Middle East was not content to remain a peripheral issue. The war shook many foundations, and solutions for repairing those foundations laid the groundwork for the implementation of mandates for the Middle East. A mandate bonds three parties: the creator of the mandate, the executor, and the lesser party whom the mandate is designed to protect. It is a commission from a higher authority to carry out an injunction on behalf of a lesser nation.

The war drove back the once flourishing Islamic Turkish Ottoman Empire and left huge areas of the borderless desert sands wiped clean like a slate. The powers that were suddenly in command after the war unrolled their maps on the tables and began to draw new boundary lines. On the one hand, the lines drawn in the settling sands of the Middle East by Western powers were simply arbitrary guess work. The accusation of many Arab nations in recent days is that those Western powers had no right to "draw the lines."

On the other hand, some of the lines were not man-made, but decrees from heaven. They lay just beneath the sand and needed simply to be brushed off and reinstated from ancient times. The nation of Israel lay veiled in Islamic dust, awaiting God's perfect timing. A new chapter of spiritual history opened as the breath of His Spirit blew away the covering.

With that unveiling, many biblical references demanded rethinking, fresh interpretation, and resolution. From those biblical references, an ancient mandate, whose time had come to fruition, emerged. It could not have been written for any other time period—it is for us, now! It is recorded in the book of Isaiah, and its components are unlike any other:

*. . . You who call upon the L*ORD*, give yourselves no rest, and give Him no rest till He establishes Jerusalem and makes her the praise of the earth.*

Isaiah 62:6b,7

Jerusalem had almost been forgotten. Liberal theology had almost succeeded in relegating Jerusalem to the archives of ancient literature, never to rise again. However, the above mandate is from God, given through the prophet Isaiah to all who call upon the Lord on behalf of Jerusalem. Ceaseless beseeching of the Almighty to make Jerusalem *the* praise in the earth.

Prior to several events, this mandate could not even be considered more than folk literature by liberal expositors of the Bible. Prior to the British defeat of the Turks in 1917 and the ensuing years which became the window of opportunity for the dispersed Jewish people to begin the return to their homeland, God's mandate in Isaiah was mere fiction.

The League of Nations, formed after WWI, issued mandates to protect people groups not yet equipped to govern themselves independently. Many of the Middle Eastern areas taken out from under the umbrella of the Ottoman Empire were not able to formulate an infrastructure successfully enough to assure them safety and independence from larger and more powerful surrounding neighbors.

The above-mentioned biblical mandate evokes some degree of apprehension. A commission to irritate a figure of immeasurable might and authority seems like something from a bad fairy tale. Yet, Isaiah delivers a mandate of irrevocable authority. It is easy to have this short section of Scripture escape our attention. Perhaps the extreme cost of taking the mandate seriously is too high.

Christian history boasts a long list of predecessors who saw the mandate as incumbent upon themselves. It is all too true that Christianity persecuted Jewish people over the centuries, but there were some who clearly saw the mandate I speak of. Some saw Israel's rebirth even before the Jews themselves were interested.

These Christian men and women, and their acts of valor on behalf of Israel, punctuate history books with selfless stories of aid to an oppressed people, desperately searching for a haven they could call home. Their involvement spans several centuries. They include the following men and women:

Sir Henry Finch

Sir Henry Finch, a British Christian steeped in the knowledge of the Bible and the Hebrew language, served several terms as a member of Parliament and was a jurist of considerable renown. In 1621, he published a treatise, called *The World's Great Restoration*, with the subtitle, *The Calling of the Jews*. It is a veritable classic of early Christian pro-Zionist literature.

This angered King James I, and Finch and his publisher were arrested in April 1621 and thrown into jail.

It was the first time in the history of Zionism that an outspoken supporter of the idea of "the return" was to pay with his liberty for his ideas. He was ultimately released.

Oliver Cromwell

In 1656, Oliver Cromwell delivered a "Zionist" speech at the Little Parliament, having been influenced by the many Christian Zionists cropping up all over England.

Holger Paulli

During this same period, a Dane, Holger Paulli, not only believed wholeheartedly in the Jewish return to the Holy Land, but he worked intensively for the establishment of a Jewish monarchy in Palestine. He published books and memoranda, which he dispatched to the kings of England and France, calling on them to go forth and conquer Palestine, so that the Jews might regain their state.

Napoleon Bonaparte

In 1799, Napoleon issued his Manifesto on the return of the land to its lawful heirs, the Jews.

U.S. President John Q. Adams

In 1826, U.S. President John Q. Adams wrote, "I sincerely wish the Jews a State in Judea."

John Nelson Darby

In 1830, John Nelson Darby founded the Plymouth Brethren. Through their publication, *Christian Witness*, he expounded his views on Israel and his doctrines on dispensationalist pre-millennialism!

George Gawler

George Gawler was an English Christian who produced a practical plan for resettlement in Palestine and then set out to implement it.

159

Unholy War for An Islamic Empire

The Jewish population of Jerusalem was hesitant, but the Montefiore-Gawler projects, including the community of Yemin Moshe, the first neighborhood outside the walls of the Old City of Jerusalem, went ahead. Modern Jewish agricultural communities in Palestine owe their beginnings to these two men.

Lord Shaftesbury

In 1840, Lord Shaftesbury drew up a plan for the resettlement of the Jews in Palestine and Lord Palmerston pledged the power of England to secure their protection. They even wrote the Turkish Sultan with their plan.

Lawrence Oliphant

In 1880, Lawrence Oliphant wrote a plan, *Land of Gilead*, which outlined Jewish settlement in Palestine, then encouraged Jewish organizations to begin settlement. This time, the Sultan of Turkey actually accepted the plan, and then rejected it as a British political ploy.

William E. Blackstone

In 1891, William E. Blackstone obtained public backing for a petition to U.S. President Harrison on *Palestine for the Jews,* which resulted in an American appeal to major European powers for the realization of that goal.

Frederick the Great was reported to have said to him: "Doctor, if your religion is a true one, it ought to be capable of very brief and simple proof. Will you give me an evidence of its truth in one word?" The good man answered—"Israel."

William H. Hechler

William H. Hechler was a British clergyman, whose parents were German. Born in South Africa, he studied theology and was ordained as a Protestant pastor.

Following the fierce pogroms in Russia in 1881, Hechler participated in a meeting in London of Christian notables which considered possibilities for settling Jewish refugees from Russia and Rumania in Palestine. He wrote a treatise, *The Restoration of the Jews to Palestine According to the Prophets,* in which he foresaw, on the strength of biblical prophecies, that the Holy Land would be restored to the Jewish people within the years 1897-98. (If the date of the First Zionist Congress, which assembled in 1897, is taken as the starting point of the modern restoration of Israel, then Hechler's prediction was indeed accurate.)

Hechler's treatise is a model Christian testimonial to Zionism. Along with a description of biblical prophecy, Hechler included a chronological calculation, which pointed to 1897 or 1898 as the beginning of Jewish restoration. Stressing the prospect of reuniting the first dispersed Jews in their ancestral land, Hechler said, "The Zionist return of the Jews would become a great blessing to Europe," and urged "an end to the anti-Semitic spirit of hatred, which is detrimental to the welfare of all our nations."

Hechler managed to convince the German Emperor that he should back the Jewish return to Zion. He succeeded, which amounted to a clear act of recognition of the Zionist Movement by the sovereign of a crucially important Protestant European power, who was about to enter the walled city.

Needless to say, Hechler was a very special guest at the First Zionist Congress in Basle, Switzerland. He also attended a number of subsequent congresses and continued to stand by the Zionist Movement long after Herzl's death in 1904.

Lord Arthur Balfour and David Lloyd George

In 1917, there was a major breakthrough in the quest for Jewish statehood. Both British Prime Minister David Lloyd George and his War Secretary, Lord Arthur Balfour, worked to get the approval for what has become known as the Balfour Declaration. Their friendship with Dr. Chaim Weizmann and Weizmann's contribution to the British War effort brought about an understanding of the desire of the Jews to return to Palestine as a religious and historical right. Both Balfour and Lloyd George were deeply religious and were steeped in the Bible. They were very much in favor of implementing this plan. The Balfour Declaration called for "the establishment in Palestine of a national home for the Jewish people."

Orde Wingate

Orde Wingate was a strong Bible-believing Christian and officer in the British army, stationed in Palestine in 1936. The Jews had taken a completely passive, defense-only stance, placing the situation of the Arab uprising of 1936-1939 firmly in the hands of the Arab rioters. In fact, their attacks increased on Jewish settlements to the point of guerrilla warfare.

Wingate singlehandedly trained special night squads of Jewish volunteers to protect themselves from Arab attacks.

Orde Wingate wrote to the Jews of Israel:

161

I count it as my privilege to help you fight your battle. To that purpose I want to devote my life. I believe that the very existence of mankind is justified when it is based on the moral foundation of the Bible. Whoever dares lift a hand against you and your enterprise here should be fought against. Whether it is jealousy, ignorance or perverted doctrine such as have made your neighbors rise against you, or "politics" which make some of my countrymen support them, I shall fight with you against any of these influences. But, remember that this is your battle. My part, which I say I feel to be a privilege, is only to help you.

For his pro-Jewish stand, the British removed Orde Wingate from Palestine and sent him to Burma. Unfortunately, he was killed in WWII. Had he lived, Ben Gurion said he would have headed the Israel Defense Forces when Israel became a state.

Corrie ten Boom

During WWII, Corrie lived in Holland with her sister, brother, and father. They were a Bible-believing Christian family who prepared a hiding place for Jews of their community. The ten Boom family all died in concentration camps. Only Corrie lived to tell their story.

Raoul Wallenberg

Raoul Wallenberg was a Swedish diplomat during WWII, who worked feverishly to save the lives of thousands of Hungarian Jews. He was arrested by the Russians—never to be heard of again.

The list of Christian Zionist supporters is even longer, but these serve to illustrate the point.

Are You on the List?

Just reading history is not enough. The mandate applies to us today. There are many ways of fulfilling the mandate which we will discuss later, but participation at some level is incumbent upon us.

The first verse of Isaiah 62 is not written in the same commanding structure as verse seven, where we are instructed to "give Him no rest," but yet, it seems to be the cry of those, who through the ages have recognized this verse as God's mandate for His people's homeland, Zion:

For Zion's sake I will not keep silent, for Jerusalem's sake I will not remain quiet, till her righteousness shines out like the dawn, her salvation like a blazing torch.

v. 1

This mandate is detailed in other scriptures as well. Some are straightforward, while others are veiled in stories and historical incidents left as examples to us by men who were inspired by the Holy Spirit and recorded them in our Bible. These sections of the Bible make very clear that the end of the age here on earth centers around Jerusalem. It will not be a quiet, happy time. On the contrary, it will be a time of upheaval and extreme pressure. What do the Scriptures tell us about the future? The past will tell us. Repeat performances abound in biblical accounts. Daniel repeated Joseph's Egypt experiences in Babylon. Joseph's story undoubtedly encouraged Daniel time and time again.

How are we, as Gentile Christians, to conduct ourselves during this time? The tales and mentoring examples recorded for us in the First Covenant will give us the flow chart of the mandate given us. What a glorious commission! There is no time for boredom in the Kingdom at this late stage of history. We live in an era that I am certain the prophets looked forward to, and according to Hebrews 12:1, they are gathered around to cheer us on. Let's charge ahead into God's future in full assurance that He has prepared all things ahead of us. This is Jesus' greatest hour. How long He has waited for the wrap-up of the ages, so that He can be united with His bride. The pressure is on, but it signals periods of great joy and expectation as we head toward His second coming.

Let's accept the mandate given us and "give Him no rest."

My own early experience with God paved the way for personal involvement in that mandate. It began in 1970.

A Threefold Cord

My friend and I were intently engaged in a Japanese strategy game called "GO" on a large blanket in an uncrowded section of the beach in Venice, California, where we both lived. Though a dangerous beach in the 1970s, residents knew which areas were safe and which areas were not. The warm sun washed over us and illuminated the focus of our attention. Black and white game pieces covered the board on which we played. Chess had given way to more exotic games in those years of rebellion. The object was to surround your opponent's game pieces and occupy as much of the board as possible until your pieces prohibited further acquisition of space.

Mindful only of our game, I didn't notice that a crowd was gathering around us until a shadow fell across the board. By that time, my blanket was fenced in by a sea of legs on all four sides. I looked up, trying to assess what was happening. We were not the focus of their attention. Without my noticing, my friend stood up and disappeared through the crowd. I began trying to gather up game pieces and retrieve my blanket, but feet tacked it to the ground in enough places on its perimeter that my attempt was in vain.

A young man noticed my attempt to gather my belongings and sat down on my blanket to help me gather game pieces and put them in the box.

"What is going on here?" I questioned.

"Oh, this is our church, and we have come to the ocean to baptize new believers," he replied. "Four hundred of us came to watch today," he added.

"You came to Venice Beach to baptize people?" I responded incredulously. "People get murdered here!" I warned.

"Oh, God protects us," he offered. "Do you know how much God loves you?" he asked.

My heart pounded like a drum in my chest. I was sure he could hear it. It was a moment of extreme irony. God had been playing a game of strategy with me for several months, but there was no way this young man could possibly know what had transpired.

God had been busy surrounding my defenses and conquering territory in my life one play at a time. A few weeks before this sunny day on the beach, I had been reading *Autobiography of a Yogi*, by Paramahansa Yogananda, founder of the Self Realization Fellowship. I was proud of my spiritual search in Eastern religion, and Christianity took a backseat in my life. Paramahansa's Indian flavored self-realization teachings and other meditation philosophies fit the times I lived in and filled the void in my life— or so I convinced myself. I had worked hard to silence the still small voice that had kept reminding me, "You are wrong!"

A passage in Paramahana's autobiography brought my house of cards crashing to the ground. In it he described the universality of the concept of reincarnation. In support of reincarnation, Jesus was quoted from the New Testament book of John, chapter three.

Paramhansa made Jesus' conversation with Nicodemus strongly support his point. Joyfully, I located a copy of the Bible and in great triumph prepared myself to confirm the yogi's interpretation. As I read, my heart sank. The biblical passage said just the opposite. It was more than clear that spiritual transformation, not reincarnation was the subject matter.

Ironically, a week before, in a brilliant preemptive play, God had begun to surround my defenses on the game board. My sister, whom I loved greatly, and her daughters, my three nieces, were attending a Jesus People coffeehouse ministry regularly in La Habra, California. All of them had received Jesus as their Saviour. They were aglow with new life and love that reached out to everyone. An invitation to their house resulted in a polite but firm confrontation on spiritual issues. They were silenced by my convoluted esoteric mumbo-jumbo and a promise to "meet them there" as "we all have our own ways to get to God," I explained. On my way home that night, I remember thinking, *God, if they know something that is vitally important for me, You have to do something to show me!*

Another meeting with the "glowing converts" took place the following week, but my day in the sun on Venice Beach fell between those two meetings.

"God wants you to live in heaven with Him someday," my beach blanket intruder said.

"Is that right!" I sneered. "I have read somewhere that you can measure heaven with a measuring rod. If that's the case, there is no way everyone in history can fit there—and if that is the kind of God you serve, I want no part of His heaven." In triumph I continued gathering my things and left the beach, but dogging my path home was the feeling that I had just experienced the "show-me" request I had made of God.

The following weekend was my birthday and a party was planned at my sister's home. After the celebration, I was cajoled into attending "The Vine," the coffeehouse ministry with my sister and nieces and some other friends. Still resistant to their newfound joy and unable to extricate myself, I determined that if I had to go, I would be sure to blend in and avoid more theological confrontations.

Sit in the back and draw no attention to yourself, I instructed myself silently.

God placed more white stones on the playing board. My nieces, whom I love dearly and have trouble saying "no" to on most any topic, dragged me close to the front! The first half of a three-hour meeting was a concert with some surprisingly good Christian music. Subconsciously my defenses were weakening. *After all, stupid people could not play great music.*

The first half of the meeting ended with a break where everyone stood together, placed their arms around one another's shoulders, and sang the Lord's Prayer. Not wanting to stand out, and being right up front, I knew I had to sing and sway to the music of the prayer just like everyone else. More white stones were placed on the board.

I knew the words of the Lord's Prayer and parroted the words with those around me. I was smug, knowing that I was cleverly disguised. We came to the last line of the prayer—". . . *for Thine is the Kingdom, and the Power and the glory forever . . .*" —and the room changed. It seemed as if I was in outerspace—alone. It was dark and I saw no one. A gentle voice, filled with authority, above my head said, "The words that are coming out of your mouth are true. Do you want to be part of that Kingdom?"

I don't remember audibly saying "Yes," but my entire being submitted and I began to weep—not just tears running down my face—wracking sobs convulsed my body, and it felt as if tears shot out of my eyes. I could not imagine what was happening to me, but in the next few minutes, waves of God's power washed over me again and again. Such "perspective." All my opposing philosophies and theological arguments melted away to nothing. I was dumfounded at how such a thing could happen.

That night changed everything. Later my niece confided to me that I was not "blending in" at all. It was actually a conspiracy. Everyone knew who I was when I came in, because they had been praying—and some even fasting—for me the week before that meeting. I was embarrassed, but the embarrassment was seasoned with gratefulness for a virtual spiritual intervention that pulled me from the gates of the kingdom of darkness.

The purpose of relating this testimony is to underscore the importance of the Lord's Prayer in my life. You might imagine that the game I was engaged in with God was over, when He so obviously won. The reality is that the game is still being played, and to this day, territory is being surrounded and conquered—territory so vague that at times I am unaware of its very existence. That first conquest was to bring me into His Kingdom, but the extent to which that Kingdom stretches is still being unveiled. God is not in a hurry to clarify life-changing aspects of the Scriptures and bring them into focus. God has continued our game of "GO," surrounding me, capturing territory, and startling me with new facets of His amazing never-ending Kingdom.

Over thirty years later, I am based in Jerusalem, Israel, with my wife Carol, raising three children, and have been working many years with Bridges for Peace, a Christian ministry aiding Jewish people coming from various nations to their homeland. Carol's worship ministry has reached nations from Jerusalem, the center of the earth. Though very busy, we could not be more fulfilled in the what God has given us to do for Him. The full extent of His end-time program—whose stage is the city where we live and work—continues to unfold before our eyes. I marvel that the game that God used to hedge me in all those years ago was called "GO."

Solomon's Prayer

The second facet of the mandate was revealed because of a relative's illness.

I had received an unsettling e-mail message. Chap, the husband of my niece, Kathy, had been taken to a hospital in Denmark, suffering from a serious heart condition. Almost a decade before, they had moved from the United States to work with a Danish Bible School. This sweet niece was one who intervened in my spiritual bankrupt state earlier. Her husband, Chap had undergone several back surgeries for deteriorating discs, and the lengthy recuperation time had affected his heart. My own heart was heavy with concern for his situation.

Inspired by King Solomon's prayer for Gentiles at the dedication of the First Temple in Jerusalem, I determined to go to the Western Wall, which is close to my home, to intercede on his behalf, trusting Solomon's request that God would . . .

> . . . hear from heaven, Your dwelling place, and do whatever the foreigner asks of You, so that all the people of the earth may know Your Name and fear You, as do Your own people Israel . . .
>
> II Chronicles 6:33

I certainly fit the picture. I was the foreigner Solomon had seen down those corridors of time thousands of years before.

At that moment, Solomon's petition to God really had overpowering appeal to me—a blank check from heaven. Standing there at the only remaining structure of the ancient Temple, the Wailing Wall, I asked for healing in the stead of my nephew-in-law. My heart and spirit were in pain, and I needed a contact point more tangible than just my prayer closet to meet with the Lord in intercession.

The Western Wall is the western-most remaining perimeter wall that supported the platform on which two Temples, holy to the people of Israel, stood. King David's son, Solomon, built the first, and the Jewish people returning from captivity in Babylon in 543 B.C. built the second. God has said that His presence would always be there.

A small and very unique prayer area is joined fast to this wall of the outer courtyard of the ancient Jewish Temple. This prayer area is a makeshift synagogue, tucked under one of the arches of an ancient Roman bridge which connected the upper city to the Temple Mount in Jesus' time. The small area has retained its roughhewn first century flavor.

It is customary in Israel to slip a written prayer into a crack of this wall. Desperate petitions are treated in this special method. I had come to collect, in a sense, on the promise that God would do anything the foreigner asked.

After placing my note in the Wall and praying for a time, I sat quietly inside the small prayer area on a hard-backed chair, just gazing at the amazing stonework and wondering what stories those warm, cream-colored stones would tell, if they could. Limestone, darkened with age, layer upon layer—books with no words. Various time periods have left their marks on these stones—chisels have etched the stones almost as clearly as the pen of a writer. The rough hewn stones of Solomon's crafting stand as neighbors to pristinely dressed stones from King Herod's era, wearing a sharp hand-tooled margin. Between those two time periods came the Macabees, those mighty warriors who resisted the Syro-Greek Empire in 160 B.C. Their valiant resistance ushered in the Festival of Hanukkah. These stones incorporate the margined edge that Herod perfected but with a rough bulging center much like King Solomon's era. Ancient stories have been etched here for centuries.

After the '67 War, Israel regained access to the Old City, which had been lost in 1948 and had fallen under Jordanian rule. With the reunification of Jerusalem, came access to the Western Wall of the Temple Mount for the Jewish people, after nearly two thousand years. In great gratitude to God for allowing them access to the Wall that surrounded their holy Temple, the authorities quickly designated this small area as a synagogue and roughly furnished it thus. Jewish prayers are offered there day and night. Some of the prayers recited there today from the distant past— some thousands of years old—still reverberate from the stones, lifted by the voices of pious men.

As I sat there, those voices were lifted in prayer from several different areas of the synagogue. My introspective "reading of the rocks" was arrested by a chorus of hearty "Amens." There is no sound that compares with a chorus of men responding in prayer together. Snapped out of my daydream, I focused my attention on the men. A very ancient prayer was being recited. Not in Hebrew but Aramaic. Its roots, at least its language, can be traced all the way back to Babylon. The prayer is now called the Mourner's Kaddish. It is the prayer used today in synagogue services for mourners in remembrance of deceased loved ones.

I found myself participating in the proper places. I was familiar with the Mourner's Kaddish, but God saved an awakening for me for this moment in time. The Kaddish is not about death. As a matter of fact, death is never mentioned in the prayer. Neither is the life of the one being mourned. The Kaddish is a proclamation of the greatness of God in the highest order. The Kaddish was not always used as a mourner's lament. In earlier times, it was recited after the study of Torah (the first five books of Moses, Genesis through Deuteronomy) for centuries to proclaim the greatness of the God from whom the Torah came. Such a proclamation! Such a powerful prayer!

The Kaddish begins:

Yit-Gadal, Ve'Yit-Kadesh, Shema rabbah . . .

Magnified and sanctified be the Name of God throughout the world which He hath created according to His will.

The Kaddish continues:

May He establish His kingdom during the days of your life and during the life of all the house of Israel. May He make His salvation closer and bring His Messiah near, speedily, yea soon; and say ye, "Amen."

At this juncture in the prayer all the hearers, not just those standing signaling their active participation, respond:

May His great Name be blessed forever and to all eternity, Amen!

Then like a string of costly pearls, the prayer provides a running list of high praise descriptions, which exalt the Name of God. It is a level of praise that is rare. The rhythm of the Aramaic itself is like music.

Yit-barach, v'yish-tabach, v'yit-pa-ar, v'yit-romam, v'yit-na-say, v'yit-hadar, v'yit-alleh, v'yit-hallel sh'mey de-kud-sha bereck Hu le-ella kol min bir-chata. . .

Blessed, praised, and glorified, exalted, extolled, and revered,
Highly honored, and lauded, be the Name of the Holy One,
Blessed be He, Whose glory transcends,
Yea, is above and beyond all praises, hymns, and
Consolations that are uttered in the earth,
And say ye, "Amen."

"Amen," is again the response.

The one reciting the prayer is proclaiming the mighty sovereignty of God over all flesh—dead or alive—and that His glory is above all praise and above all that we can possibly express in worship, and yet, He receives our worship.

The prayer then comes to a conclusion:

May there be abundant peace from heaven and life for us and for all Israel; and say ye, "Amen."

"Amen," the hearers respond again.

May He establish peace in the heavens, grant peace unto us and unto all Israel, and say ye, "Amen."

One of the most beautiful and soul-stirring songs in the Hebrew language is taken from the last few lines of this prayer, *"Oseh Shalom."* It is an ode to Him who makes peace in the heavens and for us on the earth.

The Kaddish is not a prayer for the soul of the departed, but for the magnification of the name and character of God Almighty. This indeed is "peace in the heavens" but also one that sweeps down to earth below, healing hearts and spirits.

Man is obliged to praise God for the evil that befalls him, even as he gives praise for the good. In that proclamation and giving of praise, daily for eleven months after a Jewish person has lost a loved one, is one of the greatest healing balms known to man.

That day, the striking similarities to "The Lord's Prayer," the prayer Yeshua (Jesus) taught His disciples. ". . . Hallowed be Thy name . . ." dawned on me.

The word "hallowed" is a verb. It is something that you do.

Here, God began braiding these prayers together in my mind. Surprisingly, reading the *Encyclopedia Judaica* about the Mourner's Kaddish, the scholar who submitted that section to the book drew a correlation between the Kaddish and the Lord's Prayer. Unusual for a Jewish author in such a volume, but confirmation for me that God was demarcating more of His Kingdom territory in my mind.

For the Sanctity of God's Name

A threefold cord is not easily broken. God was strengthening the two prayers with a another Scripture from the Prophet Ezekiel. The third concept came while reading Ezekiel 36, 37, and 38 in Hebrew.

The chapters that we read with our spirits trembling at our prophetic future, Ezekiel speaks of the past, as well as the dispersion of God's people from His promised land.

> *Son of man, when the people of Israel were living in their own land, they defiled it by their conduct and their actions. Their conduct was like a woman's monthly uncleanness in My sight. So I poured out My wrath on them because they had shed blood in the land and because they had defiled it with their idols. I dispersed them among the nations, and they were scattered through the countries; I judged them according to their conduct and their actions. And wherever they went among the nations they profaned My holy name, . . .*

> Ezekiel 36:17-20a

171

Unholy War for An Islamic Empire

I stopped reading mid-sentence. I knew this description was early in prophecy, before the Babylonian captivity, and it left me wondering what line of thinking was being used in accusing those exiled to Babylon of profaning the name of the Lord there. Daniel, the book which details the Jews' time there, is about God's protection of His people, their promotion to high places in that empire, and their ushering several Babylonian and Persian kings into the very presence of God Almighty—so gloriously, that binding decrees were written about the sovereignty of this powerful God.

The still small voice urged me to read on:

> . . . for it was said of them, "These are the LORD's people, and yet they had to leave His land."

v. 20b

The fog began to clear. The Babylonians believed in local gods that protected individual cities from attack. This would have caused the Babylonians to accuse the captured Jews of serving a weak god. Therefore, the God of Israel seemed small to the Babylonians. He was not a glorious being in their minds. His useless guard over the Hebrews reduced Him to almost nothing in their eyes.

But the Scripture continues:

> "I will show the holiness [sanctity] of My great Name, which has been profaned among the nations, the Name you have profaned among them. Then the nations will know that I am the LORD," declares the Sovereign LORD, "when I show Myself holy through you before their eyes.
> For I will take you out of the nations; I will gather you from all the countries and bring you back into your own land."

vv. 23-24

Reading in Hebrew tied the two prayers together, because the same Hebrew word that is used in the first verse of the Kaddish is used here. God would sanctify His name. Once again my attention was arrested. Not only that, but He would be sanctified in them before the eyes of their captors and oppressors.

> I will sprinkle clean water on you, and you will be clean; I will cleanse you from all your impurities and from all your idols.
> I will give you a new heart and put a new Spirit in you; I will

remove from you your heart of stone and give you a heart of flesh.
And I will put My Spirit in you and move you to follow My decrees and be careful to keep My laws.
You will live in the land I gave your forefathers; you will be My people, and I will be your GOD.

vv. 25-28

The Jews return from dispersion was spelled out and the exact location, *"the land that I gave your forefathers,"* was delineated as the place. He proclaimed that He would be their God once again. Now, the threefold cord was taking shape in my mind. I had read "hallowed be Thy Name" and let it go over my head for so many years. Now, like a lightning bolt, the concept was made clear; in 1948, when God began to bring His people back to His land, no longer could the heathen say, "These are the LORD's people, and yet they had to leave His land."

We know the path will be wrought with trouble, and, according to Zechariah, Jerusalem will become a cup of trembling to all nations. Nevertheless, regardless of what the news media report about Israel, once again it is God's people in God's land experiencing His miracles of protection and blessing. Therefore, I realized that "hallowing" His name means being involved in His end-time program of repopulating the Land of Israel with His scattered people.

We stand on the shoulders of those who came before us. Those who saw God's plan before it began and who acted with faith as if it were already fact. They were men who knew that even in the face of liberal theologians' ideas about the fallacy of the Scriptures, God would still fulfill His Word.

We now live on the other side of Isaiah's prophecies of a nation being "born in a day." We live with the reality of Israel as a nation, walking out the pages of Scripture before our very eyes, as a participant in the mandate. We must not give God rest until He makes Jerusalem, not just "a" praise in the earth, but "the" praise in the earth (Hebrew includes the definite article, singling Jerusalem out for special attention).

This is the mandate that God has set before us, to "hallow" His name, to participate in His ingathering of the tribes of Israel to their ancient homeland. We really are in the last chapter of God's drama. The story began here in Israel long ago and is making the full circle once again to the place it where it began.

"The Lord rebuke you Satan!
The Lord, who has chosen Jerusalem,
rebuke you!"

—Zechariah 3:2

Jewish Agency poster from circa 1930. Even then the Jewish land was referred to as Palestine,
having nothing to do with the Arabic population who disdained the name Palestinian.

He Who Chose Jerusalem

I stood in the Los Angeles area shopping mall listening to a young woman clad in an orange sari. She was a devotee of the Indian god Hari Krishna. She was not from India, but rather, an American, and very obviously a new convert to the trendy discipleship. In what seemed to be a somewhat rehearsed speech, she related the bliss of submitting to the will of Krishna. She then described her sense of fulfillment and the mental images of beauty that came from chanting the god's name over and over again.

I remained quiet, letting her speak, but thinking all the while about how to answer her about my faith in Jesus. It is amazing how one can listen on two levels simultaneously—my physical ears were tuned to her, but my spiritual ears were alert for God's instruction. An impression I was sure was from above came, *Ask her about prophecy and Israel.* In obedience I asked, "Does the *Bhagavad-gita* (their holy book) have anything prophetic to say about the rebirth of Israel?"

"What does that mean?" she queried.

"Well, we know the Bible to be true because Isaiah's predictions that Israel would become a nation again came to pass in 1948," I informed her.

"I suppose you are a Christian?" she sneered.

"Yes, I am," I answered.

She moved away from me with clear body language that the conversation was over. I stood looking after her, praying that God would intervene in her quest for truth. I remembered the days when someone like her would argue with a Christian about theology, but the constant "word of testimony" from many Christians like me had forced the leadership of many Eastern cults to issue a decree to their devotees not to waste time on us, but to move away and approach more "likely" candidates to whom to hawk their spiritual wares.

Israel and prophecy are two inseparable concepts. In fact, in tandem, they are the acid test of the truth of our Scriptures. In reading the First Covenant, there is a clear standard for prophecy and how it relates to Israel.

Islamist's vision for revolution is worldwide, but the pivot point will always be Israel. Geographically, it is also the focal point, because it sits in the midst of Islamic nations; politically, it is central because Allah's land has been "invaded;" but most importantly, it is central spiritually, because it is the starting and ending point of God's universal plan for mankind.

The Beginning and the End

There is a verse in Isaiah that is tremendously faith-building:

Remember the former things; those of long ago; I am God, there is no other. I am God, there is none like Me. I make known the end from the beginning; from ancient times what is still to come. My purpose will stand; I will do all that I please.

46:9

No other religion's sacred books contain specific information about future events that validate their claims. There is no prophecy in the Koran, neither does the Bhagavad-gita concern itself with end-time events. I would say, in any crisis of faith, this verse serves as the clincher. The Bible is the final authority on spiritual life and contains proof texts to support its claims.

God's program for earth has a distinct geographical focal point. All gripping events on the face of the earth will center around that point. Actually, it is already happening in as much as the ratio of news coverage that centers on Israel outstrips other nations by a measurable proportion. The wrap up of the age will have an ending destination—the focal point for the beginning and the focal point for the end are one and the same.

The good news is that the undue media focus on the Middle East has a pre-determined purpose from antiquity. Ezekiel tells us that in the end of time, hoards from the north will come down to take a spoil from Israel. In this verse, Jerusalem is referred to as the "center of the earth." In this case, English is anemic compared to the original language, Hebrew.

To seize spoil and carry off plunder; to assail the waste places that are now inhabited, and the people who were gathered from the nations, who are acquiring cattle and goods, who live at the center of the earth.

Ezekiel 38:12 (NRSV)

The Hebrew word *tabur* טבור (center) means navel. A physically personal mental description is given to the prophet to describe the city. Nevertheless, Jerusalem is center indeed. It was in the past and will be in the future (see map page 7).

Zechariah, What's the Point?

What is the point of a section on prophecy in a book like this? I believe Zechariah has some important points for us for just such a time as this.

Three important things stand out in Zechariah in relation to the subject of this book:

1. The man with the measuring line (2:3,4)

2. God's rebuke of Satan (3:2)

3. The flying scroll (5:1-4)

The Man with the Measuring Line

Zechariah sees a man heading for Jerusalem with a measuring line in his hand. He was stopped by a heavenly decree from completing his task. This vision is of our present day:

> *Then the angel who was speaking to me left, and another angel came to meet him and said to him: "Run, tell that young man, 'Jerusalem will be a city without walls because of the great number of men and livestock in it.'"*

2:3, 4

Not until the middle of A.D. 1800s did the populace of Jerusalem live outside its walls. Sir Moses Montefiori, a wealthy Dutch philanthropist, who read that in the latter times before Messiah came, Jerusalem would be an unwalled city. He paid for the construction of a suburb, called Yemin Moshe, and coaxed the inhabitants of Jerusalem to live in the new neighborhood by paying them stipends.

They would live in the new houses by day but run into the safety of the walls of the city at night. Montefiori was ahead of his time, but he saw the future.

Jerusalem is now over ten times the size of the walled section of the Old City of Jerusalem. That small area could never hold all the city's inhabitants today.

God's Rebuke of Satan

Yes! Only one God ever "chose" Jerusalem. That God is Jehovah, the God of the Hebrews. The Hebrews followed One God in the midst of surrounding kingdoms, who were given to the worship of many gods.

In chapter three, the Lord Himself addresses Satan with a strong rebuke:

> The LORD rebuke you Satan! The LORD, who has chosen Jerusalem, rebuke you!
>
> v. 2

This verse is specifically indicative of Jehovah speaking. The Lord is identifying Himself by something He did—He chose Jerusalem. This was vital for Zechariah's time, but has once again become vital for our time, since much of the world has grown confused about who God is. The line describes Jehovah, the God who chose Jerusalem above all other cities.

Allah, the God of the Muslim world, and late comer to the Mesopotamian pantheon of gods, never chose Jerusalem. The proof is that Jerusalem is not mentioned once in the Koran. The times that it is mentioned in the Hadith, (sayings of Mohammed related by others) are rarely to designate it as a holy site. Whereas, the Bible speaks of the chosen city of Jerusalem, 811 times.

The Muslims chose different cities to serve as their capitals at different times. They chose Baghdad, they chose Damascus, they sacked and destroyed Alexandria and shunned Memphis, creating Cairo as a new Egyptian capital. Finally they settled on Constantinople, and its Christian Byzantine name they changed to Istanbul. They never once chose Jerusalem. It has been said that Jerusalem was third on the Islamic list of places of importance to their faith, after Mecca and Medina. That, too, is not true, since capital cities of successive empires never took Jerusalem into consideration. In fact, just the opposite is true. Below are Muhammed's true feelings about Jerusalem:

Ibn 'Umar relates the story:

"While some people were offering morning prayer at Quba' a man came to them and said, "A Koranic Order has been revealed to Allah's Apostle tonight that he should face the Ka'aba at Mecca (in prayer), so you too should turn your faces towards it." At that moment their faces were towards Sham (i.e., Jerusalem) (and on hearing that) they turned towards the Ka'aba (at Mecca)." [1]

We must also remember that the two most important cities to Muslims, Mecca and Medina in Saudi Arabia, are totally off limits to non-Muslims, including the entire surrounding nation.

Unlike the West, that has welcomed Muslims to build mosques all over the world, Christianity in Saudi Arabia is illegal. Owning a Bible could send you to jail. There are no churches in the whole of the desert peninsula, unlike other Muslim nations that coexist with their Christian population.

If Jerusalem became Islamized, would there be any difference between it and Mecca and Medina, since they now claim that Jerusalem is one of Islam's holy sites? It is noteworthy that since the al-Aqsa Intifada began September of 2000, the Temple Mount has been closed, for the most part, to non-Muslim visitors. It was regularly open, during certain hours of each day, before the uprising.

The fact that God chose Jerusalem is a powerful facet of Zechariah's message. The prophet whose name means "God remembers" is very relevant for our day.

The Flying Scroll

Finally, the message of the flying scroll is now of modern importance. I believe it to be a directive for intercession.

I looked again—and there before me was a flying scroll!

He asked me, "What do you see?" I answered, "I see a flying scroll, thirty feet long and fifteen feet wide." And he said to me, "This is the curse that is going out over the whole land; for according to what it says on one side, every thief will be banished, and according to what it says on the other, everyone who swears falsely will be banished.

The LORD Almighty declares, 'I will send it out, and it will enter the house of the thief and the house of him who swears falsely by My name. It will remain in his house and destroy it, both its timbers and its stones.'"

Zechariah 5:1-4

Writing on scrolls of parchment in antiquity was done on one side only. Parchment has a face and a backside. The face is smooth and will accept ink without bleeding and causing each letter to blur illegibly. Writing on both sides of a scroll would have been unthinkable in antiquity.

In the larger picture of the history of writing, two-sided writing is a much later invention. For all intents and purposes, that makes Zechariah's vision of the flying scroll dated more for our time than for the time in which he received it.

The large scroll, lifted up above the earth and written on both sides, held a sentence of judgment against wrongdoers.

It is recorded that the scroll would enter the house of the transgressor and destroy it, both timbers and stones. The scroll, searching out the house of the evildoer, rather than the evil doer being brought to the house of the scroll (i.e., courts of law) to be judged, may speak of a time when justice and civil authorities have become corrupted, or crippled by convoluted laws, or stretched thin by terrorism.

Yet, a heavenly law exists that rules us all. Ministers of jurisprudence may miss the mark, but as in the story of Paul on the island of Malta, men know that there is justice above the sceptered sway of kings and potentates.

Once safely on shore, we found out that the island was called Malta. The islanders showed us unusual kindness. They built a fire and welcomed us all because it was raining and cold. Paul gathered a pile of brushwood and, as he put it on the fire, a viper, driven out by the heat, fastened itself on his hand. When the islanders saw the snake hanging from his hand, they said to each other, "This man must be a murderer; for though he escaped from the sea, justice has not allowed him to live." But Paul shook the snake off into the fire and suffered no ill effects. The people expected him to swell up or suddenly fall dead, but after waiting a long time and seeing nothing unusual happen to him, they changed their minds and said he was a god.

Acts 28:3-6

As we have seen in myriad negotiations with the Palestinian Authority, justice is a matter of viewpoint. The PA's imprisoning of terrorists was nothing more than a revolving door for the sake of saying that they had done something. But, it is not only Arafat that bends justice to his own ends. The PA acts ruthlessly against Palestinians suspected of "collaborating" with Israelis. We have seen their public executions in town squares on our televisions.

Intercessory prayer against terrorism should include God's justice that exceeds the reach of civil authorities.

Eternal Jerusalem

So, let's talk about a God who chose Jerusalem and His people to whom Jerusalem is at their very heart.

Jerusalem lives in the heart of every Jew throughout the world. It weaves its presence through all their feasts, fasts, and festivals. Jerusalem was center stage from the beginning and is now spotlighted once again at the end. The national anthem of Israel, *Ha Tikvah*, tells of the centrality of Jerusalem in the heart of every Jew.

Jerusalem—unlikely to be chosen for exalted destiny—is center stage for all that is to come in the future for the follower of Yeshua, the Jewish Messiah.

Perched high in the desert mountains of Israel, Jerusalem sits cradled upon a ridge that that is a watershed directing rainfall both east and west. The east side of the city channels precipitation to the Dead Sea. West Jerusalem's rain water rushes to the Mediterranean. From certain areas of Jerusalem's east side, you can see all the way to Amman, Jordan. From some western

181

vantage points, you can see all the way to the Mediterranean Sea.

This perch in the mountains would have made Jerusalem an illogical choice for the capital of any successful kingdom. The access roads leading from commercial trading centers ran miles both east and west of Jerusalem. The Via Maris, the main ancient north-south highway, ran through Israel on the coastal plain. The Kings' Highway ran north and south through the Jordan River Valley some sixty miles east, a mountain range dividing the two. Jerusalem was not a "stop-off" on trade routes. To visit Jerusalem, one had to ascend twenty-six hundred feet on twisting mountain roads from either direction.

Though out of the way, the centrality of Jerusalem in God's plan begins with the Genesis account of Abraham's sacrifice of Isaac on Mount Moriah and, later, he and the King of Salem breaking bread and sharing a communal cup of wine. History is punctuated regularly with Jerusalem thereafter. Finally brought to its heavenly appointed destiny under King David, who moved Israel's capital city from Hebron up to the crystal clear air of Jerusalem, the cycle that will end with Jerusalem as center stage began in earnest.

The world in the first century centered around Jerusalem. In fact, the ancient pinwheel map proves God to be the universe's grandest advertising campaign manager. He specifically placed His people at the hinge of history where all trade routes would converge. Far enough removed for her safety, yet central enough to influence a world-gone-wild after multiple gods, Jerusalem stood as a standard, raised to the glory of the One Supreme God of the universe.

No matter that His people had to sojourn in Egypt because of famine, Jerusalem waited patiently for her people to return. Each time Jerusalem became bereft of her children, she languished in sorrow and poverty. Like a seed falling into dry ground, she waited for the dew of heaven to cause her to spring to life once again. The return of God's chosen was the moisture of life, and Jerusalem always responded.

Jerusalem was the hub of a Jewish population that spread out like the spokes of a wheel in all directions. The account of Jesus' disciples in the book of Acts documents the nations from which Jewish worshipers traveled on the three pilgrimage festivals, where they were commanded to "come up to Jerusalem" to present themselves before the Lord.

Jesus' directive to His disciples to fulfill the Great Commission had at its center, none other than Jerusalem:

> *But you will receive power when the Holy Spirit comes on you; and you will be My witnesses in Jerusalem, and in all Judea and Samaria, and to the ends of the earth.*

Acts 1:8

Living in Israel was not mandatory for Jews, according to Scriptures, but the three pilgrimage festivals were mandatory. Passover, Shavuot (Pentecost), and Sukkot (Tabernacles). During those festivals, Jerusalem's population grew to astounding proportions. The city became a bustling center of worship, sacrifice, and thanksgiving to God.

Each of these festivals fell during the busiest seasons for merchant travelers, i.e., spring and fall. Camel caravans, at times as many as two thousand camels strong, brought spices and frankincense, peacocks and exotic nuts from the southern reaches of the Arabian Peninsula worth as much as $12 million in modern currency. From the silk route, as far as China, the caravans traveled to Europe, laden with costly cargos of silk fabric, costly dyes, and fine china vessels. The common denominator was that they all had to skirt the area close to Jerusalem.

Israel's influence was vitally important in order to fulfill God's command of being a light to the world:

> *It is too small a thing for you to be My servant to restore the tribes of Jacob and bring back those of Israel I have kept. I will also make you a light for the Gentiles, that you may bring My salvation to the ends of the earth.*

Isaiah 49:6

It has never been popular that the Jewish nation should be centrally located. The Jebusites resisted Israel's taking Jebus under King David, the Canaanites waged stiff warfare against Israel, and the Philistines were always challenging Israel and their God, whom they thought to be a local god whose might was confined to the mountains. The surrounding nations were terrified of the Jews as they came out of Egypt, returning to their homeland.

183

A Nation Within Nations

A polarization is taking place within the nations of the earth. Countries are taking sides in the battles of the Middle East. The media is reporting misinformation and disinformation regarding Israel.

A polarization is taking place in the body of believers as well. At one pole are those who believe that, somehow, Christians have replaced Israel in God's plans.

At the other pole are evangelical believers, who carefully read God's Word and know His covenant-keeping character. They believe His promises to Israel are eternal. Between those two poles is a sea of people without enough information to make intelligent decisions about where to stand in regard to Israel. We, as believers, must know where we stand and how to answer those with whom we have contact regarding the present situation. As Christians, we constitute a nation within nations. Though we are scattered throughout many nations across the earth, yet we are unified ambassadors of His coming Kingdom.

Israel is conscious and appreciative of recent evangelical Christian support. For over twenty years, thousands of Christians have been coming to Jerusalem to celebrate Sukkot, the Feast of Tabernacles. When the late and former Prime Minister of Israel, Menachem Begin, announced in 1982 that Jerusalem had been the capital of Israel for three thousand years and would continue to be the undivided capital, all but two foreign embassies pulled their headquarters and staff out of Jerusalem in protest.

At that time, an enterprising group of Christians moved to show Israel that although secular embassies might protest the declaration, Christians all over the world felt differently. That year, the International Christian Embassy Jerusalem (ICEJ) was born. Its mandate: to stand in solidarity with Israel in her lonely fight for existence.

Israeli Jews watched in amazement as visitors to the yearly celebration, sponsored by the ICEJ, grew in numbers. From a mere two hundred the first year, the celebration has hosted as many as six thousand from one hundred thirty different nations. Israeli rabbis finally admitted that they saw this phenomena as the beginnings of the fulfillment of the book of Zechariah:

> *Then the survivors from all the nations that have attacked Jerusalem will go up year after year to worship the King, the* LORD *Almighty, and to celebrate the Feast of Tabernacles.*
>
> *If any of the peoples of the earth do not go up to Jerusalem to worship the King, the* LORD *Almighty, they will have no rain.*
>
> *If the Egyptian people do not go up and take part, they will have no rain. The* LORD *will bring on them the plague He inflicts on the nations that do not go up to celebrate the Feast of Tabernacles.*
>
> 14:16-18

When Yeshua touches down upon the Mount of Olives at His second coming, all will not be bliss. An important point that is easy to forget, in our anxious expectation of the return of the Messiah, is that He returns to make war with those who have fought against Jerusalem:

> *Then the* LORD *will go out and fight against those nations, as He fights in the day of battle.*
>
> *On that day His feet will stand on the Mount of Olives, east of Jerusalem, and the Mount of Olives will be split in two from east to west, forming a great valley, with half of the mountain moving north and half moving south.*
>
> vv. 3, 4

The city He so determinedly chose will be the site where all battles, kingdoms, and empires end. A great thousand-year reign will begin, and all peoples of the earth will come to Jerusalem to worship the one God and King. The present political objectives of Islamists will again die ignominiously in the ashes of the final war.

Notes

1. Volume 6, Book 60, Number 17.

Appendices

Appendix A
Chronology of Islamic Rule

The Arab Caliphs conquered Jerusalem and governed the Palestine region first from Ramla, later from Damascus, and finally from Baghdad. Initially, most of the Caliphs tolerated non-Muslims, such as Jews and Christians, but in the eleventh century, the Seljuks from Turkey invaded Palestine. Their brutality toward Christian pilgrims brought about the Crusades. Jerusalem was *never* an Islamic capital city.

Jerusalem taken (A.D. 638)
The Patriarch Sophronius surrenders Jerusalem to the Caliph Omar.

Damascus becomes Islamic capital (A.D. 661-750)
The Omayyad Caliphs rule the Islamic empire from Damascus.

Dome of the Rock built (A.D. 700)
Caliph Abd el Malik builds the Dome of the Rock on the site of the Temple. Jerusalem now becomes third most important city in Islam.

Abbasides supersede the Omayyads (A.D. 750)
The new dynasty moves the Islamic capital from Damascus to Baghdad.

Fatimids take rule (A.D. 977)
Arab Caliphs who conquered Egypt in 696 now rule Palestine.

Persecution of non-Muslims (A.D. 1004)
Al Hakim, the new Caliph, whom the Druze make supreme leader of their religion persecutes those living in Palestine who are not Muslim.

Church of the Holy Sepulcher destroyed (A.D. 1009)
One of Christianity's most revered sites is destroyed by Muslims.

THE CRUSADES (A.D. 1099-1291)
In 1078, Turkish Seljuks attack Christian pilgrims from Byzantium and Europe. Their acts of brutality lead to the launching of the Crusades.

First Crusade - (A.D. 1096)
  Knights Templar (1119)
    Hugo Von Payen founds a protective order to oversee safe pilgrimage to Jerusalem.
Second Crusade - (1147-49)
Third Crusade - (1189-92)
Fourth Crusade - (1202-04)
Fifth Crusade - (1228-29)
Sixth Crusade - (1248-54)
Seventh Crusade - (1270)

Rule of the Mamelukes (A.D. 1291-1517)
Freed slaves of Turkish or Circassian origin came to power in Egypt and extended their rule to all the territories, ending Christian rule.

Spain's Inquisition (A.D. 1492)
Many Jews fleeing from the Inquisition in Spain come to their homeland, Israel.

Ottoman Empire (A.D. 1517-1917)
The Mamelukes are defeated, and Palestine is swallowed by the Turkish Ottoman Empire under Sultan Selim I. In 1520, Selim's son, Suleyman the Magnificent, oversees a period of growth and internal consolidation of the empire in which Palestine has a degree of peace. The Dome of the Rock is renovated and covered with faience, the blue ceramic material.

JEWISH ALIYAH (A.D. 1882-present day)
Aliyah is a Hebrew word meaning "to go up." Since Jerusalem's altitude is some twenty-six hundred feet and is nestled in the mountains of Israel, the secondary meaning of aliyah is to immigrate to Israel. Here it specifically indicates Jewish people coming back to their homeland from the nations where they had been scattered.

First Aliyah
The first great wave of immigrants, mostly from Poland and Russia, arrive on Israel's shores under the support of the Baron Edmond de Rothschild. Yemenite Jews also come from the south. Egypt is occupied by the British.

Herzl publishes his treatise, "The Jewish State" (A.D. 1896)
The dream is born of a Jewish State in Palestine. Zionism is born.

Second Aliyah (1904-14)
The second wave of Jewish immigrants arrive in Palestine.

Tel Aviv founded (1909)
Tel Aviv is founded north of Jaffa, on the Mediterranean sand dunes, as the first purely Jewish city.

Kibbutz system inaugurated (1910)
Pioneers from Russia set up the first collective settlements for protection from Arab attacks against their presence.

World War I (1914)
The assassination of heir to the Austrian throne in Sarajevo (June 28) sets the stage for WWI. Turkey allies itself with the Central Powers (Germany, Austria, and Hungary).

Hussein of Mecca promised Kingdom (1915)
The British High Commissioner in Egypt assures Abdullah Hussein of an Arab kingdom in the event of victory over the Turks.

Sykes Picot Agreement (1916)
"Spheres of influence and territorial acquisition" of the Allies (Britain and France) addressed in Turkey. This led to Palestine being subjected to an international administration.

Balfour Declaration (1917)
British Foreign Minister Arthur Balfour heads a committee to draw up the Balfour Declaration, handing to the Jewish people a national homeland.

BRITISH MANDATE (1920-1948)
A newly formed League of Nations begins to carve up the Ottoman Empire. Promises to Arab leaders of kingdoms, after their help winning the war against Turkey (Ottoman Empire), led to arbitrary lines being drawn in the desert sand.

The years between 1920 and 1948 were volatile. Arabs, seeing more Jews come home than they expected resulted in violent attacks against them to scare them off.

In self-defense, Jewish organizations were formed for protection against Arab terror attacks. The Haganah and the Irgun both had their origins here.

The Peel Report (1939)
A British attempt to divide Palestine between Arabs and Jews, giving them both independent status, was rejected by the Arabs.

White Paper (1939)
A British attempt to restrict Jewish immigration into Palestine.

Partition Plan of the United Nations (1947)
The United Nations adopted a plan for the division of Palestine into two states, one Jewish and one Arab. The vote in the General Assembly passed, but the Arabs rejected it out of hand.

State of Israel Declared (1948)
Four wars in twenty-five years followed the declaration of statehood by Israel.

War of Independence - 1948
Upon declaration of statehood, seven Arab nations attacked Israel and called for all Arab citizens to leave their homes in Israel until the Jewish people could be defeated. This created a continuing refugee problem, in which Arab nations refuse to absorb refugees from 1948 and use them, instead, as political pawns. In that same time period, Israel absorbed more than four million Jewish immigrants from many different nations, without refugee camps remaining in existence.

Suez War - 1956
Egyptian President Abdel Nasser nationalized the Suez Canal, and both France and Britain took military action. Terror infiltrations over the borders and Egyptian anti-Israel rhetoric caused Israel to take Gaza and the Sinai Peninsula for her own security.

Six Day War - 1967
Israel is attacked by Egypt, Syria and Jordan simultaneously and defeats all three, taking the Golan Heights from Syria, the West Bank, and the Old City from Jordan, and further territory into the Sinai up to the Suez Canal.

Yom Kippur War - 1973
On the holiest day of the Jewish calendar, Israel was attacked by surprise by Egypt and Syria. Egyptian troops penetrated deep into the Sinai Peninsula, while the Syrians concentrated on the Israeli positions along the Golan Heights.

Israel - Egypt Peace Treaty (1979)
Anwar Sadat, Menachem Begin, and Jimmy Carter meet at Camp David and sign a peace treaty stipulating Israel's phased withdrawal from the Sinai Peninsula. The Treaty is boycotted by most Arab states and the Palestinians.

Arabs adopt term "Palestinians" (1967)

Between 1949 and 1967, Jordan ruled the area called Palestine without any recognition of Palestinians as an independent entity. In fact, until 1967, the term "Palestinian" was denied by the Arab populace living in Israel. Esteemed Arab historian, Philip Hitti, stated before the Anglo-American Committee of Inquiry in 1946, "There is no such thing as Palestine in [Arab] history, absolutely not." Actually several Arab historians accused the Jews of inventing the term. "Palestine is alien to us; it is the Zionist who introduced it," Auni Bey Abdul-Hadi said to the Peel Commission.

The first Jewish newspaper was called *The Palestine Post*. It later became *The Jerusalem Post*. The Israel Philharmonic Orchestra was also first called the Palestine Philharmonic Orchestra.

Nevertheless, when the term Palestine became a useful tool in international negotiations, it suddenly had historical roots; and a nation and their people came into being overnight.

The Uprisings - Intifada(s) (1987, 1996, 2000)

Having succeeded in securing Western favor for the myth of a historical Palestinian entity, the ensuing years of Islamic struggle against Israel and moving toward statehood have been difficult. The Palestinians have fine-tuned the institution of *intifada* or "uprising" against Israel.

Appendix B documents how the Palestinians evolved into terror groups and how their agenda changed over the years, becoming increasingly violent.

Each uprising has its own specialities. In the most recent *intifada*, children have been used as front-line fighters. Arab mothers who are interviewed, say that they just cannot keep their children from going to throw rocks at Israeli occupiers. From PA-controlled television programs, school books, and hate-filled summer camps, which train kids how to use guns, it is safe to say that their street demonstrations are often a show for the cameras.

Appendix B

Significant Dates of PLO and Other Terrorist Attacks

In 1993, Anthony Reuben compiled, for the *Jerusalem Post*, a chronology of the PLO, and subsequent terrorist attacks. Reuben's account ends there, but from that date on, it is impossible to focus on the PLO alone. Arafat's need for plausible deniability was met by factionalization and the involvement of several other violent terror groups.

The 1960s

• **May-June 1964:** PLO founded at a conference in Jerusalem under the auspices of the Arab League. Ahmen Shukeiri nominated as chairman of the executive, but is seen as ineffective.

• **December 1967:** Yahya Hamuda takes over as head of a collective leadership.

• **July 1968:** In Cairo, National Charter is completed, which declares, "The liberation of Palestine is a national duty to repulse the Zionist, imperialist invasion. . ."

• **February 1969:** At Fifth Council session, "guerrilla" groups take over control of executive, with Fatah dominating. Yasser Arafat becomes Chairman.

The 1970s

• **May 1970:** Israeli bus is attacked by bazooka fire, killing nine pupils and three teachers from Moshav Avivim.

• **September 1970:** Palestinians hijack three airplanes to Jordan. Shortly thereafter, King Hussein ejects the PLO from the country. The incident becomes known as "Black September," which gave birth to the terrorist organization by the same name.

• **September 1972:** Eleven members of the Israeli delegation at the Munich Olympics are murdered by the "Black September" terrorist group.

• **1974:** Arab summit at Rabat recognized the PLO as "the sole and legitimate representative" of the Palestinian people. The United Nations recognized the PLO as "the representative of the Palestinian people."

- **May 1974:** Three terrorists hold pupils hostage in a Ma'alot school (Jerusalem). In the course of events, twenty-four people are killed and sixty-four wounded.

- **November 1974:** PLO takes responsibility for the PDFLP's Beit She'an murders in which four Israelis are killed. Also in that month, Arafat addresses the U.N. General Assembly with a gun in one hand and an olive branch in the other. He warns the assembly "not to let the olive branch fall from his hands." Amazingly, the U.N. recognizes the PLO as the representative of the Palestinians.

- **1975:** The civil war of Lebanon begins with the PLO acting to destabilize the delicate balance of the coalition government of Lebanon.

- **March 1975:** Members of Fatah attack the Tel Aviv sea front and take hostages in the Savoy Hotel. Three soldiers, three civilians, and seven terrorists are killed.

- **July 1975:** Nine Jews and four Arabs killed when a booby-trapped refrigerator explodes at Zion Square in downtown Jerusalem.

- **July 1976:** Four Israelis and seven terrorists killed as Israeli forces rescue over a hundred hostages from the Entebbe Airport in Uganda.

- **March 1978:** "Coastal road massacre" leaves twenty-one Israelis dead after Fatah terrorists commandeer a bus on the Haifa-Tel Aviv highway. Terrorists shoot randomly at passing cars from the bus and then explode the bus with hand grenades.

- **April 1979:** Four Israelis are killed in their home after seaborne attack on Nahariya.

The 1980s

- **June 1982:** Arafat expelled from Lebanon. After bloody battles, the Syrian-controlled wing of Fatah forces Arafat's forces back to Tripoli.

- **August 1982:** Six killed when terrorists attack the Joel Goldenberg Restaurant in Paris.

- **October 1983:** A large cargo truck loaded with explosives rammed the U.S. Marine command center in the precincts of the Beirut International Airport. The following blast took the lives of 241 American Marines, leaving scores more disabled for life. Islamic Jihad took responsibility—later to be deemed under

Arafat's direction.

- **May 1984:** National Alliance and Democratic Alliance set up by anti-Arafat factions of the PLO.

- **October 1985:** Israeli jets attack Tunisia, bombing PLO Headquarters, but fail to kill Arafat, the presumed target.

- **October 1985:** Palestine Liberation Front hijacks the Italian cruise ship, Achille Lauro. Leon Klinghoffer, a handicapped Jewish man, is thrown overboard in his wheelchair.

- **November 1987:** Members of the Popular Front for the Liberation of Palestine General Command use hang gliders to enter northern Israel and kill six Israeli soldiers.

- **December 1987:** An Israeli driver of a semi-trailer swerves across a line of oncoming traffic and collides with two vans, taking Palestinian workers back to the Gaza District. This incident sparked the violence that evolved into the first *intifada*.

- **November 1988:** Arafat proclaims "the establishment of the State of Palestine" in a ceremony near Algiers, where he is in exile.

- **December 1988:** Arafat addresses the United Nations in Geneva. The U.S. decides to talk to the PLO, after it is made clear in a press conference that it had recognized Israel's right to exist, renounced terrorism, and endorsed U.N. resolutions 242 and 338.

- **April 1989:** Arafat declared President of Palestine.

The 1990s

- **May 1990:** IDF forces thwart PLO terrorist attempt to land on the beach in Tel Aviv.

- **June 1990:** U.S. President Bush, Sr. suspends talks with the PLO until it takes action against terrorism within its ranks.

- **September 1990:** Arafat's support of Saddam Hussein after Iraq's invasion of Kuwait causes many Arab countries to withdraw funding from the PLO.

- **October 1991:** Madrid peace talks begin. Israel demands the right to approve the Palestinian delegation before the talks start. Although the PLO is not permitted to take part, the Palestinian delegation admits that it is in contact with PLO leadership.

- **June 1992:** Yitzhak Rabin wins the Israeli election and declares that his government will be able to come to an autonomy agreement with the Palestinians within a year.

- **January 1993:** Secret negotiations begin between the Israeli government and the PLO. Fourteen meetings take place before August 20.

- **June 1993:** Arafat resigns from Fatah but recants the following day.

- **August 1993:** Foreign Minister Shimon Peres meets with PLO official Mahmoud Abbas in Norway, making him the highest ranking Israeli official to talk to the PLO. Israeli officials announce on the 26th that there have been secret meetings with the PLO.

- **August 30, 1993:** "Gaza-Jericho first" plan ratified by Israeli cabinet moves toward a Palestinian state.

- **January 1993:** Israel lifts a ban on personal contacts with the PLO.

- **September 1993:** Arafat's Fatah faction approves the "Gaza-Jericho first" plan.

- **September 10, 1993:** PLO executive committee agrees in the early hours to allow Yasser Arafat to sign a letter to Yitzhak Rabin, recognizing Israel's right to exist in peace and security, denouncing violence, calling on the Palestinian people in the territories to refrain from violence, and removing all clauses in the PLO covenant that refer to the destruction of Israel.

- **September 13, 1993:** The Oslo Agreement is signed in Washington between Israel and the PLO. The Gaza Strip and the West Bank are to be transferred to a governing body of Palestinians.

Significant dates including other terrorist groups:

From this point on, terrorism in Israel included many more organizations than just the PLO. In order to give a comprehensive picture of the situation, these organizations must be taken into account as well.

The 1990s (cont'd)

- **April 6, 1994:** Eight people were killed in a car bomb attack on a bus in the center of Afula. Hamas claimed responsibility.

- **April 13, 1994:** Five people were killed in a suicide bombing attack on a bus in the central bus station of Hadera. Hamas claimed responsibility for the attack.

196

• **May, 1994:** Israel withdraws from most of the Gaza Strip and Jericho. The Palestinian State comes closer to reality under the temporary name of Palestinian National Authority.

• **September 24, 1995:** "Oslo Two" is concluded and signed in Washington, D.C. This agreement was a follow-up and some renegotiation of the initial Oslo Agreement from two years earlier.

• **Oct 19, 1994:** In a suicide bombing attack on the No. 5 bus on Dizengoff Street in Tel Aviv, twenty-one Israelis and one Dutch national were killed.

• **Nov 11, 1994:** Three soldiers were killed at the Netzarim Junction in the Gaza Strip, when a Palestinian riding a bicycle detonated explosives strapped to his body. Islamic Jihad said it carried out the attack to avenge the car bomb killing of Islamic Jihad leader Hani Abed on Nov 2.

• **Jan 22, 1995:** Two consecutive bombs exploded at the Beit Lid Junction near Netanya, killing eighteen soldiers and one civilian. The Islamic Jihad claimed responsibility for the attack.

• **Apr 9, 1995:** Seven Israelis and one American were killed, when a bus was hit by an explosives-laden van near Kfar Darom in the Gaza Strip. The Islamic Jihad claimed responsibility for the attack.

• **Jul 24, 1995:** Six civilians were killed in a suicide bomb attack on a bus in Ramat Gan.

• **Aug 21, 1995:** Three Israelis and one American were killed in a suicide bombing of a Jerusalem bus.

• **January 20, 1996:** Elections in Palestine among non-Israeli residents, for a National Council and a President of the Council. Yasser Arafat gets 88 percent of the ballots in the presidential election. Dr. Fathi Shikaki, leader of Islamic Jihad, is assassinated in Malta. Yehya Ayyash, "The Engineer" (recruiter and trainer of suicide bombers pitted against Israeli civilians) is killed when Israel sent him a booby-trapped cell phone.

• **Feb 25, 1996:** In a suicide bombing of bus No. 18, near the Central Bus Station in Jerusalem, twenty-six were killed (seventeen civilians and nine soldiers). Hamas claimed responsibility for the attack.

• **Feb 25, 1996:** One Israeli was killed in an explosion set off by a suicide bomber at a hitchhiking post outside Ashkelon. Hamas claimed responsibility for the attack.

- **Mar 3, 1996:** In a suicide bombing of bus No. 18, on Jaffa Road in Jerusalem, nineteen were killed (sixteen civilians and three soldiers).

- **Mar 4, 1996:** Outside Dizengoff Center in Tel Aviv, a suicide bomber detonated a 20-kilogram nail bomb, killing thirteen (twelve civilians and one soldier).

- **Mar 21, 1997:** Three people were killed, when a suicide bomber detonated a bomb on the terrace of a Tel Aviv cafe. Forty-eight people were wounded.

- **Jul 30, 1997:** Sixteen people were killed and 178 wounded in two consecutive suicide bombings in the bazaar-like Mahane Yehuda Market in Jerusalem.

- **Sep 4, 1997:** Five people were killed and 181 wounded in three suicide bombings on the Ben-Yehuda Pedestrian Mall in Jerusalem.

- **Oct 29, 1998:** One Israeli soldier was killed when a terrorist drove an explosives-laden car into an Israeli army jeep, escorting a bus with forty elementary school students from the settlement of Kfar Darom in the Gaza Strip.

The 2000s

The Palestinian Authority gave permission for Ariel Sharon to visit the Temple Mount during the high holidays of Tabernacles in September 2000. Yet, they used his visit as an excuse to begin the al-Aqsa Intifada.

- **Nov 2, 2000:** Ayelet Shahar Levy, 28, and Hanan Levy, 33, were killed in a car bomb explosion near the Mahane Yehuda Market in Jerusalem. Ten people were injured. Islamic Jihad claimed responsibility for the attack.

- **Nov 20, 2000:** A roadside bomb exploded, at 7:30 in the morning, alongside a bus carrying children from Kfar Darom to school in Gush Katif. Miriam Amitai, 35, and Gavriel Biton, 34, were killed and nine others, including five injured children, some of them seriously.

- **Nov 22, 2000:** Shoshana Reis, 21, of Hadera, and Meir Bahrame, 35, of Givat Olga, were killed, and sixty wounded, when a powerful car bomb was detonated alongside a passing bus on Hadera's main street, when the area was packed with shoppers and people driving home from work.

• **Dec 22, 2000:** Three soldiers were injured in a suicide bomb attack at the Mehola Junction roadside cafe in the northern Jordan Valley. The terrorist, who detonated a belt of explosives strapped to himself, was killed in the blast.

• **Jan 1, 2001:** A car bomb exploded near a bus stop in the shopping district in the center of Netanya. About sixty people were injured, most lightly. One unidentified person, apparently one of the terrorists involved in the bombing, died of severe burns. Hamas claimed responsibility for the attack.

• **Feb 8, 2001:** A powerful car bomb exploded at 4:40 pm in the ultra-Orthodox neighborhood of Beit Yisrael in Jerusalem, causing mild injuries to four people.

• **Feb 14, 2001:** Eight people were killed and twenty-five injured, when a bus, driven by a Palestinian terrorist, plowed into a group of soldiers and civilians waiting at a bus stop near Holon, south of Tel Aviv.

• **Mar 1, 2001:** One person was killed and nine injured, when a terrorist detonated a bomb in a Tel Aviv to Tiberias service taxi at the Mei Ami Junction in Wadi Ara.

• **Mar 4, 2001:** Three people were killed and at least sixty injured in a suicide bombing in downtown Netanya.

• **Mar 27, 2001:** A car bomb exploded at 7:40 in the morning in the Talpiot Industrial/commercial Zone in Jerusalem. Seven people were injured, one moderately. The Islamic Jihad has claimed responsibility for the attack.

• **Mar 27, 2001:** Twenty-eight people were injured, two seriously, in a suicide bombing directed against a northbound No. 6 bus at the French Hill Junction in Jerusalem. Hamas claimed responsibility for the attack.

• **Mar 28, 2001:** Two teenagers were killed and four injured, (one critically), in a suicide bombing at the Mifgash Hashalom "peace stop" gas station, several hundred meters from an IDF roadblock near the entrance to Kalkilya, east of Kfar Saba. Hamas claimed responsibility for the attack.

• **Apr 22, 2001:** A terrorist detonated a powerful bomb he was carrying near a group of people, waiting at a bus stop on the corner of Weizmann and Tchernichovsky streets in Kfar Saba. One person was killed and about sixty injured in the blast, two severely. The terrorist was also killed in the explosion, for which Hamas claimed responsibility.

199

- **Apr 23, 2001:** Eight people were lightly hurt in a car bombing in Or Yehuda, a few kilometers north of Ben Gurion Airport. Senior police officers said it could only be described as a "miracle" in an area packed with pre-Independence Day shoppers.

- **Apr 29, 2001:** A car bomb blew up close to a school bus traveling near the West Bank city of Nablus. There were no injuries in the attack. The body of the suicide bomber was found in the car. Hamas claimed responsibility for the attack.

- **May 18, 2001:** A Palestinian suicide bomber, wearing an explosive vest, detonated himself outside the HaSharon Shopping Mall in the seaside city of Netanya. Five civilians were killed and over one-hundred wounded in the attack. Hamas claimed responsibility for the attack.

- **May 25, 2001:** Sixty-five people were injured in a car bombing in the Hadera Central Bus Station. The two terrorists were apparently killed in the explosion. The Islamic Jihad claimed responsibility.

- **May 27, 2001:** A car bomb exploded in the center of Jerusalem shortly after midnight. There were no injuries. The Popular Front for the Liberation of Palestine claimed responsibility. A bomb exploded at 9:00 in the morning near the intersection of the capital's main Jaffa Road and Heshin Street. The bomb included several mortar shells, some of which were propelled hundreds of meters from the site of the explosion. Thirty people were injured, most suffering from shock. The Islamic Jihad claimed responsibility.

- **May 30, 2001:** A car bomb exploded shortly before 4:00 pm outside a school in Netanya, while a number of students were still in the building studying for matriculation exams. Eight people were injured, suffering from shock and hearing impairment. The Islamic Jihad claimed responsibility.

- **June 1, 2001:** Just before midnight along Tel Aviv's sea front promenade, twenty-one youth were killed, and 120 wounded when a suicide bomber, standing in a large group of teenagers waiting to enter the Dolphinarium Disco, blew himself up.

- **June 22, 2001:** Sgt. Aviv Iszak, 19, of Kfar Saba and Sgt. Ofir Kit, 19, of Jerusalem, were killed near Dugit in the Gaza Strip as a jeep with yellow Israeli license plates, supposedly stuck in the sand, blew up as they approached. Hamas claimed responsibility.

- **July 2, 2001:** Two separate bombs exploded at about 8:20

Monday morning in cars in the Tel Aviv suburb of Yehud. Six pedestrians were lightly injured. Police sources say the bombs were set by the Popular Front for the Liberation of Palestine, PFLP, a radical PLO faction, who claimed responsibility.

- **July 9, 2001:** A Palestinian suicide bomber was killed in a car-bombing attack near the Kissufim crossing point in the southern Gaza Strip, causing no other casualties. Disaster was averted as the bomb exploded without hitting any other vehicles. Hamas claimed responsibility for the attack.

- **July 16, 2001:** Cpl. Hanit Arami, 19, and Staff Sergeant Avi Ben Harush, 20, both of Zichron Yaakov, were killed and eleven wounded, three seriously, when a bomb exploded in a suicide terrorist attack at a bus stop near the train station in Binyamina, halfway between Netanya and Haifa, at about 7:30 pm Monday evening. Islamic Jihad claimed responsibility for the attack.

- **Aug 8, 2001:** A suicide bomber was killed when he detonated his car bomb, lightly wounding one soldier, at a roadblock near the B'kaot Moshav in the northern Jordan Valley shortly after 9:00 am. One soldier was lightly wounded.

- **Aug 9, 2001:** Fifteen people were killed, including seven children, and about 130 injured in a suicide bombing at the Sbarro Pizzeria on the corner of King George Street and Jaffa Road in the center of Jerusalem. Hamas and Islamic Jihad claimed responsibility for the attack.

- **Aug 12, 2001:** Twenty-one people were injured in a suicide bombing in the Wall Street Cafe in the center of Kiryat Motzkin at 5:30 pm. The terrorist was killed. Islamic Jihad claimed responsibility for the attack.

- **Aug 21, 2001:** A bomb placed under a car exploded at 2:15 pm near the Russian Compound in downtown Jerusalem; one woman was treated for shock. A second, very large, unexploded bomb was discovered inside the car and dismantled.

- **Sept 4, 2001:** Twenty people were injured when a suicide terrorist exploded a powerful charge on Ha-Nevi'im Street, near Bikur Holim hospital in central Jerusalem, shortly before 8:00 am. The terrorist, disguised as a Jew in ultra-Orthodox clothing, aroused the suspicion of passersby due to the large backpack he was wearing. As two Border Police officers approached the man, he detonated his shrapnel-packed bomb. Both officers were wounded, one critically. The terrorist was killed in the blast. To the students horror, his head flew over the wall into the courtyard of a French High School. Hamas claimed responsibility.

- **Sept 9, 2001:** Three people were killed and some ninety injured, most lightly, in a suicide bombing near the Nahariya train station in northern Israel. The terrorist, killed in the blast, waited nearby until the train arrived from Tel-Aviv and people were exiting the station, and then exploded the bomb he was carrying. Hamas claimed responsibility for the attack.

- **Sept 9, 2001:** A car bomb exploded at the Beit Lid Junction near Netanya, injuring seventeen people. One person killed in the explosion was believed to be the terrorist bomber.

- **Oct 1, 2001:** A large car bomb exploded in the Talpiot neighborhood of Jerusalem. Several people were lightly injured.

- **Oct 7, 2001:** Yair Mordechai, 43, of Kibbutz Sheluhot, was killed, when a Palestinian suicide terrorist, affiliated with the Islamic Jihad, detonated a large bomb strapped to his body near the entrance of the Kibbutz in the Beit She'an Valley.

- **Nov 26, 2001:** A Palestinian suicide bomber killed himself and lightly wounded two border policemen at the Erez crossing point in the Gaza Strip. The bomber joined workers waiting to be cleared for entry into Israel. Hamas claimed responsibility for the attack.

- **Nov 29, 2001:** Three people were killed and nine others were wounded in a suicide bombing on a No. 823 bus en route from Nazareth to Tel Aviv near the city of Hadera. Islamic Jihad and Fatah claimed responsibility for the attack.

- **Dec 1, 2001:** Eleven people were killed and about 180 injured when explosive devices were detonated by two suicide bombers. It was close to 11:30 pm Saturday night on Ben Yehuda Street Mall, in the center of Jerusalem. A car bomb exploded nearby 20 minutes later. Hamas claimed responsibility for the attack.

- **Dec 2, 2001:** Fifteen people were killed and forty injured, several critically, in a suicide bombing on an Egged bus No. 16 in Haifa shortly after midday. Hamas claimed responsibility for the attack.

- **Dec 5, 2001:** A suicide bomber exploded a powerful bomb shortly after 7:30 am on King David Street in Jerusalem. A number of people waiting at a nearby bus stop were lightly injured. The terrorist was killed in the blast. Police suspect that the bomb, packed with nails and shrapnel, went off prematurely.

Islamic Jihad claimed responsibility.

• **Dec 9, 2001:** A suicide bomber exploded a powerful bomb near a bus stop at the Checkpost Junction in Haifa shortly after 7:30 am. About thirty people were injured, most lightly and suffering from shock. A second explosive device was found and detonated nearby. The terrorist was killed.

• **Dec 12, 2001:** Four people, traveling in two cars, were lightly wounded in an attack at 6:00 pm by two suicide bombers near the Gaza Strip community of Neve Dekalim.

• **Jan 25, 2002:** Twenty-five people were wounded when a Palestinian suicide bomber detonated explosives outside a cafe on a pedestrian mall near Tel Aviv's old central bus station at 11:15 am on Friday.

• **Jan 27, 2002:** Pinhas Tokatli, 81, of Jerusalem, was killed and over 150 people were wounded (four seriously), in a suicide bombing on Jaffa Road, in the center of Jerusalem, shortly before 12:30 pm. The female terrorist, (the first female suicide bomber ever) identified as a Fatah member, was armed with more than ten kilos of explosives.

• **Feb 16, 2002:** Two teenagers were killed and about thirty people were wounded, six seriously, when a suicide bomber blew himself up on Saturday night at a pizzeria in the shopping mall in Karnei Shomron in Samaria. A third person subsequently died of his injuries. The PFLP claimed responsibility for the attack.

• **Feb 18, 2002:** Policeman Ahmed Mazarib, 32, of the Bedouin village Beit Zarzir in the Galilee, was killed by a suicide bomber whom he had stopped for questioning on the Ma'ale Adumim-Jerusalem road. The terrorist succeeded in detonating the bomb in his car. The Fatah al-Aqsa Martyr's Brigade claimed responsibility for the attack.

• **Feb 20, 2002:** A Palestinian gunman opened fire with an M-16 at a crowded bus stop on Jaffa Road in central Jerusalem. A personal friend of our family lost a lung in the attack.

• **Feb 27, 2002:** A Palestinian suicide bomber blew herself up at the Maccabim roadblock on the Jerusalem-Modi'in highway, injuring three policemen.

• **Mar 2, 2002:** Ten people were killed and over fifty were injured, four critically, in a suicide bombing at 7:15 pm on Saturday evening near a Yeshiva in the ultra-Orthodox Beit Yisrael neighborhood in the center of Jerusalem, where people had gathered for a *bar-mitzva* celebration. The terrorist detonated the bomb next to a group of women, waiting with their baby carriages for their husbands to leave the nearby synagogue. The Fatah al-Aqsa Martyrs Brigade took responsibility for the attack.

• **Mar 5, 2002:** Maharatu Tagana, 85, of upper Nazareth was killed and a large number of people injured, most lightly, when a suicide bomber exploded in bus No. 823, as it entered the Afula Central Bus Station. Islamic Jihad claimed responsibility.

• **Mar 7, 2002:** A suicide bomber blew himself up in the lobby of a hotel in the commercial center on the outskirts of Ariel in Samaria. Fifteen people were injured, one seriously. The PFLP claimed responsibility for the attack.

• **Mar 9, 2002:** Eleven people were killed and fifty-four injured (ten of them seriously), when a suicide bomber detonated himself at 10:30 pm, Saturday night, in a popular crowded cafe at the corner of Aza and Ben-Maimon streets in the Rehavia neighborhood in the center of Jerusalem. Hamas claimed responsibility for the attack.

• **Mar 17, 2002:** A suicide bomber exploded himself near bus No. 22 at the French Hill Junction in northern Jerusalem. Twenty-five people were lightly injured.

• **Mar 20, 2002:** Seven people, four of them soldiers, were killed and about thirty wounded (several seriously), in a suicide bombing of bus No. 823, traveling from Tel Aviv to Nazareth at the Musmus Junction on Highway 65 (Wadi Ara) near Afula. Islamic Jihad claimed responsibility.

• **Mar 21, 2002:** Three people were killed and eighty-six injured, three of them seriously, in a suicide bombing on King George Street in the center of Jerusalem. The terrorist detonated the bomb, packed with metal spikes and nails, in the center of a crowd of shoppers. The Fatah al-Aqsa Brigades claimed responsibility for the attack.

• **Mar 27, 2002:** Twenty-nine people were killed and 140 injured (twenty seriously) in a suicide bombing in the Park Hotel in the coastal city of Netanya, during the evening Passover Seder with 250 guests. Hamas claimed responsibility for the attack. The terrorist was a member of Hamas from Tulkarem, on the list of "wanted" terrorists Israel had requested be arrested.

• **Mar 29, 2002:** Two people were killed and twenty-eight injured (two seriously), when a female suicide bomber blew herself up in the Kiryat Yovel supermarket in Jerusalem. The Fatah al-Aqsa Martyr's Brigade claimed responsibility for the attack.

• **Mar 30, 2002:** One person was killed and about thirty people were injured in a suicide bombing in a cafe on the corner of Allenby and Bialik streets in Tel-Aviv. The Fatah al-Aqsa Martyrs Brigades claimed responsibility for the attack.

• **Mar 31, 2002:** Fifteen people were killed and over forty injured in a suicide bombing in Haifa, in the Matza restaurant of the gas station near the Grand Canyon Shopping Mall. Hamas claimed responsibility for the attack.

• **Mar 31, 2002:** An MDA paramedic (Magen David Adom [Israel's Red Star of David]), was very seriously injured along with three other people at 5:00 pm Sunday afternoon in a suicide bombing at the Emergency Medical Center in Efrat, in the Gush Etzion bloc south of Jerusalem.

• **Apr 1, 2002:** A police officer was killed in Jerusalem, when a Palestinian suicide bomber, heading toward the city center, blew himself up in his car after being stopped at a roadblock. The Fatah al-Aqsa Martyrs' Brigade claimed responsibility for the attack.

• **Apr 10, 2002:** Eight people were killed and twenty-two injured in a suicide bombing on bus No. 960, en route from Haifa to Jerusalem, which exploded near Kibbutz Yagur, east of Haifa. Hamas claimed responsibility for the attack.

• **Apr 12, 2002:** Six people were killed and 104 wounded, when a woman suicide bomber detonated a powerful charge at a bus stop on Jaffa Road at the entrance to Jerusalem's Mahane Yehuda Market, just prior to the Jewish Shabbat. The al-Aqsa Martyrs' Brigade claimed responsibility for the attack.

• **May 7, 2002:** Sixteen people were killed and fifty-five wounded in a crowded game club in Rishon Lezion, southeast of Tel Aviv, when a suicide bomber detonated a powerful charge in the third floor club, causing part of the building to collapse. Hamas claimed responsibility for the attack.

• **May 19, 2002:** Three people were killed and fifty-nine injured (ten seriously), when a suicide bomber, disguised as a soldier, blew himself up in the market in Netanya. Both Hamas and the PFLP took responsibility for the attack.

• **May 20, 2002:** A suicide bomber, apparently bound for Afula, killed himself after border policemen approached him for questioning at a bus stop. There were no other casualties.

- **May 22, 2002:** Two people were killed, and about forty wounded when a suicide bomber detonated himself in the Rothschild Street downtown pedestrian mall of Rishon Lezion.

- **May 23, 2002:** A bomb planted by terrorists exploded underneath a fuel truck at the Pi Glilot fuel depot north of Tel Aviv. The truck burst into flames, but the blaze was quickly contained. A second bomb planted on the same truck failed to detonate.

- **May 24, 2002:** A security guard opened fire on a terrorist attempting to ram a car bomb into the Studio 49 Disco in Tel Aviv. The terrorist was killed and five Israelis slightly injured, when the bomb exploded prematurely.

- **May 27, 2002:** A grandmother and her infant granddaughter were killed, and thirty-seven people were injured, some seriously, when a suicide bomber detonated himself near an ice cream parlor, outside a shopping mall in Petah Tikva. The Fatah al-Aqsa Martyrs' Brigade claimed responsibility for the attack.

- **June 5, 2002:** Seventeen people were killed, and thirty-eight injured, when a car, packed with a large quantity of explosives, struck bus No. 830, traveling from Tel Aviv to Tiberias at the Megiddo Junction near Afula. The bus, which burst into flames, was completely destroyed. The terrorist was killed in the blast. The Islamic Jihad claimed responsibility for the attack.

- **June 11, 2002:** A fourteen year-old girl was killed, and fifteen others were wounded, when a Palestinian suicide bomber set off a relatively small pipe bomb at a *shwarma* restaurant in Herzliya.

- **June 18, 2002:** Nineteen people were killed, and seventy-four injured (six seriously) in a suicide bombing at the Pat Junction on Egged bus No. 32A, traveling from Gilo to the center of Jerusalem. The bus, which was completely destroyed, was carrying many students on their way to school. Hamas claimed responsibility for the attack.

- **June 19, 2002:** Seven people were killed, and fifty injured (three of them critically), when a suicide bomber blew himself up at a crowded bus stop and hitchhiking post at the French Hill intersection in northern Jerusalem, shortly after 7:00 pm, as people were returning home from work. The Fatah al-Aqsa Martyrs' Brigade claimed responsibility for the attack.

- **July 17, 2002:** Seven people were killed, and twenty wounded, when a terrorist cell group, disguised as Israeli soldiers, ambushed a bus from a Tel Aviv suburb to the Immanuel settlement, which is mostly ultra-Orthodox residents. The bus was initially stopped by a bomb which blew out the front tires. When passengers exited the bus, they ran toward Palestinians disguised as Israeli soldiers, who fired on them killing seven. Four Palestinian organizations took responsibility for the attack, according to Qatar's Al Jazeera television station: Fatah, the al-Aqsa Martyrs' Brigade, Hamas, and the Democratic Front for the Liberation of Palestine.

• **July 18, 2002:** Three people were killed, and forty wounded, when two suicide bombers, standing fifteen meters away from each other, blew themselves up at a Tel Aviv cafe. The first bomber detonated himself, and the other one waited for a crowd to gather, then detonated himself. Islamic Jihad claimed responsibility for the bombing.

This list is not complete, but hopefully, conveys the horrors of Islamic terrorism. There is also not room to list the almost daily shooting attacks, as well as the attacks on the southern Jerusalem suburb of Gilo from Bethlehem and Beit Jalla.

The attacks will, undoubtedly continue. As I write this today, a forty-three year old rabbi was shot to death as he drove his automobile, near Alei Zahav.

Hundreds have died and perhaps thousands have been wounded, some of those will be crippled or deformed for life.

Since Israel's Operation Defensive Shield in 2002, Arafat is now known to be behind many of the other organizations besides his own Fatah. The charade provided him deniable plausibility until his computers and documents were confiscated by Israeli authorities.

As the numbers of incidents increase, international media sources have grown weary of covering them all. This list is an attempt to show the severity of the daily crisis Israel faces. There is a very high percentage of families personally affected by terrorist acts in such a small nation. Almost everyone knows someone personally who has been touched by Islamic terrorism here.

Appendix C

How to be Active Against Terror
and
Help Israel At the Same Time

Below are suggestions of how you can become involved, should you choose to do so. Most of the items are from **www.aish.com**, a Jewish site—with some of my own additions on how we can help Israel in practical ways. The suggestions closely mirror the agenda of the **Israel Hasbara Committee**, which has members of all faiths in 61 countries and works to educate people about Israel and the Jewish people. You can help Israel by challenging Islamic and Muslim propaganda with solid facts.

For many around the world, one of the most frustrating aspects of the violence in Israel and the growing possibility of terror in their own countries is the seeming inability to help—even in some small way. And while we may not be able to stop the suicide bombers, we can still take action to lift Israel's spirits and help them contend with an increasingly uncertain situation.

• **Let Bridges for Peace be your hands to bless Israel** — Contact Bridges for Peace at **www.bridgesforpeace.com** to see the many social assistance projects that you can take part in. A large variety of programs are offered that are designed to help immigrants come home to Israel and to aid them in their adjustment to a new life once they arrive.

• **Buy Israeli products and services** — With the Israeli economy suffering, go out of your way to support Israel's export trade. **www.shopinisrael.com, www.usaisrael.org, and www.israeliwishes.com** allow you to buy Israeli products directly. **www.shorashim.net** is an online tourist gift shop.

When in the grocery store, look for brands like Elite, Telma, Osem, and Ahava beauty products. Even if you have to pay a few more dollars for Israeli olives or juice, do it! Ask the supermarket manager to order these items specifically. Buy Jaffa oranges, even if you hate citrus fruits. (You'll find someone to give a present to.) Home Depot and other stores have many made-in-Israel products. **www.israelexport.org** lists the names of products sold in the U.S.A.

• **Speak out** — The next time you hear something negative against Israel, don't wonder to yourself, "What is anyone going to do about it?" No Jewish organization or Israeli Consulate can fight the propaganda war on every front, so don't assume they will. You be the "anyone" and pick up your pen or sit at your keyboard and start writing. Write a piece you for local newspaper, set up information tables at your high school or college, or simply talk to people. Be a roving ambassador for Israel by explaining the true facts to everyone you meet. Even the cashier in the supermarket needs good information. You never know how your contribution may affect someone else's views. The possibilities are endless. The worst thing that one can do is to remain quiet in times like this. So do something!

• **Get the facts** — The Internet is a great resource for getting an accurate picture of what is really happening in the conflict. For daily news, visit the *Jerusalem Post*, **www.jpost.com**, **www.israelinsider.com**, and *Independent Media Review Analysis*, IMRA, **www.imra.org.il**. For crucial background information, read *Israel: A History* (by Martin Gilbert), *From Time Immemorial* (by Joan Peters), and *Myths and Facts* (by Mitchell G. Bard) — online at: **www.us-israel.org/jsource/myths/mftoc.html**.

• **Pray** — Psalm 122:6 *"Pray for the Peace of Jerusalem."* Pray to God to bring peace to the land. Pray for Israel's leaders who need wisdom. Pray that they continue to do what is best for Israel in spite of international pressure. Pray for the safety of Israeli civilians who are targeted by suicide bombers.

Pray Scripture against terrorism from Proverbs 26:2 *"Like a fluttering sparrow or a darting swallow, an undeserved curse does not come to rest."*

Pray for the protection of IDF soldiers as they root out every last terrorist. Ask God to heal Israel's wounded soldiers and civilians and to thwart future terrorist attacks. And pray for the Arabs to realize the true nature of their leadership and doctrines that teach hate and murder. Regardless of your level of observance, you can add a request for Israel to your regular (or even irregular) prayer regimen. No prayer goes to waste. You can send prayers via the Western Wall at **www.thewall.org.** Cry out for God's compassion—because the gates of tears are never closed. And remember: God is in ultimate control. He has done miracles before and will do them again.

- **Phone Israel** — Pick up the phone and make a solidarity call to your Israeli friends and relatives. If you don't know someone personally, ask someone who does. Call that person in Israel and assure them that you share their pain and understand what they're going through. Commend that person for having the courage to live in Israel now. Let them know they are not alone!

- **Protest bias in the media** — The media has a powerful influence on public opinion and government policy. When you discover a piece of bias, immediately contact the news agency and complain. Keep your remarks respectful and stick to the facts. Build a list of e-mail addresses of friends and colleagues, so when you discover bias, you can alert others to also file a complaint. There is power in the number of responses, even if your specific letter is not printed. You can join a media watch e-mail list at **www.HonestReporting.com**, which gives guidelines for how to be effective in contacting the media, and has over 25,000 subscribers protesting biased news against Israel.

- **Give Charity** — Give some charity every day for Israel. Encourage others to give charity for Israel, too. A list of worthy causes is online at: **www.jewishcharitiesonline.com**. One person wrote; "Because our church has been forced to cancel their annual trip to Israel, we are sending our money anyway to the tour guides and bus driver."

- **Empathize with terror victims** — As you are lying in bed at night, imagine what it's like to be the sister, child, or parent of someone who yesterday was full of life, and today is nothing but scattered bones and flesh. It's a *mitzvah* (a charitable deed) to cry and feel another's pain. Send an e-mail to **Prayers-InjuredVAT@yahoogroups.com**, and they will send you regular updates with the names and status of people who have been injured in attacks. A full listing of terror victims—and suggestions to help—is online at:
www.walk4israel.com and www.projectonesoul.com

- **Visit Israel Anyway** — Bridges for Peace offers "Solidarity Mission Tours" to Israel yearly. Contact them through the previously mentioned website for details. Go to Israel on vacation, to study, or to visit family. Encourage your local organizations to sponsor trips—study tours, religious tours, *bar/bat mitzvah* tours. It can be for three days or ten days. Spend as much money as you can afford in order to help the economy. Hotels, stores, and restaurants are lacking tourists—precisely what the terrorists seek! Talk to others about the beautiful landscape of Israel, about the unique feeling of thousands of years of Jewish existence in Israel. Visiting Israel will show Israelis that you really care and will make a tremendous difference to your own sense of connection. Make your motto: "Tourism against Terrorism!"

• **Fly the Israeli flag** — Put an Israeli flag in front of your home, church, etc. Let everyone know that you are proud of Israel. Put an "I Support Israel" bumper sticker on your car. Wear a combined American/Israeli flag pin on your lapel. If you can't find an Israeli flag, make one yourself or ask your kids to draw one and display it in your car window or office.

• **Conserve energy** — Dependence on Arab oil drives much of the pro-Arab sentiment throughout the world. American foreign policy is also heavily influenced by the need for imported oil. To conserve energy, take simple measures like making sure your tires are properly inflated, using compact fluorescent light bulbs in your home, and buying energy-efficient cars and appliances. What about hanging up those car keys and walking or riding your bicycle for a change? If millions would cut down on fuel consumption, the Arab clout would change. Also, don't visit gas stations that import oil from Arab countries. On a public policy level, urge your political representatives to allow the reopening of our own oil fields.

• **Recognize the God factor** — With all the practical efforts to help Israel—media watch, education, economic assistance, political lobbying, etc., don't forget the spiritual component! The very existence of the Jewish people after 3,500 years and the return to the land after a long exile is miraculous. Understand the significance of Abraham's covenant with God. Each of us, on whatever level of observance, must strive to connect.

• **Send flowers** — You can show family and friends in Israel that you are thinking about them by sending flowers. This is a double-*mitzvah*—it can also save a flower shop from going out of business because of the weakened Israeli economy. You can pay by credit card over the phone or via e-mail. One Jerusalem florist, an *oleh* (new immigrant) from the U.K., can be contacted at **simikov@zahav.net.il**. You can find other Israeli florists on the web.

• **Rally for Israel** — Hold a rally in your city. When thousands of people turn out for a public display of support, it affects all segments of your community—the politicians, the media, general public opinion. And most importantly, it engenders unity and pride within the Jewish and pro-Israel community.

• **Know your enemy** — The Arab world tends to say one thing in English, but a very different message in Arabic. Blood libels and fabrications of Israeli-sponsored massacres are common. **Memri, www.memri.org** provides important translations of the Arabic media. And the Center for Monitoring the Impact of Peace, **www.edume.org**, tracks Palestinian compliance with peace agreements.

The Bridges for Peace website has regular quotes from the Arabic press under "Notable Quotes" **www.bridgesforpeace.com**.

• **Holocaust education** — With the rise of anti-Semitic incidents around the world and the state-sponsored anti-Semitism in Arab countries, it is important to see the warning signs before a crisis happens. Learning about the Holocaust helps us appreciate the depth of anti-Semitism and its root causes. Excellent information is online at **www.anti-semitism.com**. Squelch all anti-Semitic language everywhere you are. Stand up against this terrible hatred—no matter what the consequences.

• **Repentance and Return** — Known in Hebrew as *teshuva*, the reviving of our devotion to the Almighty is going to bring about the reviving of our land and our people as a whole. If we can humble ourselves even a little, it can arouse the Almighty's compassion and lives can be spared. Each individual who does *teshuva* brings Israel one step closer to redemption.

• **Post on the web** — There are hundreds of Palestinian websites devoted to spreading propaganda—with pictures of starving Palestinian children and sites with blood dripping down your screen, describing the "horror of massacres orchestrated by the fascist Israelis." Pro-Palestinian activists have flooded chat rooms, bulletin boards, and online comments sections. Speak up against individuals who spread lies, against the mobs who bomb synagogues in Europe, and against those who preach intolerance in our schools and universities. Be strong and take heart in the knowledge that all decent people are on Israel's side.

• **Restitution** — It is a rarely talked about spiritual exercise in our day and age. It means making things right with those you have wronged. If you've had an argument with someone, stolen something, done some other wrong deed, seek to make it right. Then forgive those you feel have done such things to you. Also ask God to forgive His people.

• **Fight child abuse** — Palestinian children are being brainwashed into sacrificing their lives for the promise of "martyrdom." A group called SICK—Stop Inciting Children to Kill, **www.opsick.com** is trying to stop this child abuse.

• **Support Israeli citizens** — Show Israelis your support, love, and friendship by writing letters, postcards, and e-mails to everyone you know. Become an e-mail pen pal to someone in Israel.

• **Thank God for His many miracles** — Read the Jerusalem Post, **www.jpost.com** to see how, almost every day, suicide bombers and attacks are averted. And thank God! Also pray daily for terrorists' plans to be thwarted.

• **Organize an Israeli products fair** — In Denver, Christians and Jews have come together under "ActionIsrael" to sponsor what is called "Ben Yehuda Street in Denver." Shop owners in Jerusalem send some of their inventory and it is sold for them. This helps Jerusalem merchants keep their shops open and provide a living for their families during this terrible time. Thousands turned out to show their support.

Yearly, Faith Bible Chapel, in Denver, Colorado, sponsors a special "Israel Awareness Day" and is joined every other year by Bridges for Peace for a full four-day conference. Information can be obtained at **www.bridgesforpeace.com**.

• **Support Magen David Adom** — Israel's medical emergency service is severely financially strapped and in need of ambulances. Months of terror have stretched MDA to its maximum capacity, while exposing its rescue workers to extreme danger and great sacrifice. Get your synagogue, church, or school, to start a campaign to defray the cost of an ambulance. Or contribute online at: **www.magendavidadom.org**. Jewish lives depend on it.

• **Aliyah! If You Are Jewish, Make Israel Your Home** — You can have a great effect on what happens in Israel by living there. A large influx of educated, entrepreneurial Jews from Western countries will give Israel a major boost. Israel is the place where a

Unholy War for An Islamic Empire

Jew is truly at home and can maximize his/her Jewish potential. Start making plans to move when things quiet down (or even now if you're brave.) If you are Gentile, support *aliyah* in as many ways as possible.

• **Learn Hebrew** — Call your local synagogue, or Jewish Community Center, or seminary, and find out about Hebrew classes. This will build your bond with the Jewish people and the Land of Israel.

• **Get the Israeli side** — There's a lot of misinformation out there. When an incident happens in Israel, visit the websites of the Israeli Ministry of Foreign, Affairs, **www.mfa.gov.il** and the Israeli Defense Forces, **www.idf.il/newsite/english/main.asp** to get the Israeli side of the story.

• **If Jewish, Learn Torah** — Through the learning of Torah, the Hebrew Bible, the world is brought to its senses, and the Jewish people are protected. Make a commitment to a specific increase in the amount of time you learn each day. Attend a class about Judaism or pick something from the recommended reading list at **www.aish.com/literacy/reference/recommended_books.asp**.
The impact of even a few extra minutes of Torah learning is enormous. And teach Torah to your children!

• **If Christian, Study the Bible** — The above exhortation is applicable for us as Christians as well. Studying of the Word of God is vital. Coupled with prayer, it is a powerful offensive weapon against our formidable enemy.

• **Contact the President** — Call or e-mail the U.S. President daily or weekly, to commend his support for Israel in the common fight against terrorism, and respectfully urge him to allow Israel to take vigorous action to defend itself. Write a short, personal e-mail with a subject line like: "Thank you for standing with Israel." Every call, letter, and fax is counted. Send e-mail to: **president@whitehouse.gov**, or call the White House comment line at: **202-456-1111**, or **202-456-1414**.

• **Support Israeli soldiers** — Write a letter and express appreciation for their self-sacrifice in valiantly defending our people and our land. You can even send a care package to a soldier with a holiday gift, etc. How to do this can be found on the Jerusalem Post website **www.jpost.com**.

- **Fight terror** — For the civilized world to survive, terrorism must be stopped. Some would appease Arab countries that supply oil. Call on your government leaders to make policy decisions based on what is morally correct, not economically expedient. Order the documentary by PBS called: "Jihad in America" by Steven Emerson. Show it to friends. It's a real eye-opener.

- **Distribute literature on college campuses** — There is an urgent need to counter the virulent wave on anti-Semitism and pro-Palestinian activism on college campuses. Print and distribute literature on campuses highlighting Israel's humanitarian achievements, democracy and ethnic diversity. One group working on this front is **www.israelactivism.com**.

- **Proclaim the Psalms** — There is a time-honored custom for Jews to gather and recite Psalms in times of distress. King David wrote stirring words that seem to be written for our exact situation today! You can set up a schedule to say a few Psalms every day (recommended are Psalms 20, 83, 121,130 and 142) or organize a group of friends to read aloud the entire book together. Rabbi Elyashiv in Israel has requested that all Jews worldwide take fifteen minutes out of their hectic daily schedules to say Psalms. You can say them in Hebrew or English, and a free downloadable translation is available at **www.artscroll.com**.

- **Order Derek Prince's Book** - *Power of Proclamation* — There is tremendous power released through proclaiming the Word of God. Many Christians are not aware of the amazing potential available to them through proclamations. **www.derekprince.com**
- **Reach out** — At such difficult times, people need to reach out to one another. Invite a friend to dinner. Especially now, people feel the need to connect and discuss the world situation.

- **Register and vote** — Elected officials analyze voting registration and voter turnout carefully and make decisions accordingly. If you are not already registered to vote, contact your local Board of Elections. Ask for a voter registration application, and be sure to vote in the upcoming elections.

- **Invest** — Buy stocks on the Tel Aviv Stock Exchange. Help Israeli companies obtain venture capital funds. You can even buy an Israel Bond for as little as $136.

- **Sponsor educational forums** — If you are qualified, offer a crash course in the Mideast conflict at your local library, community center, church or community college.

• **Hold governments accountable** — Write and call (and boycott if necessary) any governments that are complicit in anti-Semitic and anti-Israel activities. Educate the public about the inconsistency of the European Union stand. Why would democracies who support human rights not speak out against virulent Arab hate speech? Protest at the consulates of those countries that have minimized the problem of anti-Semitic activities taking place in their countries.

• **Help Israel get better spokespeople** — Palestinian spokespeople are persuasive and articulate, but Israeli spokespeople are sometimes less so. Compile a list of Israeli spokespeople, and run an online poll, asking people to vote for their favorite. Then inform the Israeli government of the results, so they know who to get the networks to interview in the future. Israelis need to know how they come across to the American TV viewer!

• **Hold prayer rallies** — Communal prayer is more powerful than any individual can muster. Bridges for Peace holds "*Chai* Nights" (*Chai* is Hebrew for "life") in many cities in the U.S. These are evenings to show support for Israel with detailed information about how you can be involved on a level that suits your abilities.

• **Send for the video "Jihad in America"** — Produced by The National Unity Coalition for Israel and aired on PBS in the U.S.A. Call their toll free number - 1-800-688-2204.

Bibliography

Bishop, Joseph W. "Legal Measures to Control Terrorism in Democracies," in Benjamin Netanyahu, ed., *International Terrorism: Challenge and Response* (New Brunswick, NJ: transaction, 1981), p. 301.

Bodansky, Yossef. *Target America: Terrorism in the U.S. Today.* S.P.I. Books, a division of Shapolshy Publishers, Inc. 1993.

Graves, Robert. *Lawrence and the Arabs.* Athena Books, Paragon House, 1927, 1955, 1991.

Katz, Samuel. *Battleground.* *Fact and Fantasy in Palestine.* Bantam Books, 1973.

Mostyn, Trevor. Executive Editor, Hourani, Albert. Advisory Editor. *The Cambridge Encyclopedia of The Middle East and North Africa.* Press Syndicate of the University of Cambridge, 1988

Netanyahu, Benjamin. *A Place Among the Nations.* Bantam Book, May 1993.

Netanyahu, Benjamin. *Fighting Terrorism; How Democracies Can Defeat Domestic and International Terrorism.* Farrar Straus Giroux, 1995.

Sasson, Jean P. *Princess.* Avon Books, New York, 1992.

Sela, Avraham, Editor. *Political Encyclopedia of the Middle East.* The Jerusalem Publishing House, 1999.

Internet Websites Sources

C.I.A. *The World Fact Book.*
   http://www.odci.gov/cia/publications/factbook/

Koranic references are from the searchable Koran and "Al-Koran" translated by Ahmed Ali.
   http://www.hti.umich.edu/k/koran/simple.html

The Hadith is a compilation of the sayings of Muhammed from those close to him. The Hadith site is:
   http://www.usc.edu/dept/MSA/reference/searchhadith.html

I have listed two websites here that have much more information about Hasan and the assassins:
   http://www.alamut.com/subj/ideologies/alamut/hitti_Ass.html
   http://homepage.ntlworld.com/anthony.campbell1/assassins/

BRIDGES FOR PEACE – is a Jerusalem-based, Bible-believing Christian organization supporting Israel and building relationships between Christians and Jews worldwide through education and practical deeds expressing God's love and mercy.

It is our desire to see Christians and Jews working side by side for better understanding and a more secure Israel. Founded in 1976, Bridges for Peace seeks to be a ministry of hope and reconciliation. Through programs both in Israel and worldwide, we are giving Christians the opportunity to actively express their biblical responsibility before God to be faithful to Israel and the Jewish community.

For too long, Christians have been silent. For too long, the Jewish community has had to fight its battles alone. It is time Christian individuals and congregations speak up for the people who gave us the Bible.

We are committed to the following goals:

❖ To encourage meaningful and supportive relationships between Christians and Jews in Israel and around the world.
❖ To educate and equip Christians to identify with Israel, the Jewish people, and the biblical/Hebraic foundations of our Christian faith.
❖ To bless Israel and the Jewish people in Israel and worldwide through practical assistance, volunteer service, and prayer.
❖ To communicate Christian perspectives to the attention of Israeli leaders and the Jewish community-at-large.
❖ To counter anti-Semitism worldwide and support Israel's divine God-given right to exist in her God-given Land.

We are accomplishing this through a variety of programs:

❖ *Dispatch from Jerusalem:* A bi-monthly publication with pertinent and positive news from Israel and informative insights into the hopes and aspirations of the Israeli people, all in a prophetic context.
❖ *Israel Teaching Letter:* Monthly in-depth studies bringing to light the fuller meanings of biblical concepts from the Hebraic roots of the Scriptures.
❖ *Non-English Publications:* Israel Teaching Letter available in Spanish, Portuguese, Japanese, and German.
❖ *Jerusalem Mosaic:* A dynamic television series, shot on location in Israel, which brings the Land of the Bible and her people direct from Israel to you.

❖ *Update From Jerusalem:* Weekly e-mail update with prayer focus. To subscribe, visit our website at www.bridgesforpeace.com and sign up on the right hand column of our front page.

❖ *Chai Night* **Prayer and Study Groups:** A monthly intercessory prayer program sponsored by individuals and churches around the world who desire to *"Pray for the Peace of Jerusalem."*

❖ **Bridge-Building Projects:** Promote better Christian-Jewish understanding and support for Israel on the local and regional level around the world. Projects such as Hebrew classes, film series, Israel Awareness Programs, speakers bureau, study seminars, etc., are offered.

❖ **Operation Ezra:** A vital social assistance program providing a channel of practical help to a variety of worthy projects in Israel utilizing cash contributions and gifts-in-kind from Christians to bless Israel. Through our Food Bank, food gifts are channeled to help Israel's needy (both Jews and Arabs). Currently, we are assisting Jewish immigrants to Israel, Israel's elderly and poor, and Arab believers.

❖ **Project Rescue/Project Hope:** These programs help the poorest Jews, from the countries of the former Soviet Union, prepare to immigrate to Israel (Project Rescue), and helps sustain those who cannot come, the elderly and the sick (Project Hope). Without our help, most would find the cost of passports, visas, ground transportation, lodging, etc., out of their reach.

❖ **Short Term Service:** A wonderful opportunity for Christians to build sincere relationships by volunteering to serve as short term staff assisting Israel's poor and new immigrants directly via our BFP Food Bank/Distribution Center, Gleaning Program, and Home Repair Project.

❖ **Bridges for Peace Forest in Israel:** Located on Mt. Tabor, this forest gives Christians the opportunity to participate in the greening of Israel and the fulfillment of the prophecies about the restoration of the Land.

❖ **Bible Study Tours in Israel:** Bridges for Peace provides a variety of travel opportunities and lectures to help you or your tour group gain a deeper understanding of Israel, the Jewish people, and the Jewish roots of our Christian faith in light of the Bible, history, archaeology, and current events. An extensive pre-travel study manual is a part of all BFP tours and is also available for purchase to individuals or tour groups coming to Israel.

FOR MORE INFORMATION, write to any of our national offices. We are also available to help you plan activities in your area. When you come to Israel, we would like to meet you or speak for your group. Please contact us in advance to visit our International Headquarters in Jerusalem. Phone: 972-2-624-5004, FAX: 972-2-624-6622

We invite you to join us in a practical expression of this desire to bless Israel by becoming an active Bridge-builder and participating in fulfilling biblical prophecy through the vital and important work of Bridges for Peace.

www.bridgesforpeace.com   1-800-566-1998

Other Books by Ron Cantrell

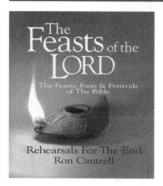

The Feasts of the LORD

119 pages; fully illustrated.

The feasts outlined in the book of Leviticus chapter 23 are "Feasts of the LORD." These feasts are rehearsals for end-time events.

What should we expect in the future? The past will tell us. This book provides priceless insights into the plan of God that is unfolding before our eyes.

The Final Kingdom

240 pages

The book of Daniel recounts the protection and promotion of God's people, who led Babylon to the throne of God Almighty three different times.

- When was the return from Babylon completed?
- Why was the den of lions punishment for Daniel and not the fiery furnace?
- How did "playing king" as a boy set the stage for Darius?

This book will answer these questions as well as provide insight into the history and culture of Mesopotamia, that land between the Tigris and Euphrates rivers that still, to the present day, holds intrigue and mystery for students of the Bible.